KU-499-716

Michael Tracker
1986

CAMBRIDGE COMMENTARIES ON
WRITINGS OF THE JEWISH AND CHRISTIAN WORLD
200 BC TO AD 200
VOLUME 6

# Jews and Christians:
# Graeco-Roman Views

CAMBRIDGE COMMENTARIES ON
WRITINGS OF THE JEWISH AND CHRISTIAN WORLD
200 BC TO AD 200

General Editors:

P. R. ACKROYD

A. R. C. LEANEY

J. W. PACKER

# JEWS AND CHRISTIANS: GRAECO-ROMAN VIEWS

## MOLLY WHITTAKER

*Formerly Senior Lecturer in Classics*
*The University of Nottingham*

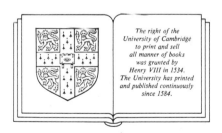

The right of the
University of Cambridge
to print and sell
all manner of books
was granted by
Henry VIII in 1534.
The University has printed
and published continuously
since 1584.

## CAMBRIDGE UNIVERSITY PRESS

Cambridge
London   New York   New Rochelle
Melbourne   Sydney

Published by the Press Syndicate of the University of Cambridge
The Pitt Building, Trumpington Street, Cambridge CB2 1RP
32 East 57th Street, New York, NY 10022, USA
296 Beaconsfield Parade, Middle Park, Melbourne 3206, Australia

© Cambridge University Press 1984

First published 1984

Printed in Great Britain by the
University Press, Cambridge

Library of Congress catalogue card number: 84-1880

*British Library Cataloguing in Publication Data*
Whittaker, Molly
Jews and Christians.–(Cambridge commentaries on writings
of the Jewish and Christian world 200 BC to AD 200; v 6)
1. Church history–Primitive and early church, ca 330–600–Sources
2. Judaism–History–Greco-Roman period, 332 BC–210 AD–Sources
1. Title
200    BR167
ISBN 0 521 24251 7 hard covers
ISBN 0 521 28556 9 paperback

# Contents

# General Editors' Preface

The three general editors of the Cambridge Bible Commentary series have all, in their teaching, experienced a lack of readily usable texts of the literature which is often called pseudepigrapha but which is more accurately defined as extra-biblical or para-biblical literature. The aim of this new series is to help fill this gap.

The welcome accorded to the Cambridge Bible Commentary has encouraged the editors to follow the same pattern here, except that carefully chosen extracts from the texts, rather than complete books, have normally been provided for comment. The introductory material leads naturally into the text, which itself leads into alternating sections of commentary.

Within the severe limits imposed by the size and scope of the series, each contributor will attempt to provide for the student and general reader the results of modern scholarship, but has been asked to assume no specialized theological or linguistic knowledge.

The volumes already planned cover the writings of the Jewish and Christian World from about 200 BC to AD 200 and are being edited as follows:

1 *Jews in the Hellenistic World* – J. R. Bartlett, Trinity College, Dublin
2 *The Qumran Community* – M. A. Knibb, King's College, London
3 *Early Rabbinic Writings* – H. Maccoby, Leo Baeck College, London
4 *Outside the Old Testament* – M. de Jonge, University of Leiden
5 *Outside the New Testament* – G. N. Stanton, King's College, London
6 *Jews and Christians: Graeco-Roman Views* – M. Whittaker, University of Nottingham

A seventh volume by one of the general editors, A. R. C. Leaney, *The Jewish and Christian World 200 BC to AD 200*, examines the wider historical and literary background to the period and includes tables of dates, relevant lists and maps. Although this companion volume will preface and augment the series, it may also be read as complete in itself and be used as a work of general reference.

P. R. A.    A. R. C. L.    J. W. P.

# Author's Foreword

The aim of this volume is to give access to sources which illustrate Graeco-Roman views of Judaism and Christianity from 200 BC to AD 200. Almost all the authors quoted are pagan, a word used here and throughout the book as a convenient term to cover any religion other than Judaism and Christianity, without implying any value-judgement. The translations are my own, except for translation from the Arabic of Galen and the biblical passages which are from the New English Bible. Sometimes passages survive only in quotation by a Jewish author such as Josephus or by a later Christian writer. Occasionally Christian writers, e.g. Prudentius, have been cited to give evidence for practices which were current earlier, but for which we have no contemporary literary attestation.

Pagan references illustrating attitudes towards Judaism are of two kinds, the historical and the incidental. Tacitus prefaces his account of the siege of Jerusalem with a sketch of the origins, customs, geography and history of the Jews. This has been quoted in full. Strabo, the historian and geographer, devotes a section to the Jews and so, briefly, does Dio Cassius. These are valuable, not only for the information which they contain but also for the light they throw on the writer's view of the Jews in the context of his own period.

Rather different are historians whose works only survive in quotation. Here, information about the author who quotes them and his date and background is essential. The original author might be outdated, but the fact that he was named and quoted shows that he still carried weight and could influence the opinions of those who might read him, albeit in quotation, a century or so later. An instance is Hecataeus who, though strictly speaking before our period, was quoted at length by Diodorus Siculus and Josephus and is valuable as a counterbalance to later Alexandrian anti-Jewish propaganda. There are several accounts of the Exodus, varying in length, but all deserving reproduction because of their differences.

Equally valuable perhaps are the incidental references (here the date and background of the author are particularly important), which show how such external marks of Judaism as circumcision, sabbath-observance and food laws are taken for granted as being well known to the reader. Most of these are brief and best related to separate sub-sections within which they are given in chronological order. A page reference in brackets after an author's name gives a cross-reference to the page on which his biographical details are to be found.

For Christianity in its early stages literary evidence of pagan views is necessarily more scanty. The New Testament throws some light on contemporary feelings. Records and unofficial accounts of persecutions have their value. There are some incidental references to be found in pagan authors, but only towards the end of the period was there sustained anti-Christian polemic by such an author as Celsus.

The third section of this book, 'The Pagan Background', is not a collection of sources but an attempt to sketch the cults and superstitions and general climate of thought. Passages have been chosen to illustrate the practices and beliefs which would influence men's reactions to such strange and alien cults as Judaism and Christianity.

A Chronological Chart (pp. 269–72) is given to put authors in historical perspective and to list, in one column, a few outstanding persons and events of importance in the Graeco-Roman world and, in another column, those which were of particular relevance for Jews and Christians. G (Greek) and L (Latin) mark the language used, but this is not necessarily a clue to the author's nationality. Many dates are approximate, as shown by the conventional abbreviations *c.* (*circa*, 'about') and *fl.* (*floruit*, 'flourished'). Usually an author has connections with some period, or at least with some century. When even this is speculative (?) has been added.

The maps (pp. x–xiii) have the primary aim of showing authors' nationalities and the centres where they worked. Maps should also enable the reader to identify most places mentioned in the book. In the text and commentary places are usually linked with some larger and better-known areas, so it should not be too difficult to locate them. Map 1 gives the eastern regions of the Mediterranean and Map 2 gives Asia in more detail. Map 3 shows the extent and provinces of the Roman Empire in the second century AD. In the Index map references are added to place-names.

I should like to thank the three general editors, Professor Leaney, Canon Packer and Professor Ackroyd, for much detailed and constructive criticism; also the staff of CUP for their insistence on trying to achieve clarity, accuracy and consistency in the presentation of so much fragmentary material.

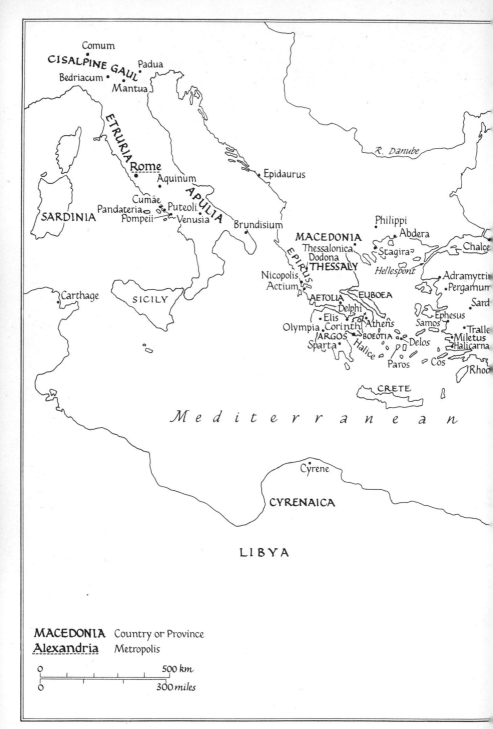

Comum
CISALPINE GAUL
Bedriacum
Padua
Mantua
ETRURIA
Rome
Aquinum
APULIA
Cumae
Pandateria
Puteoli
Pompeii
Venusia
Brundisium
SARDINIA
SICILY
Carthage
R. Danube
Epidaurus
Philippi
Abdera
MACEDONIA
Thessalonica
Stagira
Chalce
Dodona
Hellespont
THESSALY
EPIRUS
Nicopolis
Actium
Adramytti
Pergamum
AETOLIA
EUBOEA
Delphi
Sard
Elis
Athens
Ephesus
Olympia
Corinth
Samos
Tralle
ARGOS
BOEOTIA
Delos
Miletus
Sparta
Halice
Halicarna
Paros
Cos
Rho
CRETE
Mediterranean
Cyrene
CYRENAICA
LIBYA

**MACEDONIA**  Country or Province
<u>Alexandria</u>  Metropolis

0       500 km
0       300 miles

Map

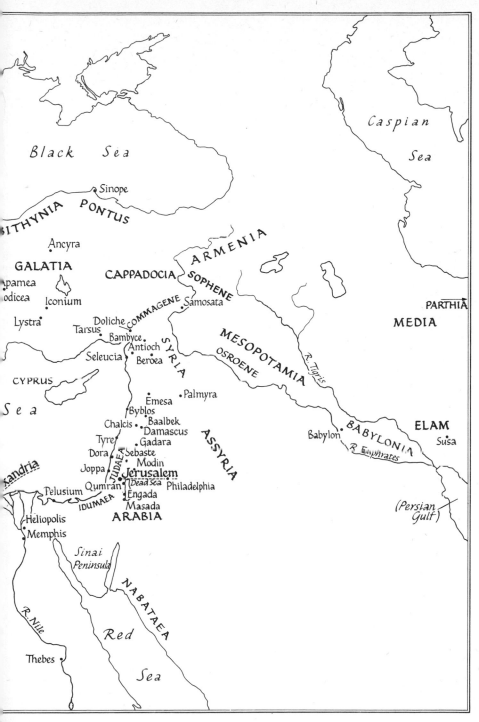

The Diaspora

Map 2    Asia Minor

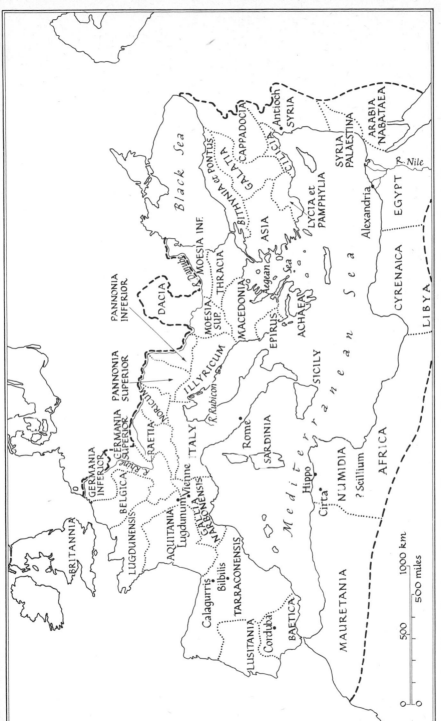

Map 3  Provinces of the Roman Empire AD 161 (Scillium was in Numidia, but its exact location is unknown)

# PART I

# Judaism

# Judaism

## Early History of the Jews

Some knowledge of Jewish history is necessary and the following brief sketch is given to put the Jews in perspective, not as they saw themselves, but as they and their history might appear, rightly or wrongly, to an outsider.

The Jews were a small and obscure Semitic people with legendary association with Egypt, which they left under the leadership of Moses, who in part at least devised their particular institutions. Jerusalem was built as their capital city and was a natural fortress. Later it became famous for its Temple. Tiny Judaea was continually harassed by its more powerful neighbours and eventually many of the inhabitants of the northern part of the land (by then a separate kingdom) were led into captivity by the Assyrians (721 BC). The Babylonians who succeeded the Assyrian empire carried out a similar deportation from the southern kingdom (597, 587). When the Persians took Babylon, some of the exiles were permitted to return (c. 538), although many remained and formed a permanent outpost of Judaism in Babylon or in Mesopotamia. Jerusalem was inhabited once more and the Temple and its worship restored.

The Persian rule lasted until 333 BC, when Alexander the Great led his forces from Macedon in Greece on a triumphant course as far as India to the east and Egypt to the southwest, absorbing and organizing the lands through which he passed into one vast empire. On his death in 323 this was partitioned among his generals, often known as the Diadochi (Successors). Egypt with Judaea fell to Ptolemy, the eastern part of the empire to Seleucus. For a time Judaea was a battleground between the rival Ptolemies and Seleucids until the decisive defeat of Ptolemy at Panion in 200 BC. When our period begins in 200 BC Judaea, under the rule of its high priest and aristocratic families often at odds among themselves, had come under the control of the Seleucids. Jewish religious institutions were respected, but in general the Seleucids pursued a policy of hellenization, trying to bring the benefits of Greek civilization to those whom they saw as backward peoples. This was

3

welcome to some Jews, who hankered after the delights of the gymnasium and theatre, but repugnant to traditionalists. Judaea itself suffered from intrigues among the dominant high-priestly families and their alignments with the rival powers of the Seleucids in Syria and the Ptolemies in Egypt.

One deposed high priest, Jason, drove the Seleucids out of Jerusalem but in 169 Antiochus IV Epiphanes regained the city, plundered the Temple and desecrated it by setting up an altar to Olympian Zeus on the altar of sacrifice. This led to the Maccabaean revolt in 168, started by Mattathias, a priest from Modin, and taking its name from one of his five sons, Judas, who was nicknamed Maccabaeus, perhaps meaning 'Hammer'. This dynasty is also called Hasmonaean after an ancestor of Mattathias. The Seleucids were divided among themselves, which facilitated the struggle of the rebel Maccabaeans. In fact the latter felt strong enough to send an embassy to the senate at Rome, which supported John Hyrcanus (high priest and virtual ruler 135–104) and his successors as a counterpoise against the Seleucids.

## Judaea in the Roman Period

Rome now enters the scene and something must be said of its previous history. (For a more detailed account see A. R. C. Leaney, *The Jewish and Christian World 200 BC to AD 200*, vol. 7 in this series.) Traditionally the small settlement on seven hills dated its foundation to 753 BC. Legendary kings had been succeeded by a republic. This was ruled by a senate of elders, patricians (i.e. of noble birth); there was also in course of time a popular assembly. Magistrates were elected annually, the chief being the two consuls, who acted each as a check upon the other. In times of national emergency a dictator with supreme power could be appointed for a limited period. Other magistrates, in ascending order of importance, all elected for one year only, were the aediles supervising the markets, the quaestors connected with the Treasury and the praetors dealing with legal affairs. Originally these magistracies were open only to patricians. The plebeians, common folk, had after much contention obtained the right to elect plebeian tribunes, who could veto any senatorial proposals. Intermediate between patricians and plebeians were the equites (knights), originally those who were sufficiently well off to supply and maintain a horse for military service. A young Roman who wanted a public career would perform some military service and pass through the various grades of magistracies (cursus honorum), culminating with the consulship and an influential voice in the senate. It was an admirably balanced constitution for a small city-state, for the class distinctions had gradually become less rigid.

Rome however was destined to become something more. Her influence and power were extended throughout the Italian peninsula. She came into conflict with the great African city of Carthage in the third century BC and narrowly survived an invasion by Hannibal. Then came a third Punic War and the complete destruction of Carthage in 145 BC. These wars had entailed contacts with Carthage's overseas allies. Consequently Rome found herself mistress in the first place of Sicily, an island containing old Greek colonies and Carthaginian outposts in the west, then of Greece proper. So magistrates, after their year of office in Rome, could now be sent abroad for a year to govern a province in a rapidly extending empire. It was not that Rome was deliberately following a policy of imperialism. Sometimes she was attacked and after subjugating the aggressors annexed their land as a province. Parthia was becoming a threat on the Empire's eastern frontiers so, after the collapse of the Seleucid dynasty, Rome took over Asia Minor and Syria. Client kingdoms were encouraged to act as buffer states on the Empire's borders, but could be treated as hostile and annexed if they were suspected of treacherous sympathies.

Such was the position of Judaea at this time, by now a small, virtually independent kingdom which had come under Roman protection. The Pharisees, as upholders of the Law, were becoming a recognizable group over against the wealthy aristocratic families, later to be known as Sadducees. There were internal squabbles over the succession to the priesthood, which led to an appeal to Pompey in 63 BC. This great Roman general had been sent by the senate to defeat Mithridates of Pontus, which he did in 66. Mithridates' ally, Tigranes I of Armenia, had also been involved and Pompey undertook mopping-up operations in Syria. Unfortunately for the Jews, Aristobulus, favoured by Pompey, started rebellious activities during the latter's absence. Thereupon Pompey besieged and took Jerusalem and entered the Temple, probably unaware how grievously he was affronting Jewish religious sensibilities. He did not loot the Temple, but to his great surprise he found no image there.

Pompey now organized an eastern settlement in which Judaea became part of the province of Syria. The high priest was to oversee the worship of the Temple, but had no political power, which was entrusted to an aristocratic council, the Sanhedrin. Pompey himself became increasingly involved in Roman politics. He and Julius Caesar and the wealthy Crassus formed the so-called First Triumvirate (three-man junta) to obtain military commands for themselves and opportunities for acquiring prestige and power. This affected Judaea in that Crassus became governor of Syria in 55 BC and in preparation for an ill-fated attack on Parthia despoiled the Temple of all its treasures.

In the following Civil Wars Caesar, returning from a triumphant conquest of Gaul, overcame Pompey (murdered on landing in Egypt in 48) and the last remnants of senatorial opposition. He was preparing for an expedition against Parthia when in 44 he was murdered by Brutus and Cassius and other conspirators, who saw in him a threat to the Republic. He was avenged by the Second Triumvirate, a coalition of a politician called Lepidus, Caesar's close friend and follower Mark Antony, and Octavian, then a mere youth, Caesar's great-nephew and adopted as his heir. Brutus and Cassius were defeated and met their death at Philippi in 42. Antony then took the East as his sphere and with his mistress, the Egyptian queen Cleopatra, formed grandiose schemes of conquest. In the clash with Octavian that followed they were defeated at Actium in 31, and in 30 committed suicide.

Octavian, given the title of Augustus in 27 BC, was now in full control, for Lepidus had been forced to retire into private life. The senate and the magistrates continued their administration at home and abroad, but the Emperor had overall charge of the army and finance and undertook responsibility for the government of provinces which by their situation and internal instability might offer particular dangers. To these, which included Syria, he nominated his own governors. Octavian and his successors always regarded Egypt as their own personal domain because its corn harvest was vital for supplying the populace at Rome; therefore control of this supply was an essential element in maintaining power. A period of peace and stability followed for the world at large with the beginning of the era of the Roman Empire.

During the Civil Wars Jewish contestants for power supported opposing parties, intrigued with Parthia and dexterously changed sides as occasion arose. By 37 BC Parthia had been defeated, a campaign in which the Roman forces had received considerable help from Herod, an Idumaean who aspired to become ruler of Judaea. He won the favour of Mark Antony and with Roman aid was able to besiege and capture Jerusalem. In this way he imposed himself as ruler, though without the support of the people in general and in the face of the antagonism of the great aristocratic families. When Antony's fortunes waned he had no scruples in abandoning him and supporting Octavian.

Herod's reign lasted from 37 to 4 BC. He enjoyed imperial favour and was particularly intimate with Marcus Agrippa, the son-in-law of Augustus and his most trusted lieutenant – hence the adoption of the surname Agrippa in the Herodian dynasty. Herod's private life with its domestic intrigues and murders was probably seen as typical of an oriental despot, but he presented the public image of a civilized hellenistic monarch, uninhibited by what was regarded as that odious Jewish exclusiveness. He made generous gifts to Greek cities and at home his building activities were prodigious. Besides various fortresses he rebuilt Samaria, henceforth called Sebaste (the Greek for Augusta), and Caesarea, the great coastal city which later became the Roman administrative capital. He tried to put down banditry and to ensure peace and stability. In spite of his patronage of many pagan buildings, he also tried to conciliate the Jews and to defer to their religious scruples; in particular, he rebuilt the Temple on a most magnificent scale, but counteracted this by having an eagle (emblem of the Roman army) carved over the gateway. Jewish protests led to cruel martyrdoms.

Herod's will divided his lands among three sons. Archelaus was to rule Judaea, Idumaea and Samaria, Antipas (the Herod of the Gospels) to be tetrarch of Galilee and Peraea and Philip to be tetrarch of Gaulanitis, Trachonitis, Batanaea and Panias in the north. Revolts broke out, some thoroughly nationalistic and against foreign rule of any sort, others against the hated Idumaean dynasty. Archelaus went to Rome and appealed for Roman support. Augustus through Varus, the legate of Syria, quelled this rebellion with great severity.

Archelaus ruled for ten years, but was both incompetent and cruel. Finally complaints to the Emperor led to his banishment. His kingdom was then put in the charge of a procurator, the Emperor's personal agent, subordinate to the governor of Syria, Quirinius. The latter held a census in AD 6 (cp. Luke 2:1–5), which provoked an armed protest by Judas of Galilee, chiefly on the religious grounds that a census was offensive to God. To the government such religious scruples must have been incomprehensible; for them this was just another outburst of Jewish turbulence fostered by superstition.

Antipas reigned until AD 39. His relationship with Rome was satisfactory until 37 when his brother-in-law Agrippa I, a favourite of the new Emperor Gaius (or Caius) (37–41), was given the territory of Philip who had died in 34. Intrigues followed, Antipas was banished and in 41 Agrippa became king of Judaea, under Roman suzerainty but once more a kingdom in itself. In the meantime, from AD 6 to 41 Judaea had been governed by a series of procurators of whom the one best known to us was Pontius Pilate. In provinces governed by the Emperor's own nominees it was not uncommon for a man to hold office for a long period. Pilate was in Judaea from 26 to 37, when complaints of misgovernment caused his recall to Rome, where the death of Tiberius in 37 prevented his being brought to trial.

The next Emperor Gaius (37–41), a megalomaniac, in retaliation for a Jewish attack on a Greek altar in Jamnia, ordered Petronius, legate of Syria, to arrange for the Emperor's own statue to be set up in the Temple at Jerusalem. Petronius reported to Gaius that this could only be done at the cost of terrible bloodshed. Agrippa as a personal friend of Gaius added his entreaties and Gaius actually rescinded the order. His assassination in 41 prevented further outrages.

His successor Claudius (41–54), on the death of Agrippa in 44, returned Judaea to rule under Roman procurators. These ruthlessly put down 'bandits', often like Theudas (Acts 5:36ff.) religious fanatics. There are sorry tales of bribery and disregard of Jewish religious scruples, although freedom of worship had long been guaranteed to all Jews throughout the Empire. Claudius wanted good government; in 52 he sent Cumanus (procurator 48–52) into exile. Felix (52–60) was recalled to Rome under Nero (54–68) and stood trial; he was acquitted, probably because of influence in high places.

Corrupt and inefficient government finally led to the First Jewish Revolt in AD 66. Other factors were religious fanaticism and nationalistic fervour. There were also opposing factions among the Jews themselves and terrible internecine strife. Rioting and minor pogroms took place in some neighbouring cities where the Jews lived on uneasy sufferance (cp. p. 86). The Roman legate in Syria was slow to take action and was defeated when he attacked Jerusalem. Nero then appointed Vespasian, an experienced and reputable general, who with his son Titus began his successful Jewish campaign. Meanwhile Nero in 68, when assailed by Galba, committed suicide. The so-called year of the Four Emperors followed in which Galba, Otho and Vitellius quickly succeeded one another by force of arms and finally Vespasian emerged as victor; he reigned until 79 and established the Flavian dynasty.

Tacitus' sketch of Jewish history begins at this point (see p. 16) when Vespasian, departing to assume imperial power at Rome, left his elder son Titus to finish off the Jewish war. Jerusalem was taken with fearful slaughter and the Temple was looted and destroyed. From now on Jews throughout the Roman world had to pay their annual Temple tax into a fund for the maintenance of the temple of Jupiter on the Capitol at Rome. Vespasian tried to rehabilitate Judaea by appointing good governors, founding cities and allowing the establishment of a seminary of rabbinic learning at Jamnia. High priest, the Temple sacrificial system and the Sanhedrin – all had gone.

Under Trajan (Emperor 98–117) there was unrest and some sporadic revolts among the Jews of the Diaspora from 115–17 (see p. 12), but no real evidence for similar activity in Judaea. In Judaea however, under Hadrian (Emperor 117–38), came the Second Jewish Revolt, 132–5. Hadrian was a great traveller, a great builder and restorer of buildings. He saw himself as bringing the civilizing benefits of the Roman way of life throughout the Empire. Most of his subjects saw him in the same light and accepted gratefully, but not the Jews. They were utterly opposed to the proposed rebuilding of Jerusalem as Aelia Capitolina, the plans for which included a pagan temple. The leader of the revolt was a Messianic pretender, Bar Kokhba, and he was supported by the famous rabbi Akiba. It was a guerilla war and its length shows that Rome found it difficult to suppress the rebels. Aelia Capitolina was now built as a Roman colony, complete with circus, baths, amphitheatre, theatre, temples of Jupiter and Hadrian. Jews were rigorously excluded, except on one day in the year when they were allowed in to conduct a ritual lamentation. Judaea ceased to be a danger to Roman rule.

### The Jews of the Diaspora

The foregoing has concentrated on the Jews of Judaea who, for the government, represented the Jewish nation, but the Jews of the Diaspora (Dispersion) were far more numerous. The first major dispersion of the Jews came with the Exile in 597 BC. When Jews were permitted to return to Jerusalem many preferred to remain in Babylon. These had their links with Jerusalem, the spiritual centre of the Jewish world, but otherwise were cut off. Academically Babylon became most important for Jewish scholarship and the study of the Law. The Jews there succeeded in accommodating themselves to their various rulers, even when the Jews of Judaea had perforce to support their Roman masters in the spasmodic conflicts with Parthia. Apart from this toleration of Judaism by the Babylonian authorities, we do not have sufficient evidence to assess the native viewpoint.

The extent of the Diaspora at the beginning of our era is attested by Acts 2:9–11: 'Parthians, Medes, Elamites; inhabitants of Mesopotamia, of Judaea and Cappadocia, of Pontus and Asia [our Asia Minor], of Phrygia and Pamphylia, of Egypt and the districts of Libya around Cyrene; visitors from Rome, both Jews and proselytes, Cretans and

Arabs.' The contemporary Philo (p. 35) in his *Legatio ad Gajum* (*Leg. Gaj.*), 281–2, gives more detail: 'Egypt, Phoenicia and Syria, Pamphylia, Cilicia, most of Asia as far as Bithynia and remote corners of Pontus; and similarly in Europe, Thessaly, Boeotia, Macedonia, Aetolia, Attica, Argos, Corinth and most of the Peloponnese. Islands also contain colonies, e.g. Euboea, Cyprus, Crete. I say nothing about the regions beyond the Euphrates.' Nor does Philo mention Rome; perhaps he took knowledge of its Jewish community for granted. The infiltration into the Mediterranean world is impressive. Jews would also find their way into such Romanized western provinces as Gallia Narbonensis (southern France) and Spain.

In the ancient world citizenship was a jealously guarded privilege. The Greek city-states and their colonies (around the Black Sea, on the coastal fringe of Asia Minor, the Aegean islands, Sicily and southern Italy) followed a certain pattern. Each was totally independent, a law unto itself. Its citizens had political privileges and obligations dependent on its constitution, whether oligarchic or democratic. Trading communities such as Athens welcomed foreigners to keep up business links. There was even a technical term *metics* for resident aliens. These were subject to clearly defined conditions and liable to special taxes, but their own rights were safeguarded. When these cities became units in a much larger empire they lost their complete independence, being under the control of a governor, but retained their own form of municipal administration. The Jews ranked as *metics* and, as such, had their rights, the most important of which for them was their freedom of worship. In some cases these rights were infringed but, from the time of Julius Caesar, Rome by a series of enactments confirmed certain rights for all Jews (see pp. 92ff.). There is archaeological evidence for many synagogues. Paul's missionary journeys, as described in Acts, took in cities and towns where there were Jewish communities and synagogues, in some of which the Jews were quite influential (e.g. Pisidian Antioch 13:50, Iconium 14:5, Thessalonica 17:5–9, Corinth 18:12–17). One gets a general impression that the Jews were a recognized part of the community and eager to show their loyalty to Rome, even if only to get an advantage over the Christians – perhaps a prejudiced imputation.

Elsewhere, in Egypt there was constant immigration, as Judaea was so near a neighbour, particularly into the great city of Alexandria, founded by Alexander in 332 BC. Here according to the pattern usual in Greek cities the Jews were numerous enough to form a *politeuma*, a corporate body of resident aliens with their own rights. There was some inter-racial feeling, for Egyptian Jews helped the Roman invaders in 55 and 48 BC, but it is only in the period of Roman rule that there is evidence of positive acts of hostility. One of the five 'quarters' of the city was called Jewish and they were a privileged community by comparison with the native Egyptian population. Augustus however introduced a capitation tax to which all non-Greeks were liable, so that in this respect Jews and the despised native peasantry were on the same level. Ill-feeling seems to have arisen because some Jews tried to worm their way into the *ephebate*, an organization for the education and athletic training of Greek youths, partly to enjoy its facilities, partly to be ranked as Greek citizens and so escape payment of the capitation tax.

Matters came to a head in AD 38 when Flaccus, the prefect appointed by Tiberius in 32, fearing deposition by the new emperor Gaius, accepted Greek support in exchange for the 'surrender' of the hated Jews. Philo in his *Against Flaccus* (*Flacc.*) and *Legatio ad Gajum* (*Leg. Gaj.*) gives a detailed account of the whole affair, in which the Alexandrian mockery of Agrippa I (p. 7) who had briefly passed through the city, was followed by riots. Flaccus was persuaded to declare that the Jews were aliens, devoid of any citizen rights at all. This led to a long and bloody pogrom. Eventually Flaccus was arrested and sent to Rome and the new Emperor Claudius in 41 explicitly re-affirmed Jewish rights, while recommending to both parties a policy of 'live and let live' (p. 99). Hostilities still smouldered and in 115 for no clearly known cause the Jews staged a rebellion, primarily against the Greeks. This was completely suppressed by the Romans in 119 and for the rest of our period no more is heard.

In another notable city, Antioch, founded in Syria by Seleucus I in 330 BC, the position of the Jews was politically the same as in the parallel Greek foundation of Alexandria. By the first century AD the Jewish community there was one of the largest in the Diaspora, to be classed along with those in Alexandria and Rome. The Jews prospered and their numbers were swelled not only by immigrants but by proselytes. There was also a Christian community (Acts 11: 19ff.), whom the Greeks may have confused with the Jews. In AD 67 an apostate Jew, Antiochus, then holding a magistracy, denounced his own father and some other Jews for plotting to set fire to the city – reminiscent of the charge brought against the Christians in Rome in AD 64 (p. 147). Lynch law followed. Some Jews were forced to offer pagan sacrifices and sabbath-observance was prohibited. This last was an illegal prohibition, but the government was preoccupied with the First Jewish Revolt. In the winter of 70/71 a great fire actually did break out. The Greeks readily believed Antiochus' renewed accusations of the Jews and were prepared for immediate reprisals, but the governor intervened and held an enquiry which completely exonerated the Jews. None the less at the end of the Jewish War the Antiochenes petitioned Titus against them, but he confirmed for the Jews the rights guaranteed to all the Jews of the Diaspora.

A third important city affected by the war of AD 66–70 was Cyrene, an old Greek colony and trading centre on the north African coast, where there had long been a sizeable Jewish community (cp. Acts 11:20). Refugees from Judaea enlisted support from the poorer Jews for rebellion against Rome. The more prosperous remained loyal, but false informers in collusion (so at least Josephus alleges) with the Roman governor, came forward and many wealthy Jews were executed and their property confiscated. Later government enquiry proved their innocence, but resentment continued. It was in Cyrenaica that the rebellions of 115–17 (distinct from the Judaean Second Jewish Revolt of 132–5) began. There had been instances of bloody massacres in Syrian cities in the troubled times of the Jewish Wars, but the worst example is to be found in the revolt of 115–17 in Cyprus. Here exceptionally large numbers of Greeks were killed with the utmost cruelty.

These instances of virulent inter-racial hatred have been found in regions close to Judaea itself, regions with a largish Jewish population, where Jews and Greeks alike were provocative and, given the opportunity, massacred their opponents pitilessly. It is a relief to turn to Rome from where, geographically, Judaea was so far away as to seem only one of the many small countries on the outskirts of the Empire and where the Jews were seen as one of the Semitic peoples. The Romans were not given to colour-prejudice. It is noteworthy that the physical features of the Jews, apart from circumcision which was superimposed, are not described. A swarthy complexion would not be enough to distinguish the Jews from other Semitic immigrants who were continually flocking into Rome. As early as 139 BC they were banished for proselytizing, but must have returned. Similar edicts followed under the Empire, but were never of more than temporary effect.

Pompey's conquest of Judaea in 63 BC brought a host of Jews on the market as slaves. Again hundreds of Jewish captives were led in Titus' Triumph in AD 71, to be sold, though many would later get their freedom. This marked a nadir of the Jewish reputation in Rome. Along with the captives the golden candelabrum and other Temple furniture and much booty as well were part of the triumphal procession. The Arch of Titus with its carvings depicting the procession was a constant reminder of the Jewish humiliation, as also another arch, no longer extant, erected in the Circus Maximus in 80. Coins too were struck, a series from 71, generally showing a Jewess sitting under a palm tree and the inscription 'Judaea captured'; on the other side there is often a Jew with his hands tied behind his back or a Roman soldier on guard leaning on his spear.

On the lowest level some Jews were seen as dirty, beggars, squatters, telling fortunes and cheating silly women. In Rome itself they were seen as exciting riots; abroad they had dared to flout Roman authority and caused much bloodshed. Their plight showed how little they were actually favoured by their God, though they despised traditional religion. Their circumcision was abhorrent and their anti-social habits an affront. Yet, distinct from these imported captives, there were the Jewish families who had been settled in Rome for many generations. Their religion was legal, their sabbath–observance taken for granted. Catacombs, the earliest at Monteverde going back to the first century BC, are evidence of this Jewish presence. Most of the burials have no memorial and many of the epitaphs are cheaply executed and illiterate, which illustrates the poverty and low social status of the Jews. However, later in the period there are a few painted tomb-chambers still extant and epitaphs of good workmanship, so some Jews must have been affluent. An increase in the number of catacombs shows that there was a marked increase in the number of Jews in Rome in the second century AD.

To pagan neighbours the synagogues would be the normal sign of a Jewish residential quarter. Epitaphs giving the name of the synagogue to which the dead belonged show that this practice of differentiating the synagogues by giving them individual names began under Augustus. These buildings were different from pagan temples; they were places for educational and administrative purposes, for gathering to worship on the sabbath, but without priests, without images, without any of the apparatus of a sacrificial cult. Jewish habits might seem peculiar, but in Rome they had no aspirations as a corporate body to Roman citizenship with all its privileges nor did they offer any serious economic threat, so they could be tolerated as one among the many oriental superstitions.

## Attitudes Towards the Jews in General

The Jews saw themselves in a very different light, as a special people, God's own chosen race, set apart from the rest of mankind by their unique knowledge of the one true God and by customs and a morality that were divinely inspired. They were proudly conscious of tracing their origins to a distant antiquity, of a long and well-documented history, of a great literature compiled by poets, historians and prophets. Their difficulty lay in persuading the rest of the world to accept them at their own valuation.

First and foremost in our period was the difficulty of the language barrier. The Jews spoke in Aramaic, the common language of Palestine and the eastern regions beyond. The Greeks, for all their curiosity to explore and colonize, were not interested in learning foreign languages; all foreigners were barbarians, uncivilized by comparison with themselves. When Alexander the Great (d. 323 BC) made his conquering way even as far as India, founding cities as outposts of Greek civilization as he went, the settlers spoke Greek. This became the *Koine*, i.e. 'the common tongue', a rather simpler development of classical Greek, lacking its richness of vocabulary and the niceties of construction which gave it such elegance and flexibility. Anybody speaking the *Koine* could make himself easily understood in all the eastern Mediterranean and it was the administrative language for Alexander's empire when partitioned between his generals after his death. For Jews of the Diaspora in these parts it would be their everyday language, so that the Hebrew scriptures were gradually translated into the Greek Septuagint for their use. The Romans too saw no necessity to learn the languages of the various subject peoples who kept on coming under their sway. They could easily cope with the *Koine* in the lands where it was used, for educated Romans had Greek tutors from an early age, while subordinates could pick up enough knowledge of it for practical purposes without too much difficulty.

Granted that in time language no longer presented an insuperable barrier, there was little inducement for the non-Jew to visit Judaea with its reputation for banditry, even when the relative peace and stability of the Empire facilitated communications, unless he was a determined sightseer. Merchants used the coastal ports, but had no need to visit the hinterland or make the toilsome journey up to Jerusalem. Nor was it much easier to make contact with Jews elsewhere, as their exclusiveness prevented table-fellowship and all except the most liberal refused to take part in the many pagan festivities and holidays.

The Jewish scriptures became accessible in Greek, but such a vast and amorphous collection of books must have daunted all but devoted scholars. Only towards the end of our period is there some knowledge of them in an academic context. It was not until the Christians, claiming the Old Testament as their own inheritance, began to ransack it for Messianic proof-texts that more general interest was aroused.

How was it then that Judaism attracted sympathizers, some even becoming full proselytes and submitting to circumcision, though most remained on the fringe? For one thing, the Jews were most fervent proselytizers, which in itself accounts for much. For another thing, the synagogues were there for all to see, visible witness to the reality of Jewish worship, a focus for the community. It was clear too that the Jews had a happy and closely-knit family life, never following the pagan practice of exposing unwanted children at birth. If they were true to their own moral code (not all would be of course), they must have shone out in an environment so often corrupt and libertine. On the intellectual side their monotheism and rejection of images attracted respect. In fact many of the attractive features of Christianity were already to be found in Judaism and had brought in those Judaizers who were on the fringe and who later whole-heartedly embraced Christianity. Yet our literary evidence, while recording the growth of proselytism, does not give reasons for it. There are no pagan converts to Judaism who provide a reasoned explanation for their conversion as the Christian apologists have done. The proselytes would be a small minority by comparison with the speedily growing numbers of Christians, but their existence is not to be forgotten.

The extant references to Judaism in pagan writers are conditioned by the date and background of the authors and must be seen in the context from which they are quoted. Except for literature inspired by Alexandria, where there was a political motive for hatred of the Jews, we have no work which was written with the deliberate intention of traducing Judaism. Even Tacitus, much though he disliked and despised the Jews, tried to write with the objectivity which was his avowed aim as a historian (*Ann.* 1.1.6). As for the government, Judaism satisfied the criteria that a foreign religion must be neither politically dangerous nor morally unacceptable. It had legal status and the Jews even had certain exceptional privileges to enable them to perform their religious obligations. Rome had fine ideals of justice and impartiality; mis-government was due to the obtuseness, greed and corruption of individuals, which would have been practised in any situation, rather than to reasoned anti-Jewish prejudice.

Outstanding among Latin sources are Tacitus' sketch of the Jews and Juvenal's incidental references to the Jews in a social context. These are given here first, in their entirety. After them quotations are given under sectional headings for convenience of reference:

TACITUS (Cornelius), the great Roman historian, dates and parentage unknown, was probably born about AD 56, of Gallic or north Italian stock. He became well known as a successful advocate and passed through the usual stages of a political career; he was consul in 97 and proconsul of the province of Asia, probably in 112/113. It is clear from the letters of the Younger Pliny (p. 149) that they were friends and moved in the same literary and political circles. Apart from the considerable value of his works as history, he is noted for his style, which is brilliant and terse, his vivid descriptions, his genius for summing up a situation or a character in one telling epigrammatic phrase. He makes compulsive reading.

His works include three monographs: the *Dialogus*, a discussion on the decline of Roman oratory; *Germania*, an ethnographical treatise describing the tribes north and south of the Rhine and the Danube; *Agricola*, a biography of his father-in-law, best known for his conquests in Britain. These two latter were both published in 98.

His two major historical works were the *Histories* (*Hist.*) and the *Annals* (*Ann.*). The former begins with AD 69, the year of the Four Emperors, and presumably ended with the assassination of Domitian in 96, but we possess only the first four books and twenty-six chapters of the fifth. Book 5, introducing the events of the year 70, opens with Titus' assumption of the command in the Jewish War. Tacitus starts with a sketch of the Jewish people, their origin, laws, rites, country, Jerusalem, history, breaking off at the siege of Jerusalem to pass on to events elsewhere in the same year. He does not name his authorities. For historical facts he could rely on public records, and the Jewish War had happened within living memory, which probably contributed towards his anti-Jewish prejudices. For his account of their religion and life and thought and other aspects it is likely that he relied on Alexandrian sources, possibly Apion (p. 53). The gross errors combined with a certain amount of genuine knowledge show what a distorted view could prevail even in educated circles.

The *Annals* started with the end of Augustus' reign, AD 14. We know of sixteen books, though parts of Books 5 and 6 and the whole of Books 7 and 10 are missing and the work breaks off at 16.35, in AD 65 before the death of Nero. So Tacitus' account of the outbreak of the Jewish War is lost to us. His main concern is inevitably with the imperial government at Rome and it is in this connection that he refers to Tiberius' expulsion of the Jews in AD 19 (p. 103) and Nero's persecution of the Christians after the Great Fire of Rome in AD 64 (p. 148).

Tacitus *Hist.* 5.1–13

¶ At the beginning of the same year [AD 70], Titus[1] Caesar was chosen by his father to subjugate Judaea. When both were of private standing,[2] he was renowned as a soldier and then began to proceed with enhanced energy and reputation, for the armies and provinces vied with one another in their enthusiasm. He himself, that he might not be thought to depend on his good fortune, carried out his military duties properly and promptly. By his friendliness and affability he won men's hearts to his service and among working parties and on the march he often mixed with the common soldiers while preserving intact the respect due to a general. Three legions awaited him in Judaea, the fifth and the tenth and fifteenth, old soldiers of Vespasian. He added the twelfth from Syria and the twenty-second and the third detached from Alexandria. Twenty allied cohorts accompanied him, eight squadrons of cavalry, also the kings Agrippa and Sohaemus and the auxiliaries of king Antiochus[3] and a strong corps of Arabs hostile to the Jews because of the hatred that is usual between neighbours.[4] There were many who had come from the city [i.e. Rome] and Italy, each with his own hopes of ingratiating himself with the prince while the latter's affections were still disengaged. With these forces he entered the enemy's territory in marching order, reconnoitring all the terrain and ready to engage, and encamped not far from Jerusalem.

1. Vespasian, who had been appointed by Nero to crush the Jewish rebellion, after the death of Nero and the ensuing disorder had handed

over his command to his elder son *Titus*. He himself returned to crush
Vitellius and seize imperial power (*Hist.* 4.51). Now Tacitus returns
to the subject of the Jewish campaign. The Romans were already in
control of most of the country, but clearly felt that increased forces
were necessary against such a stronghold as Jerusalem and such fanatical
foes as the Jews, cp. *Hist.* 2.4: 'Vespasian had brought the Jewish War
to an end, except that Jerusalem remained to be besieged, a task more
laborious and difficult because of the nature of the mountain and the
obstinacy of its superstitious defenders than that the besieged had
sufficient strength left to endure the necessities of a siege.'

2. *private standing*: this is in contrast to their later imperial rank.

3. *Agrippa*, AD 27 to before 93 (cp. Acts 25–6), was the son of Herod
Agrippa I, 10 BC–AD 44 (cp. Acts 12). He was king of Chalcis (Map
1) and had been given the supervision of the Temple. His sister Berenice
was the mistress of Titus and naturally he backed the Romans. *Sohaemus*
was king of Sophene and Emesa (Map 1), *Antiochus* was king of
Commagene (Map 1), both client kings of Rome.

4. We learn from Josephus, *War* 3.4.2. (68), that the *Arabs*, sent by
the Nabataean king Malchus, comprised five thousand infantry and one
thousand cavalry.

¶ But since we are about to describe the last days of a famous city, it
seems fitting to relate its origins.[1]

There is a story that the Jews fleeing from Crete settled on the
furthest edge of Libya,[2] at the time when Saturn was forcibly expelled
by Jupiter and left his realm.[3] Proof is drawn from the name, on the
grounds that there is in Crete the famous Mount Ida, and the Idaean
inhabitants, their name barbarously lengthened, came to be called
Judaean. Some say that in the reign of Isis[4] a throng overflowed Egypt
and were sent off under the leadership of Hierosolymus and Juda into
neighbouring lands.[5] Several take them to be descended from Ethiopians
who in the reign of Cepheus were driven by fear and hate to change
their abode.[6] Some relate that Assyrian wanderers, people in want of
land, gained possession of part of Egypt and soon colonized cities of
their own and Hebrew lands and the regions nearer to Syria.[7] Others
assign to the Jews an illustrious origin, that the Solymi, a people
celebrated through Homer's poems,[8] founded the city and called it
Hierosolyma from their own name.[9]

1. It was usual for historians to preface an account of some important war by such a sketch of the people against whom it was to be waged and the fact that Tacitus devotes so much space to this account of a small obscure nation shows how dangerous a foe they had now become. He cites no authorities for the differing stories of the origin of Jerusalem, but leaves his readers to choose the one they think most credible.

2. Tacitus is the only authority for this story of a Cretan origin, which may have arisen from confusing Jews with Philistines, who do seem to have had some connection with Crete, cp. Amos 9:7, 'Philistines from Caphtor [Crete]'.

3. The Romans identified the supreme Greek god, Zeus, and his father, Kronos, with their own *Jupiter* and *Saturnus*.

4. *Isis* (pp. 248ff.) was the great Egyptian goddess around whom many myths had clustered.

5. Some such story seems to have been known to Plutarch (p. 72) who, in *On Isis and Osiris* 31, wrote: 'Those who tell that after the battle Typhon mounted on an ass fled for seven days and after reaching safety begot sons, Hierosolymus and Judaeus, are obviously dragging Jewish history into the story.' Tacitus may have derived his information from the Egyptian priests, who supplied him with details about the cult of Serapis (*Hist.* 4.83).

6. The origin of this story is unknown. In Greek mythology *Cepheus* was the father of Andromeda, whose deliverance from the dragon slain by Perseus was associated with Joppa, so this story may be a Phoenician myth.

7. The nomadic and Assyrian connections are vaguely reminiscent of Manetho (p. 38) and Nicolaus (p. 47).

8. For the Greeks and Romans any link with Homer conferred distinction, although the *Solymi* were only mentioned cursorily, twice with the stock epithet 'renowned' as a fabulous people on the borders of Lycia (*Il.* 4.184), once in connection with their mountains (*Od.* 4.282).

9. In the Septuagint *Jerusalem* (transliterated and indeclinable) is the usual form, but *Hierosolyma* became frequent both in Greek and Latin, being interpreted as 'Holy place (or Temple) of the Solymi'. The conventional translation *Jerusalem* will be found in the rest of this book.

¶ Most authors agree that when a wasting and disfiguring plague swept over Egypt king Bocchoris[1] approached the oracle of Ammon in search of a remedy and was commanded to purify the kingdom and drive away that group of men to other lands, as they were hated by the gods.

So the host was sought out and assembled together and left in the desert. The rest were spiritless and in tears, but Moyses, one of the exiles,[2] warned them not to expect any help of gods or men, as they had been deserted by both, but to trust in themselves, under the divine guidance by the aid of which they would have first rid themselves of their present miseries. They consented and in complete ignorance set out on their hazardous journey. Nothing harassed them as much as scarcity of water. Already not far from death they were sprawling all over the desert, when a troop of wild asses returning from pasture withdrew towards a rock shaded by a thicket. Moyses followed and guessing from grassy soil opened up abundant springs of water.[3] That was a relief and after journeying for six days without a break they drove out the inhabitants and took possession of lands in which a city and a temple were dedicated.

    1.  This story about *Bocchoris*, who was a historical king in the eighth century BC, was known to Lysimachus (p. 45), who particularized the pollution as due to leprosy and scurvy. Leprosy and other physical disabilities figure in most accounts, e.g. Apion (p. 54), 'Moses led forth the lepers and the blind and the lame.'
    2.  Manetho (p. 42) made their leader an Egyptian priest called Osariph. Chaeremon (p. 53) named the Egyptians Tithisen and Peteseph, whose names when they became leaders of the exiles were Moses and Joseph, and briefly described a journey without food through the Arabian desert.
    3.  Plutarch (p. 78) argued that perhaps the Jews abstain from pork because they revere the pig, 'just as they honour the ass which showed them the spring of water'.

¶ Moyses, in order to strengthen the people's loyalty towards himself for the future, gave them new rites, contrary to those of the rest of mankind.[1] With them all is profane that among us is sacred. Again, acts with them are permissible that for us are incestuous. They dedicated in their inmost shrine an image of the animal by whose guidance they had escaped from their wanderings and their thirst,[2] and slay a ram as if in mockery of Hammon.[3] The bull too is sacrificed because the Egyptians worship Apis.[4] They abstain from eating pork, thanks to the disaster of their previous disfigurement by scabies to which that animal is subject.[5] By frequent fasts[6] they still bear witness to their long former famine and retain unleavened bread[7] in token of the grain which they plundered. They say that a rest was instituted on the seventh day because that brought an end to their labours;[8] then because of the pleasures of idleness the seventh year was also given to indolence. Others say that it is held in honour of Saturn,[9] either because the Idaeans, traditionally banished with Saturn, and the founding fathers of the race, transmitted their religion; or because out of the seven stars by which mortals are ruled the star of Saturn moves in the highest orbit and is outstandingly powerful and most of the heavenly bodies complete their way and their course in periods of seven apiece.

1. Tacitus goes on to describe the rites and social customs of the Jews. These epigrammatic generalizations are followed by more specific accusations in the next chapter, but he does not particularize his charges of incest.

2. Mnaseas (p. 106), Posidonius (p. 107) and Apollonius Molo (p. 107), knew the story that the Temple contained the head of an ass.

3. *Hammon*: this god was usually represented in human form, like Zeus with whom the Greeks equated him, but with curling ram's horns.

4. *Apis*: this was a sacred bull.

5. Plutarch (p. 79), *Quaest. Conv.* 4.5 (2), attributes abstention from *pork* to purely hygienic reasons, for fear of contracting leprosy: 'The Jews apparently abominate pork because barbarians are particularly disgusted by white scales and leprous diseases and think that such diseases ravage men by contact. We see that the underbelly of every pig is full of leprous scales and scurfy eruptions.'

6. *Fasts*: these were prescribed by Mosaic Law only for the Day of Atonement (Lev. 16:29–31; Num. 29:7), but by Tacitus' time had multiplied. The Pharisees fasted twice a week (Luke 18:12). In Rome some believed that the Jews kept the sabbath as a fast, for the Emperor Augustus (p. 70) in a letter refers playfully to a 'sabbath fast' and the poet Martial (p. 70) mentions 'the stench of women keeping fast on the sabbath'.

7. *Unleavened bread*: this is mentioned here for the first time by a pagan writer. Tacitus' explanation seems to be pure conjecture; actually, unleavened bread was eaten by Jews at the Passover in memory of the haste with which they left Egypt (Exod. 12:15; Lev. 23:6).

8. *a rest*: Pompeius Trogus (p. 49) knew this explanation of the sabbath and also associated fasting with it, 36.2.14: 'they hallowed the

seventh day, habitually called sabbath by that nation, by a fast for all time to come. This was because that day had put an end to their fasting and wandering.'

9. *Saturn*: division of the month into seven-day periods named after the planets was becoming current even in the first century BC: e.g. Tibullus (p. 65), 1.3.18: 'I alleged...that the day held sacred to Saturn had held me back' (i.e. the sabbath as a day preventing activity). Dio Cassius (p. 69) also identified the two, *Epitome* 65.7.2: 'So perished Jerusalem on the very day of Saturn, which the Jews even now revere more than any other day.'

¶ These rites, however they were introduced, have the defence of antiquity. The rest of their customs, evil and disgusting, have gained ground from their depravity. For all the riff-raff[1] who scorned their native religions used to bring to them their tribute and their offerings; as a result the fortunes of the Jews prospered, also because among themselves there is unswerving loyalty, ready compassion, but hostility and hatred towards all others. Eating apart, sleeping separately, though a people most prone to lechery, they abstain from sexual relations with women of another race;[2] among themselves nothing is banned. They have instituted circumcision of the genitals, in order to be recognized by the difference.[3] Converts to their customs observe the same practice. The first thing they learn is to scorn the gods, to cast off their native country, to hold cheap fathers, children, brothers.[4] Yet they take measures for the increase of the population.[5] For it is criminal to kill any of their children and they think the souls of those killed by battle or torture are immortal. Hence their passion for procreation and their contempt of death.[6]

1. *riff-raff*: Tacitus refers contemptuously to the proselytes who, like the Jews themselves, used to pay the yearly contribution towards the upkeep of the Temple.

2. The exclusiveness of the Jews had always led to anti-Jewish comment, but the charge of *lechery* is new.

3. *circumcision*: by now this had become commonplace (pp. 80–5) as a distinguishing feature of Judaism.

4. *hold cheap fathers* etc.: this is Tacitus' rhetorical way of emphasizing that the proselyte cut himself off from contact with all non-Jews and abandoned even family ties.

5. *population*: Hecataeus (p. 38) also recognized the Jews' care for

their children: 'He obliged the inhabitants to rear their children and, as infants were reared at little expense, the Jewish people was always rich in manpower.'

6. On the contrary, the Greeks and Romans were in the habit of exposing their unwanted children at birth and no stigma was attached to the practice. It is doubtful whether at the time of Tacitus this belief in the immortality of the souls of such victims (cp. 2 Macc. 7) was held by the Jewish people at large.

¶ They bury corpses in Egyptian fashion[1] rather than cremate them and take the same care of the dead and have the same beliefs about the underworld, the opposite about the heavenly beings. The Egyptians worship many animals and images combining human and animal forms. The Jews with the mind alone conceive a single divinity and think those impious who with perishable materials fashion images of the gods in the likeness of men;[2] that supreme being is eternal, inimitable and imperishable. Therefore they allow no statues in their cities, much less in their temples. This compliment is not accorded to kings nor honour to the Emperor.[3] But because their priests used to make music with flutes and tambourines and were wreathed with ivy, and a golden vine was found in the Temple, some have thought that father Liber,[4] conqueror of the East, was worshipped, though the cults are not at all similar. Liber in fact instituted festive and joyous rites, the practices of the Jews are bizarre and sordid.

1. *Egyptian fashion*: the Jews did wrap up corpses in linen and spices, but did not mummify them.

2. *single divinity*: with all his misconceptions of Judaism Tacitus does clearly recognize their monotheism and the absence of images in their worship. He is not necessarily contradicting his previous statement that an ass's head was to be found in the inmost shrine; for this could have been a token of gratitude, not an object of worship.

3. *honour to the Emperor*: the Jews offered sacrifices for the Emperor, but not to either those dead Emperors who had been deified or the *genius* of the living Emperor (pp. 121, 209). They had been tacitly allowed this licence by law, as part of their religion, but it could be seen in some quarters as disaffection and was liable to rouse prejudice among the local populace and authorities. For the Christians, a positive refusal to sacrifice could lead to persecution (p. 151).

4. *Liber* was the Roman god identified with the Greek Bacchus or

Dionysus, whose worship was widely spread over the Graeco-Roman world. Plutarch (p. 72), *Quaest. Conviv.* 4.6.2, treats the subject in some detail (p. 127). Jewish priests were not wreathed, but he associates the ivy with the booths at the Feast of Tabernacles, which immediately followed the vintage.

¶ The country and territory eastward are bounded by Arabia; on the south lies Egypt; on the west are the Phoenicians and the sea; to the north there is a far view on the Syrian side. The men are healthy and can stand hard work. Rains are rare, the soil fertile. The crops are of the same kinds as ours, but as well as these there are balsam and palms. The palm trees are tall and graceful. The balsam is a smallish shrub. Each branch when it is swollen is opened by a bit of stone or pot; if a knife is applied, the veins suffer shock from its violence. The sap is used medicinally.[1] Chief of the mountains rises Libanus which, strange to tell, in such great heat is shady and faithful to its snows. The same mountain feeds and pours forth into the River Jordan. The Jordan does not enter the sea, but after flowing through one lake and then another without losing its identity is absorbed by a third. This lake of an immense circumference, in appearance like the sea, in taste more salty, is injurious to the inhabitants because of the fetidness of its smell. It is neither ruffled by winds nor does it tolerate fish or water-fowl. Its stagnant waters support anything thrown on them, as if on dry ground. Swimmers and non-swimmers are buoyed up alike. At a certain time of year it produces bitumen. As with other skills, experience has taught how to gather it. Of its own nature it is a black liquid and, if vinegar is sprinkled on, it solidifies and floats. Those engaged in the business catch this in their hand and draw it onto the deck of the boat; after that without any assistance it flows in and loads, until you cut it off. You could not cut it with either bronze or iron; it shrinks from gore and clothing stained with the blood of women's menstruation. So ancient authors say. But those who know the locality tell that the floating clots of bitumen are in motion and are drawn by hand to the shore; soon, when they have dried because of the heat of the ground and the strength of the sun, they are split with axes and wedges like trees or stones.

1. *balsam*: this was highly valued for its fragrance and healing qualities. The Romans thought that only Palestine and Arabia produced it. As it was so profitable, the Roman government had taken over the business of producing the shrub, cp. Elder Pliny (p. 120), *NH* 12.113.

¶ Not far away are plains which they say were once fertile, peopled with great cities.[1] These were struck by lightning and consumed by fire; traces remain and the ground itself looks dried up and has lost its productive power. For all plants, both the self-sown and those sown by hand, whether they have grown up as far as the blade or flower or up to their normal size, are black and empty and vanish into ashes. For my part, while conceding that cities once famous have gone up in flames through fire from heaven,[2] I think that the ground is infected by the exhalation of the lake, that the atmosphere which spreads over it is tainted and for this reason produce of grain and fruit putrefies, since soil and air are equally noxious. Another river, the Belus,[3] flows into the Judaean sea. Around its mouth sand is gathered, mixed with nitre and baked to make glass. There is a smallish extent of shore and yet it has not been exhausted by extraction.

1. *cities*: there had been five according to Gen. 14:2, thirteen according to Strabo 16, p. 764.

2. *fire from heaven*: cp. Gen. 19:24: 'and then the LORD rained down fire and brimstone from the skies on Sodom and Gomorrah. He overthrew those cities and destroyed all the Plain, with everyone living there and everything growing in the ground.'

3. *Belus*: Tacitus refers to the river, also called Naman, which flows into the Mediterranean Sea in northwest Judaea, near Ptolemais. Two rivers, Arnon and Zered, flow into the Dead Sea.

¶ A large part of Judaea is peopled by scattered villages; they have towns too. Jerusalem is the capital of the race. There was an immensely wealthy temple there, the city with the first fortifications, then the palace, the Temple with the inmost encirclement. Only a Jew could approach the doors; with the exception of the priests, they were debarred from passing the threshold.[1] While the East was under the dominion of the Assyrians and Medes and Persians, they were the most despised of the enslaved peoples. After the Macedonians gained power,[2] king Antiochus[3] tried to eradicate superstition and impose Greek customs, but was prevented by the Parthian War from changing a most abominable people for the better; for at that time Arsaces had revolted.[4] Then the Jews, as the Macedonians were weak and the Parthians had not yet reached their full strength (and the Romans were far away), appointed their own kings. Driven out because of the fickleness of the mob these regained their power by force of arms.[5] They exiled citizens, destroyed cities, slew brothers, wives, parents and committed other crimes usual among kings. But they fostered the superstition, because they claimed for themselves the honour of the priesthood in order to strengthen their power.

1. *threshold*: Luke 1:8–10 distinguishes between Zechariah (the priest) and the people waiting outside.

2. *Macedonians*: after the death of Alexander in 323, the Seleucid dynasty, beginning with the Macedonian general Seleucus, ruled Palestine (see pp. 3–5).

3. *Antiochus*: this was the infamous Antiochus IV (Epiphanes), who died in 164 BC.

4. *Arsaces*: Tacitus here seems to have confused Antiochus IV with his predecessor Antiochus II, for the revolt of Arsaces took place in 250 or 256 BC.

5. *mob*: this is hardly true. It was internal dissension, not popular rebellion, which caused the fall of the Maccabaean dynasty and the rise of the Herods.

¶ Gn. Pompeius was the first of the Romans to subjugate the Jews and by right of victory he entered the Temple.[1] Then it became common knowledge that there was no image of the gods inside, that the building was empty and the inner sanctuary void.[2] The walls of Jerusalem were destroyed,[3] the shrine remained. Presently when there was Civil War among us, after the provinces had passed into the power of Antony,[4] the Parthian king Pacorus took possession of Judaea. He was killed by P. Ventidius[5] and the Parthians were driven back across the Euphrates; G. Sosius[6] subdued the Jews. Herod had been given the kingdom by Antony,[7] and Augustus, when victorious, increased it. After the death of Herod, without waiting for the Emperor, a certain Simo[8] had usurped the title of king. He was punished by Quintilius Varus who held Syria [6–4 BC]. The people were reduced to obedience and the kingdom divided among the three sons of Herod.⁹ Under Tiberius there was quiet. Then on being ordered by G. Caesar to place his image in the Temple they chose rather to take up arms; Caesar's death stopped this rising. Claudius, as the kings were dead and their power diminished,¹⁰ gave over Judaea as a province to Roman knights and freedmen. One of these, Antonius Felix,¹¹ practised every kind of cruelty and debauchery and exercised regal authority with a servile natural bent. He married Drusilla,¹² the grand-daughter of Antony and Cleopatra, so that Felix was grandson-in-law of the same Antony of whom Claudius was the grandson.

1. *first*: This was in 63 BC.

2. *no image*. this lack of images made a powerful impression (cp. pp. 37, 124).

3. *walls*: Caesar later gave Antipater, father of Herod the Great, permission to rebuild them.

4. *provinces*: this does not refer to the provinces in general, but to those in the East.

5. *P. Ventidius* (Bassus) had been appointed by Antony as commander against the Parthians in 38 BC.

6. *Sosius* was a legate of Antony and governor of Syria.

7. *Herod*: this was Herod the Great, who had supported Sosius in his campaign.

8. *Simo* was a slave of Herod and for a time established himself in the hilly territory between Jerusalem and Jericho.

9. *three sons*: these were Archelaus, Antipas and Philip.

10. *kings were dead*: Herod Agrippa I, favourite of the Emperors Gaius (Caligula) (37–41) and Claudius (41–54), had died in 44 and his son, although he had the title of Herod Agrippa II, had only small powers (see above p. 18).

11. *Felix* (Antonius because he was a freedman of Antonia, Claudius' mother) was the brother of Pallas, Claudius' favourite and financial secretary.

12. *Drusilla* was a Jewess, Acts 24:24, perhaps the daughter of Agrippa I, in which case her mother must have been a daughter, otherwise unknown, of Antony and Cleopatra. Claudius was a grandson of Antony through his mother Antonia, who was the daughter of Antony and Octavia, the sister of Augustus.

❡ However the patience of the Jews[1] lasted up to the procurator Gessius Florus;[2] under him war broke out. Cestius Gallus, legate of Syria, tried to crush it and waged battles with varying fortunes, more often without success. When he died because of fate or frustration, Vespasian was sent by Nero and thanks to his good fortune, his fame and his excellent lieutenants, within two summers he held with his victorious army the whole of the plain-country and all the cities except Jerusalem. The next year,[3] occupied by the Civil War, as far as concerned the Jews passed without action. When peace was won throughout Italy, foreign cares also returned. Anger was augmented by the fact that only the Jews had not yielded. At the same time it seemed more expedient that Titus should remain with the armies to face all successes or mishaps of the new principate. Therefore he pitched camp, as we have said, before the walls of Jerusalem and displayed his legions in battle formation.

1. *patience*: although Tacitus does not go into details about the misgovernment of Judaea, the very use of this word shows that he does recognize that the Jews had some legitimate grievances.

2. *Gessius Florus* was procurator (i.e. an imperial agent appointed to govern a minor province) from 64 to 66, a Greek by birth, who won promotion because of his wife's friendship with Nero's wife, Poppaea.

3. *next year*: this was 69, the year of the Four Emperors.

❡ The Jews drew up their battle line at the very foot of the walls so as to venture further if things went well and to have a refuge ready if they were driven back. Cavalry and lightly armed cohorts were sent against them and there was an indecisive fight. Presently the enemy fell back and on the following days engaged frequently before the gates, until they were driven within the walls by their constant losses. The Romans turned to the assault, thinking it beneath their dignity to wait for the enemy to be reduced by famine. They clamoured for dangers, some because of valour, many because of savagery and desire for loot. Titus himself had Rome and wealth and pleasures before his eyes and these seemed to be delayed if Jerusalem did not fall forthwith. But the city with its steep site had been strengthened by massive fortifications which would have given adequate protection even on the level. For two hills rising to an immense height were enclosed by two walls skilfully slanted or curving inwards, so that the flanks of the assailants were exposed to attack. The edges of the rock were precipitous and towers rose sixty feet high where they had the help of the mountain, each one hundred and twenty feet high where the ground was lower, a marvellous sight, and at a view from a distance equal in height. There were other walls inside surrounding the palace, and the tower Antonia,[1], conspicuously high, named by Herod in honour of Mark Antony.

1. *Antonia*: this fortress to the northwest of the Temple area had housed the small Roman garrison and it was there that Paul was taken to face the commandant, Acts 21:34.

¶ The Temple was like a citadel and had its own walls, more laboriously and skilfully constructed than the others. The very colonnades which surrounded the Temple were an excellent defence. There was a never-failing spring, subterranean tunnels hollowed out under the mountains, tanks and cisterns for storing rain water. Because of the difference of their practices the founders had foreseen frequent wars, so there was everything to face any siege however long. After Pompey had taken the city, fear and experience[1] prompted most of their defences. Because of the greediness of the time of Claudius they bought the right to fortify[2] and in peacetime built walls as if for war, their numbers being increased by a vile rabble and the calamity of the other cities. All the most obdurate had taken refuge there and so much the more were they given to faction. There were three leaders, as many armies. Simon[3] had secured the outermost walls, the widest in extent, John[4] (whom they called Bargioras) the middle city, Eleazar[5] the temple. John and Simon had the advantage in numbers and arms, Eleazar in the site. But there were fights, treason, arson among themselves and a large amount of corn was burnt.[6] Presently John under a show of offering sacrifice sent men to massacre Eleazar and his band and took possession of the Temple. So the State was split into two factions, until with the approach of the Romans an external war was to produce agreement.

1. *experience*: in 34 BC Sosius had besieged and taken the city to

secure it for Antony, driving out Antigonus, the pro-Parthian ruler established by Pacorus, so proving that it was not impregnable.

2. *right to fortify*: Herod Agrippa I had managed to acquire this permission by using bribes.

3. *Simon*: Tacitus was misinformed, for it was Simon who was Bar Giora; he was a bandit-type leader who by his threats forced those in the city to admit him. He survived to be led in Titus' Triumph and was put to death in Rome.

4. *John*: he was John of Gischala.

5. *Eleazar*: he was the son of Simon and a Zealot leader, but distinct from the Eleazar who led the last stand at Masada.

6. *corn was burnt*: famine was the ultimate cause for the fall of the city.

¶ Portents[1] had happened which a race prone to superstition, opposed to religious observances, does not think it right to expiate either by sacrifice or prayer. Battle lines were seen to engage in the sky, flashing arms and the Temple suddenly aglow with fire from the clouds. The doors of the sanctuary suddenly opened and a superhuman voice was heard crying that the gods were departing; at the same time there was a great movement of departure.[2] Few took these as fearful omens; the majority were persuaded that in the ancient books of their priests it was written that at that very time the East would grow strong and masters of the world[3] would go forth from Judaea. This ambiguous saying had foretold Vespasian and Titus, but the common folk, as is usual with human desire, interpreted such a great destiny in their own favour; not even their own misfortunes converted them to the truth. We are told that the besieged, male and female, numbered six hundred thousand. All had arms who could carry them and a disproportionate number[4] made the venture. Men and women were equally determined. Should they be forced to change their homes they feared life more than death. Against this city and this people Titus Caesar, since the site did not permit assaults and surprises, decided to contend with earthworks and mantlets. The tasks were divided between the legions and there was rest from fighting, until all the devices for capturing cities discovered among the ancients or by fresh ingenuity could be constructed.

1. *Portents*: the Jews were forbidden to take account of omens, Lev. 19:26, 'You shall not practise divination or soothsaying'; cp. also Jer. 10:2, 'Do not fall into the ways of the nations, do not be awed by signs in the heavens.' At Rome in the case of omens affecting the State the sibylline books would have been consulted (p. 215).

2. *departure*: this reflects the common belief that the gods afforded special protection to places in which each was pre-eminently worshipped (cp. p. 197).

3. *masters of the world*: both Josephus, *War* 6.5.1, and Suetonius, *Vespasian* 4, confirm the prevalence of this belief.

4. *disproportionate*: by this Tacitus means that a greater proportion of the populace than might normally have been expected took to arms.

Tacitus' account of the fall of Jerusalem has been lost, but it has been plausibly suggested that Sulpicius Severus, a fourth century historian, in his *Universal Chronicle* followed Tacitus in describing this. So the two following fragments are given here to supplement Tacitus; both from Sulpicius Severus *Universal Chronicle* 2.30.

Fragment 1.3

¶ The Jews, confined by the siege, because no opportunity was offered for either peace or surrender, in the end were perishing through famine and the streets began to be filled everywhere with corpses, for the duty of burying had now been superseded. Indeed after venturing to eat all kinds of abominations[1] they did not spare even human bodies, except those which putrefaction had forestalled from providing such food.

1. *abominations*: Josephus describes these in some detail, *War* 5.12.3 (512–18); 13.7 (567–72), but does not mention cannibalism except for one melodramatic story of a mother who devoured her baby son (6.3–4 (201–13)).

Fragment 2.6

¶ It is said that Titus called a council[1] and first deliberated whether to overthrow such a mighty work as the Temple. Several indeed thought that a sacred building, renowned above all mortal works, ought not to be destroyed. Its preservation would bear witness to Roman moderation, its destruction would be a perpetual mark of cruelty. Others on the contrary, including Titus himself, were of the opinion that the Temple in particular ought to be destroyed, in order that the religion of the Jews and the Christians[2] might be more completely abolished, since these religions, although opposed to one another, yet had arisen from the same origins; the Christians had sprung from the Jews and if the root were pulled up the stock would easily perish.

1. *council*: Josephus gives a detailed account of this council of war preceding the actual taking of the Temple (*War* 6.4.3 (236–43)). According to him Titus strongly favoured preserving the Temple and did everything to prevent a fire, started accidentally, from spreading. Josephus however was biassed in favour of the imperial house and the story given above is more probable.

2. *Christians*: this mention of Christians is quite anachronistic and was probably inserted by Sulpicius, himself a Christian.

JUVENAL (D. Junius Juvenalis) was born at Aquinum in Italy, dates uncertain but within the second half of the first century AD and the first half of the second. He was a satirist in the tradition of Horace and Persius, but using the bitter invective which has influenced the modern conception of satire. The only contemporary reference to him is by his friend Martial (p. 70).

Juvenal clearly had no high opinion of the Jews, but he was not deliberately setting out to attack them. After the fall of Jerusalem in AD 70 many Jews had been brought to Rome as slaves. Jewish beggars thronged the streets, telling fortunes and preying on women's superstitious credulity. On a higher social level proselytism could lead to anti-social exclusiveness and contempt for Roman law. Juvenal is no historian or scholar aiming at giving information about the Jews to his readers. He simply sees the Jew as part of the contemporary social scene and, as such, fair game for scathing incidental comments. This makes his evidence all the more valuable, so it is given in full below, although detached quotations are also to be found in the sections on Moses, Sabbath, Circumcision, Food Laws and Proselytism.

Juvenal *Satires* 1.3.10–16

The poet's friend Umbricius, dissatisfied with life in Rome, is leaving and after this introduction gives his reasons:

¶ But while all his household goods were being loaded into one cart, he stood by the ancient arches and the dripping Capenian gate,[1] here where Numa[2] used to have assignations by night with his mistress, where now the grove with its sacred spring is let out to the Jews, the total of whose furniture is a basket and hay.[3] For every tree has been ordered to pay rent to the people,[4] the Camenae have been evicted and the wood practises begging.[5]

1. *ancient arches*: This refers to an aqueduct, the water from which dripped on the Capenian gate, in the eastern quarter of the city.

2. *Numa*: this legendary king of Rome was said to have been advised by the nymph Egeria, one of the *Camenae*, counterparts of the Greek Muses.

3. *basket and hay*: this may mean a haybox to keep food warm on the sabbath or a begging basket and hay for bedding.

4. *rent*: it seems that the Jews were allowed to squat in this grove, once sacred to the local nymphs, on payment of a small rent to the authorities.

5. *begging*: The Jews were noted as beggars (pp. 34, 121).

*Satires* 1.3.296
One of the perils of the Roman streets by night was the drunkard who makes you stop and asks insulting questions to provoke a brawl:

❡ Tell me where you have your stand;[1] in what prayer-house am I to look for you?

1. *stand*: the insult lies in assuming that he is a professional beggar, a Jew, for *prayer-house* is the Greek term transliterated into Latin for a Jewish synagogue.

*Satires* 2.6.156–60
The whole poem is a catalogue of the frailties of women, here extravagance in buying jewels:

❡ Next [she gets] the famous diamond, more valuable through being worn on the finger of Berenice.[1] A barbarian, Agrippa, once gave it to his incestuous sister, in the land where kings celebrate the sabbath bare-footed and long-established clemency spares pigs to grow old.

1. *Berenice*: The sister of Agrippa II (cp. Acts 25:13 when both were present at Paul's trial before Festus) was popularly supposed to have incestuous relations with her brother and was notorious in Rome, where she spent much time, as mistress of Titus (Emperor 79–81).

*Satires* 2.6.542–7

The feminine frailty satirized here is addiction to superstition and Juvenal gives a catalogue of various cults patronized by the superstitious woman:

❡ When he [an Egyptian priest] has made way, a palsied Jewess[1] leaving her basket and hay begs mysteriously in her ear, an interpreter of the laws of Jerusalem and mighty priestess of the tree[2] and faithful intermediary of heaven.[3] She too gets her hand filled, but more sparingly. Jews sell for small change any kinds of dreams you like.

    1. *palsied*: an old hag is meant.

    2. *tree*: this is probably not a reference to the Christian cross, but to the grove outside the walls where Jews were allowed to squat for a small rent. There may be a contemptuous allusion to the fact that there is no longer any Temple at Jerusalem in which a priestess could worship.

    3. *heaven*: there was a vague idea that the Jews, who were known to reject the anthropomorphic pagan gods, worshipped the sky.

*Satires* 5.14.96–106

The first half of this satire deals with the corrupting influence of parental example. The father is a god-fearer, in that he observes the sabbath and abstains from pork; the son goes further and becomes a full Jew.

❡ Some who happen to have a father who stands in awe[1] of the sabbath, worship nothing but clouds and the holy heaven and do not differentiate between human and pigs' flesh, from which their father abstained; soon they also put aside their foreskins. Moreover as they are accustomed to despise Roman laws, they learn to keep and revere whatever Jewish ordinances Moses handed down in a mysterious volume: not to show the way to any one who does not practise the same sacred rites, not to guide any one to the spring he is seeking unless he is circumcised.[2] But the father is to blame, who spent every seventh day in sloth without any contact with life.

    1. *stands in awe*: the verb literally means 'to fear' and is probably used vaguely here in its technical sense of 'god-fearers', i.e. Gentiles on the fringe, who sympathized with Judaism but were not full

proselytes (cp. Acts 10:2, 22 in reference to Cornelius and 13:16, 26 in addressing a mixed audience in Pisidian Antioch).

2. *to show the way* etc.: these were obligations commonly regarded as due to mankind in general (cp. Seneca *de Ben.* 4.29.1: 'Then...will you neither let an ungrateful man draw water nor show him his road if he goes astray?' (i.e. Is an ungrateful man not entitled to even the most elementary human rights?).

As well as the pagan authors to be cited, two Jews have been quoted when they give valuable information not available elsewhere:

PHILO JUDAEUS, *c.* 15 BC–AD 45, lived in Alexandria. He is best known as a theologian and philosopher, but also took part in politics and wrote two political pamphlets, 'Against Flaccus' (*In Flaccum*) and 'Embassy to Gaius' (*Leg. Gaj.*).

JOSEPHUS, b. AD 37–8, was an aristocratic Jewish priest who, captured by the Romans in 67, became a favourite in court circles. He settled in Rome and wrote 'Jewish War' (*War*), 'Jewish Antiquities' (*Ant.*), which was a history of the Jews from the Creation to the Jewish War (AD 66–7), an autobiography, *Life*, and a defence of Judaism, 'Against Apion' (*Apion*).

### Beliefs About Jewish Origins and Development

Our extant accounts, quoted here roughly in chronological order, vary according to their sources, the place of writing and the period. There is a strong consensus that the Jews were of Egyptian origin or foreigners, immigrants or hostile invaders settled in Egypt. They were expelled because of some pestilence, usually leprosy, and reached Judaea under the leadership of Moses. He introduced particular customs, mainly regarded as anti-social and pernicious, occasionally as wise and good. The authors quoted by Josephus in *Apion*, which he wrote to refute their allegations, had Alexandrian connections and reflect the anti-Jewish feeling in that city. The earliest and most virulent of these is Manetho, *fl. c.* 280 BC, himself an Egyptian. Yet Hecataeus, about the same period, a Greek but conversant with Alexandria, recognized Jewish monotheism and absence of images and gave Moses' institutions guarded approval. At this time little was known of the Jews outside the world of the eastern Mediterranean.

However the Jews of the Diaspora were spreading, even in Rome, where a deep impression was made by the news of Pompey's taking of the Temple at Jerusalem in 63 BC and by the information that there was no image there. In fact Strabo soon after this gave quite an idealized picture. Tacitus, writing in the aftermath of the Jewish War, AD 66–70, while clearly anti-Jewish, yet recognized Jewish monotheism and their rational basis for aversion from images. Finally Dio Cassius, at the end of our period, in his brief sketch mentioned this feature in particular, while recognizing dispassionately that the Jews practised an exclusive way of life with which his readers would be familiar.

HECATAEUS of Abdera, *c.* 300 BC, was a prolific writer, whose best-known work was *Aegyptiaca*, a history of Egypt and Egyptian culture; he had visited Alexandria. Diodorus *fl. c.* 60 BC (p. 46) expressly quotes Hecataeus' account of the Jewish emigration from Egypt, so his views would be known to later Graeco-Roman readers.

Diodorus *World History* 40.3.1–9

¶ In ancient times a pestilence arose in Egypt and the common people attributed the cause of the trouble to the gods; numerous aliens of every kind were resident, practising different customs in regard to religious observances and sacrificial rites and so the ancestral worship of the gods had been neglected. The native inhabitants imagined that unless they got rid of the foreigners there would be no solution of their problem. Straightway therefore they were banished. The most distinguished and efficient gathered into bands, which were expelled, as some say, to Greece and certain other places, under leaders of repute, the most famous of whom were Danaus[1] and Cadmus,[2] but the mass of the people emigrated to the country now called Judaea, which lies not far from Egypt and in those days was completely uninhabited.

    1. *Danaus*: in Greek legend Danaus was of Greek descent, but of a family long domiciled in Egypt. He was not banished, but fled to Greece with his daughters to find sanctuary from an enforced marriage with their cousins. There he became king of Argos.
    2. *Cadmus*: usually Cadmus is described as a Phoenician, who founded Thebes in Greece. The fact that there was also an Egyptian Thebes may have caused confusion.

¶ At the head of the colony was a man called Moses, outstanding by reason of his wisdom and courage. After taking possession of the land he founded various cities, including the one which is now the most famous, called Jerusalem. He also established the Temple which they hold in the highest honour and instituted rites and sacred observances and organized the legislation of the government. He divided the people into twelve tribes because this number was thought to be the most perfect and corresponding to the sum of months which made up the year. He did not fashion any image of the gods at all, because he thought that God had no human form, but that the sky surrounding the earth was the only God and Lord of the universe. The sacrifices and social customs which he instituted differed from those of other nations, for because of their own expulsion he introduced a way of life which was unsociable and hostile to strangers. He selected those men who were the most accomplished and would be the most capable of presiding over the whole nation and appointed them priests. He ordained that they should occupy themselves with the Temple and divine ritual and sacrifices. These same men he appointed also as judges[1] in the most important cases and entrusted to them the guardianship of laws and customs. For this reason there was never to be a king of the Jews, but authority over the people was always to be given to that priest who was reputed to excel in wisdom and goodness. They address him as *high priest* and consider that he announces God's orders. At assemblies and other gatherings, according to our author, he publishes the commands and on this point the Jews are so compliant that they immediately fall to the ground and make obeisance to the high priest who gives the exposition. At the end of the laws there is written in addition 'Moses having heard these words of God speaks them to the people'.[2] The lawgiver made provision for military matters too and enforced training for the young men in courage and hardiness and endurance in general of any distress.

1. *judges*: for the judicial duties of the priests, cp. Deut. 21 : 5.
2. *Moses having heard*. . . : similar formulas referring to Moses are to be found in Lev. 26:46; 27:34; Num. 36:13.

¶ He also campaigned against neighbouring lands, conquered much territory and distributed it by lot, equal portions to private citizens, larger ones to the priests;[1] this was in order that receiving a more considerable income they might without distraction continually attend to the divine cult. Private citizens were not allowed to sell their own portions[2] lest some should buy them up for their own selfish ends and by oppressing the poor cause the population to diminish. He obliged the inhabitants to rear their children and, as infants were reared at little expense, the Jewish people was always rich in manpower. Practices relating to marriage and the burial of the dead he regulated very differently from those of the rest of mankind. Under later empires, the Persian domination and the Macedonian which destroyed this, because of their intercourse with foreigners many of the ancestral customs of the Jews were displaced. As regards the Jews this is the account of Hecataeus of Abdera.

1. *priests*: a certain number of cities with their suburbs were assigned to the Levites (cp. Num. 35:1ff.; Josh. 21) but not a share in the land (cp. Deut. 10:9; 12:12; 18:8; Num. 18:24).

2. *sell their own portions*: the sale of any land was to be temporary and the land returnable to its previous owner in the year of Jubilee (cp. Lev. 25:13). Num. 5:3–12 records the return of mortgaged land to debtors. The alienation of land from smallholders and concentration in the possession of great landowners was a perennial problem in the ancient world.

MANETHO was a scholarly Egyptian priest of the third century BC (p. 238). He wrote a *History of Egypt* in Greek, which survives only in quotations.

Josephus *Apion* 1.14.73–91

¶ Manetho was an Egyptian, who obviously had a tincture of Greek culture, for he wrote a history of his country in Greek, translating sacred records, as he himself says. He criticizes Herodotus[1] for numerous ignorant errors about Egyptian history. This is what Manetho writes about us [i.e. the Jews] in the second book of his History of Egypt. I shall quote his own words so as to make him his own witness.

1. *Herodotus*: the famous fifth century Greek historian of the Great War between Greeks and Persians, also a traveller and anthropologist, devoted his second book to Egypt as part of the Persian empire.

¶ ⟨There was a king⟩ called Timaus.[1] In his time a storm of divine wrath broke over us, I know not why. Unexpectedly an obscure people from the East[2] boldly marched against the land and easily conquered it without a fight. They overpowered its rulers,[2] then ruthlessly burnt the cities and destroyed the temples of the gods. All the natives they treated most cruelly, slaughtering the men and enslaving their wives and children. Finally they made king one of themselves called Salatis. He lived in Memphis, exacting tribute from both Upper and Lower Egypt. He also left garrisons in the most strategic positions and made special provision for the security of the districts facing east as he foresaw that someday the Assyrians would become powerful and covet and attack his kingdom. In the Saite district he found a city very conveniently situated to the east of the Bubastite branch of the river, called Avaris from some ancient Egyptian religious tradition. He rebuilt this, fortified it strongly and installed a garrison of two hundred and forty thousand fighting men. Every summer he used to come here, partly to apportion rations and to pay his troops, partly to train them in manoeuvres so as to inspire fear in outsiders. After ruling nineteen years he died.'

1. *Timaus*: manuscripts are corrupt and some such phrase in brackets must be supplied.

2. *East*: who the Hyksos were and where they came from has been much debated. Probably they were mainly of northwestern Semitic stock. Manetho implies that they were Jews when he states that they founded Jerusalem and built the Temple (see below, p. 41). They are not mentioned by the other authors cited below. From Egyptian sources we know that the first wave of invasion began about 1720 or 1710 BC. Some thirty years later came a second wave and gradually Egypt was mastered. A capital was built at Avaris and the Hyksos domination lasted about one hundred years. After bitter conflicts under the Egyptian king Kamosis, his successor Amosis finally took Avaris in *c.* 1550, expelled the invaders and drove them to the borders of Palestine. Manetho's account, in spite of various inaccuracies in names and chronology, has some relation to historical fact.

3. *overpowered its rulers*: modern scholars see the Hyksos ascendancy as the culmination of a long period of infiltration, starting as early as the end of the eighteenth century BC, rather than Manetho's speedy conquest.

¶ After him a second king, called Beon, ruled for forty-four years and after him another, Apachnas, for thirty years and seven months, then Apophis for sixty years and Jannas for fifty years and one month. Last of all Assis ruled for forty-nine years and two months. These were the first six rulers of the dynasty and ever more and more they desired to extirpate the Egyptians. The tribe as a whole was called *Hyksos*,[1] i.e. *shepherd kings*, for in sacred language *hyk* means *king*, while in the common tongue *sos* means *shepherd*, both singular and plural. So the two combined give *hyksos*. Some say they were Arabs. In another copy it is said that not *kings* were designated by the word *hyk*, but on the contrary *shepherds* were signified as *captives*,[2] because in Egyptian *hyk* and *hok*, when aspirated, expressly denote *captives*. I think [i.e. Josephus] this more credible and in line with ancient history.

    1. *Hyksos*: the Egyptian word means *foreign princes* and had already been used to describe Bedouin Sheikhs. The composite derivations given here are dubious.
    2. *captives*: see below.

¶ Manetho says that the kings of the so-called *shepherds* named above and their successors ruled over Egypt for five hundred and eleven years. After this there was a revolt of the kings of the Thebais[1] and of the rest of Egypt against the *shepherds* and a great and protracted war broke out. In the time of a king called Misphragmouthosis the *shepherds*, he says, were vanquished, driven out of all the rest of Egypt and confined in a place called Avaris, an area of ten thousand *arourae*.[2] According to Manetho the *shepherds* enclosed the whole place within a high, strong wall in order to keep all their possessions and booty in security. Thummosis,[3] son of Misphragmouthosis, he says, tried to overpower them by siege and besieged the walls with four hundred and eighty thousand men, but raised the siege and came to an agreement that they should all quit Egypt and go unscathed where they pleased. On these terms they left Egypt with all their families and possessions, numbering two hundred and forty thousand persons and journeyed through the desert into Syria. Since they feared the power of the Assyrians, who at that time had dominion over Asia, they built in the land now called Judaea a city big enough for such huge hordes and named it Jerusalem.

In another book of his *History of Egypt* Manetho says that this race of so-called *shepherds* is termed *captives* in the sacred books of Egypt.

1. *Thebais*: this was the region of the great city of Thebes.
2. *arourae*: the *aroura* was an Egyptian land measurement, 52·5 metres square.
3. *Thummosis*: this sounds like a garbled version of Thutmosis, the name of four important Pharaohs of the eighteenth dynasty which drove out the Hyksos.

Josephus quotes Manetho for the following story too.

*Apion* 1.26.228–52

¶ This Manetho, who had undertaken to translate the history of Egypt from their sacred chronicles, related first that our ancestors, numbering many tens of thousands, came to Egypt and conquered the inhabitants and then himself agreed that some time later they were expelled, took possession of what is now Judaea, founded Jerusalem and built the Temple. Up to this point he followed the records. After that by saying that he would recount the stories and reports current about the Jews he gave himself licence to insert incredible tales, wishing to confuse us with a throng of Egyptians who because of leprosy and other ailments, as he says, were condemned to exile from Egypt. He intercalates[1] a king Amenophis, a fictitious name, which is why he does not venture to reckon the years of his reign as he did exactly for the other kings. To him he attaches certain legendary tales, having doubtless forgotten that he had put the *shepherds'* exodus to Jerusalem five hundred and eighteen years earlier.

1. *intercalates*: Josephus was much concerned with the question of chronology as a test of Manetho's credibility. He had devoted *Apion* 1.26.93–105 to examining it and now briefly inserts chronological data to show that Amenophis' reign must have been intercalated.

¶ So Manetho, after recognizing that our ancestors had left Egypt so long before, then introduces a fictitious king Amenophis[1] and says that like Or, one of his predecessors, he desired to behold the gods and revealed his desire to a man of the same name as his, Amenophis son of Paaphis, who was reputed to have a tincture of the divine nature by virtue of his wisdom and foreknowledge of the future. This namesake told him

that he would be able to see the gods if he purged the whole country
of lepers and other polluted men. The king rejoiced and collected
together from Egypt all those who were physically disfigured, to the
number of eighty thousand, and cast them into the stone quarries on
the east bank of the Nile to labour there segregated from the rest of
the Egyptians. Among them, he says, there were even some illustrious
priests infected by leprosy. As for that wise and prophetic Amenophis,
he was afraid that the gods might vent their wrath on himself and the
king, if they were forced into being seen. He prophesied that the
polluted would find allies and be masters of Egypt for thirteen years,
but as he did not dare to tell the king himself, he left a complete account
in writing and committed suicide. The king was left despondent. Then,
to quote him word for word, 'When those in the quarries had suffered
for a long time the king was asked to grant them refuge and shelter
and assigned to them Avaris,[2] at that time abandoned by the *shepherds*.'
(According to ancient theology the city is sacred to Typhon.)[3]

1. *Amenophis*: Josephus was mistaken in thinking this a fictitious
name. There were several rulers of this name, which also figures in
Chaeremon's account (p. 52).

2. *Avaris*: see above pp. 39, 40.

3. *Typhon*: this refers to the Egyptian god (p. 239), not the giant
of Greek mythology.

¶ 'After coming there they used this as a base for revolt, appointed as
their leader one of the priests of Heliopolis[1] called Osariph and took
an oath to obey him in everything. First he laid down a law that they
should cease to worship the gods and should not abstain from the
animals held particularly sacred in Egypt, but sacrifice and eat them
all. Also they were to associate with none but those under the same
oath. After enacting such laws and many others very contrary to
Egyptian customs, he ordered them in full force to fortify the city walls
and prepare themselves for war against king Amenophis. He himself
enlisted some of the other priests and of those who shared his pollution
and sent ambassadors to the city called Jerusalem, to the *shepherds* who
had been driven out by Tethmosis.[2] He described the treatment of
himself and his companions in misfortune and asked them to join him

in a common campaign against Egypt. He promised to bring them first
to Avaris, their ancestral home, to furnish their contingents with
abundant supplies, to fight on their behalf if necessary and easily bring
the land into subjection to them. They were overjoyed and to the
number of two hundred thousand men all eagerly set out together and
soon reached Avaris.'

    1. *Heliopolis*: this was a city in Lower Egypt and the chief centre
of Sun-worship. The Greek name means City of the Sun and its priests
were celebrated for their learning.
    2. *Tethmosis*: his name is given earlier as Thummosis (see p. 40).

¶ 'Amenophis, king of Egypt, when he learnt of their invasion, was
extremely disturbed, remembering the prophecy of Amenophis, son
of Paaphis. First he assembled the Egyptian people and after taking
counsel with their leading men sent for the sacred animals which they
venerate most in their temples to be brought to him. He also ordered
each body of priests to conceal the statues of the gods as securely as
they could. To his own friend he entrusted his five-year-old son Sethos,
also called Rameses after his ancestor Rapses. He himself with the rest
of the Egyptians, comprising three hundred thousand of the bravest
warriors, crossed over, but when he met the enemy he did not engage
them, as he was afraid he would be fighting against the gods. He
retraced his steps to Memphis, picked up Apis[1] and the other sacred
animals which he had ordered to be brought there and made straight
for Ethiopia with all his army and the host of Egyptians, for the king
of the Ethiopians owed him a debt of gratitude. This king welcomed
him and all his host and provided him with all such products of the
land as were fit for human food and cities and villages, sufficient to
maintain him for the destined period of thirteen years of exile from
his kingdom. Moreover he also assigned to Amenophis and his
followers an army to garrison the Egyptian frontier. So much for the
state of affairs in Ethiopia.'

    1. *Apis*: a sacred bull was venerated as the living embodiment of
the god.

¶ 'The Solymites after returning with the polluted Egyptians treated the people so impiously that the rule of the former, described above, seemed a golden age when men saw the present acts of sacrilege. For they not only burnt cities and villages, but not satisfied with pillaging temples and defacing statues of the gods they made a habit of using the sanctuaries as kitchens for roasting the animals which were objects of worship. They compelled the priests and prophets to sacrifice and slaughter the animals and drove them out naked. It is said that a priest, by birth a citizen of Heliopolis, named Osariph after Osiris the god worshipped there, established their constitution and laws and after joining this people changed his name and he was called Moses.' These then are the Egyptian stories about the Jews and there are many others which I pass over for the sake of brevity. Manetho says next that, 'after this Amenophis with a great army, along with his son Rameses who also had an army, attacked from Ethiopia. The two of them engaged the *shepherds* and the polluted, vanquished them and after killing a large number pursued them as far as the borders of Syria.' These and other such stories Manetho recorded.

POSIDONIUS, *c.* 135–51 BC, came from Apamea in Syria (map 2), but later lived in Rome. He was a Stoic philosopher with a remarkably wide range of interests, including natural science, anthropology, geography and history. His *Histories*, which started from 146 BC, where Polybius (p. 202) left off, were immensely influential, complementing his philosophic system. Only fragments, written in Greek, survive. The following excerpt from Diodorus *fl. c.* 60 BC (p. 46) is generally thought to be derived from Posidonius because it shows marked affinities with Josephus, *Apion* 2.7.79ff., where Posidonius is mentioned along with Apollonius Molo as one of the main sources for Apion's anti-Jewish slanders (p. 107).

Diodorus *World History* 34.1–3

¶ When king Antiochus[1] was besieging Jerusalem the Jews held out for a while, but when all their provisions were exhausted they were forced to send envoys to arrange for an armistice. Most of his friends advised him to storm the city and completely wipe out the Jewish race; for they alone of all nations refused to associate with any other people and considered them all as enemies. They pointed out that their ancestors, because they were impious and hateful to the gods, had been exiled from the whole of Egypt.

For all those who had white or leprous marks on their bodies were thought accursed and, to secure purification, were herded together and banished beyond the border. After their expulsion they seized the regions around Jerusalem, formed the Jewish nation and made their hatred of mankind traditional. For this reason too they instituted completely different laws, not to have table-fellowship with any foreigner nor to show any goodwill at all.

They also reminded him of his ancestors' previous aversion from this nation. For Antiochus, surnamed Epiphanes,[2] after vanquishing the Jews entered the innermost sanctuary of their god, which it was lawful only for the priest to enter. In it he found a stone statue of a man with a long beard seated on an ass and holding a book in his hands. He assumed that this was the statue of Moses who founded Jerusalem and formed the nation and also enacted for the Jews their misanthropic and lawless customs.

1. *Antiochus*: this was Antiochus VII, Sidetes, 139–129 BC, who campaigned against the Jews and took Jerusalem in 128/9.

2. *Epiphanes*: Antiochus IV, surnamed *Epiphanes*, lived c. 215–163 BC and was the traditional arch-enemy of the Jews.

LYSIMACHUS, date unknown, but probably in the first or second century BC. It is uncertain whether he was the Alexandrian mythographer of this name. He is quoted for his anti-Jewish views by Josephus.

Josephus *Apion* 1.34.304–11

¶ Next after these[1] I will introduce Lysimachus who took as they did, the fiction about the lepers and the maimed as his basic theme, but made up stories which surpass them in their incredibility and which he obviously composed because of his violent hostility. For he says: 'When Bocchoris was king of Egypt the Jewish people, who suffered from leprosy and other ailments, took refuge in the temples and begged for a living. When a very large number fell sick, Egypt became barren. The Egyptian king Bocchoris sent to Ammon[2] to consult the oracle about the barrenness and the god told him to purge the temples from men who were impure and impious by casting them out from the temples into the desert. As for the victims of scurvy and the lepers, he must drown them, since the sun was vexed that they should be alive. He must purify the temples and so the land would be fruitful.'

  1. *these*: Josephus refers to Manetho and Chaeremon.
  2. *Ammon*: this was the famous oracle situated in the Libyan desert, but under the patronage of the Egyptian god Amon-Ra.

¶ 'When Bocchoris received the oracle's reply he summoned the priests and altar-attendants and ordered them to make a list of the unclean and hand these over to the soldiers to conduct to the desert. The lepers they were to encase in plates of lead and sink them in the open sea. After the leprous and the scurvy had been drowned, the rest were abandoned in the desert to die en masse. They gathered and took counsel together and when night fell they kindled fires and torches and stood guard. All through the following night they fasted and propitiated the gods to save them. Next day a certain Moses advised them to make the venture and follow a single route until they reached inhabited regions. He urged them to show goodwill to none, to give not the best but the worst advice and to overturn any shrines and altars of the gods that they might come across. The rest consented and acting as agreed journeyed through the desert. After great hardships they came to inhabited country, maltreated the men, plundered and burnt the temples and reached the country now called Judaea. There they built a city and settled. This town was called Hierosyla[1] because of their propensity to sacrilege. Later, when their power had grown, to avoid odium they changed the name; the city was called Hierosolyma [Jerusalem] and they were called Hierosolymites.'

  1. *Hierosyla*: this was a combination of an adjective meaning 'sacred' (cp. hierarchy), from which the Greek word for temple came, and a verb meaning 'to loot'.

DIODORUS SICULUS, born at Agyrium in Sicily, flourished under Julius Caesar (100 to 44 BC) and Augustus (Emperor 27 BC to AD 14), until at least 21 BC. He wrote a *World History* in Greek in forty books of which the first five have survived complete; 6 to 10 were lost, but some fragments of other books remain.

*World History* 1.28

❡ They [the Egyptians] say that it was from Egypt that Danaus set out with his followers when they founded Argos, almost the oldest of the Greek cities. From the Egyptians came the Colchians, who settled in Pontus and the Jews who settled between Arabia and Syria. For this reason the circumcision[1] of their male children has long been established among these peoples, a custom originating in Egypt.

1. *circumcision*: Diodorus gives the same argument to prove Egyptian descent more briefly in 1.55 (see below, p. 81).

NICOLAUS OF DAMASCUS was born at Damascus *c.* 64 BC and lived on into the beginning of the first century AD. He was an orator, scholar and historian and, though not himself a Jew, diplomatic adviser to Herod the Great (*c.* 73 to 4 BC). His great work was a *World History*, written in Greek, in one hundred and forty-four books, now lost, but one of Josephus' main sources. Two quotations from Josephus are relevant to the very early days of the Jews:

Josephus *Ant.* 1.3.6 (94–5)

❡ Nicolaus of Damascus in the ninety-sixth book of his *Histories* gives the following account of them [i.e. the flood[1] and the ark]: 'Beyond Minyas in Armenia there is a great mountain called Baris, where according to tradition many took refuge and were saved at the time of the flood. One man, floating in an ark, grounded on the peak and the remains of the timbers were preserved for a long time. This man could be the one recorded by Moses[2] the Jewish lawgiver.'

1. *flood*: Nicolaus had just mentioned the Chaldaean Berossus and the Egyptian Hieronymus as referring to the flood. The tale of a great flood, sent because of the wickedness of mankind, was well known to the Greeks. In their version Deucalion and his wife Pyrrha, because of their piety, took refuge in an ark and were saved. The Jewish story comes in Gen. 6:5ff.
2. *Moses*: it is assumed that readers knew of Moses as an author.

Josephus *Ant.* 1.7.2 (659–60)

❡ Nicolaus of Damascus in the fourth book of his *Histories* states: 'Abrames,[1] a foreigner who arrived with an army from the land beyond

Babylon, called the land of the Chaldees, became king of Damascus. Soon after, he emigrated with his people from this country too and settled in the land then called Canaan, but now Judaea, he and his multiple descendants, whose history I shall recount in another book. Even now the name of Abram is famed in Damascus and a village is shown, called after him "Abram's dwelling place".'

1. *Abrames*: according to Gen. 11:31 he did come from Ur of the Chaldees, but there is no mention of Damascus. According to Pompeius Trogus (see below) both he and Israel reigned there.

POMPEIUS TROGUS was a native of southern Gaul, whose grandfather had been enfranchised by Pompey. He lived in the period of Augustus (Emperor 27 BC to AD 14) and wrote in Latin a *Universal History*, called *Historiae Philippicae*, in forty-four books. This survives only in the *Epitome* made by Justinus in the third century AD. In Book 36 he treated Jewish antiquity, the geography of Judaea and the history of the Jews from the Persian period, i.e. 539 BC onwards.

Pompeius Trogus *Universal History* 36 (Justinus *Epitome* 1.10–2.16)

¶ He [Antiochus][1] also subdued the Jews, who in the time of his father Demetrius had regained their freedom by force of arms. So great was their strength that after him [Antiochus] they brooked no Macedonian king and exercising self-government devastated Syria with great wars. For the Jews originated from Damascus, a very noble Syrian city, from which the Assyrian kings also traced their descent from Queen Semiramis.[2] The city took its name from King Damascus in whose honour the Syrians revered the tomb of his wife Arathis as a temple and from then on have considered her a goddess of the greatest sanctity. After Damascus Azelus reigned, next Adores and Abrahames and Israhel.

1. *Antiochus*: the reference is to Antiochus VII, who was killed in battle with the Parthians in 129 BC.
2. *Semiramis*: tradition associated her with the great temple at Bambyce of the Syrian goddess Atargatis, who was thought to have been born at Damascus. Semiramis herself was best known as the legendary Assyrian queen, immensely powerful, also reputed as daughter of Atargatis – hence the Damascene connection (see pp. 260ff. for the cult of Atargatis).

¶ Israhel was fortunate in having ten sons, which made him more famous than his ancestors. So he divided the people into ten kingdoms and handed them over to his sons and called them all Jews after Judah,[1] who had died after the division, and ordered all to revere the memory of one whose portion had accrued to them all. The youngest of the brothers was Joseph. His brothers were afraid of his outstanding ability and secretly kidnapped him and sold him to foreign merchants. These carried him off to Egypt where through his natural cleverness he learnt magic arts and soon became very dear to the king himself. For he was very skilled in portents and also the first to formulate the interpretation of dreams; nothing within divine or human law seemed unknown to him. So much so that he even foresaw crop failure many years beforehand. All Egypt would have died of famine, if the king had not on his advice issued an edict that crops should be conserved for many years. So often was his advice proved right that his replies seemed to be given not by a man but by a god.

1. *Judah*: the author does not know the tradition of the twelve tribes nor the separate kingdoms of Israel and Judaea.

¶ His son was Moyses[1] who besides inheriting his father's knowledge also won favour by his personal beauty. But the Egyptians, when they were suffering from scabies and skin-disease, on the advice of an oracle, to prevent further spreading of the plague expelled him along with the diseased from the frontiers of Egypt. So he became leader of the exiles and stole the Egyptians' sacred vessels.[2] Seeking to reclaim these by force of arms the Egyptians were compelled by storms to return home. Moyses, seeking to return to Damascus, their former home, took possession of Mount Sinai. When he with the people, wearied out by seven days without food, at last arrived there through the deserts of Arabia, they hallowed the seventh day, habitually called sabbath by that nation, by a fast for all time to come. This was because that day put an end to their fasting and wandering. Since they remembered that they had been expelled from Egypt for fear of contagion, so as not to incur the enmity of the natives for the same reason, they took the precaution of not associating with foreigners. This, done for a reason, he gradually changed into the way of life and a religious observance. After Moyses his son Arruas[3] was made a priest of the Egyptian cult and presently king. From then on it has always been the custom among the Jews to have the same men as kings and priests. By their combination of justice with religion they became incredibly powerful.

 1. *Moyses*: the infant Moses, who was not in fact Joseph's son, was called 'a fine child' in Exod. 2:2.
 2. *sacred vessels*: Exod. 12:35–6 relates only that the Jews absconded with the jewels borrowed from their neighbours.
 3. *Arruas*: Trogus is perhaps confusing him with Moses' brother, Aaron.

Trogus in chapter 3 added a description of the palms and balsam trees and the Dead Sea, concluding this excursus on the Jews with a brief summary of their history up to the Roman period when they gained independence from the Seleucids and had an alliance with Rome (161 BC).

STRABO, 64/3 BC to AD 21, philosopher, historian and geographer, was born at Amasia in Pontus. He wrote, in Greek, *Historical Sketches*, surviving only in fragments, covering the period from 168 BC, where Polybius' *Histories* stopped, down to Augustus (Emperor 27 BC to AD 14) and an extant *Geography*, which included an account of Judaea and the Jews in the framework of the geography of Syria.

Strabo *Geographica* 16.2.34–7, 49

¶ For the most part each region is inhabited by a mixture of tribes drawn from Egyptians and Arabs and Phoenicians, for such are those who dwell in Galilee and Jericho and Philadelphia and Samaria, which Herod called Sebaste.[1] Although they are so mixed, the predominant opinion among the beliefs concerning the Temple at Jerusalem represents the ancestors of those now called Jews as Egyptians.

 For a certain Moses, an Egyptian priest who dwelt in the region called ⟨Lower Egypt⟩, because he was disgusted with Egyptian institutions emigrated there and many who honoured the Divinity[2] emigrated with him. He said that the Egyptians and the Libyans too were mistaken in representing the Divinity in the shape of wild or domestic animals and that the Greeks were also wrong in depicting gods in human form. One thing alone could be God, that which envelops us all by sea and

land, what we call sky or universe or nature. What rational man would
be bold enough to make an image of this in the likeness of anything
existent among us? But men ought to abandon all making of images
and honour God by setting apart a worthy precinct and sanctuary
without any statue. They should sleep in the sanctuary to get
revelation[3] on their own behalf; others, who had auspicious dreams,
should do so on behalf of the rest. Those who lived a righteous and
sober life should always expect some good and gift and sign from God,
but the rest should expect nothing.

    1. *Sebaste*: the ancient city was rebuilt and renamed in honour of
Augustus by Herod the Great in 27 BC.
    2. *Divinity*: Strabo uses the neuter of the adjective so as to form
an abstract noun, of the same root as the word God.
    3. *revelation*: this refers to a common religious practice, technically
known as *incubatio* (cp. p. 212), generally used by the sick and priests
in temples of gods of healing, not attested elsewhere for the Temple
at Jerusalem. This is a good example of the way which an author might
attribute ideas of his own time to men of the past.

¶ With such arguments then he persuaded a large number of rational men
and led them away to this spot, where there is now the foundation of
Jerusalem. He easily occupied it, for the site was not one to excite envy
nor any vigorous fighting for its possession, as it is stony and, though
it has a good water-supply itself, the surrounding land is poor and arid
and within a radius of sixty stades [seven and a half miles] is rocky too.
At the same time instead of resorting to arms he put forward in his
defence his religious rites and the Divinity, claiming to seek a settlement
for the latter and promising to institute such a form of worship and
such a cult as would not burden its devotees with expense or ecstatic
possession or other absurd doings.[1] In this way then he gained a good
reputation and established an extraordinary kind of state, for all the
surrounding peoples were won over easily because of their intercourse
with him and his promises.

His successors for some time kept up the same just practices and were
truly pious. Then the priesthood was held at first by superstitious and
then by tyrannical men. From superstition arose abstentions from foods,
such as are customary even now, and circumcisions and excisions and

similar usages; from tyranny arose banditry. For rebels ravaged both
the land itself and the neighbouring territory, while the supporters of
the government plundered other people's possessions and conquered
a large part of Syria and Phoenicia. Yet the citadel[2] had a certain
prestige, for they did not abominate it as the abode of tyranny, but
reverenced and exalted it as a holy place.

1. *expense* etc.: cp. p. 247 for such accompaniments of pagan
religions.
2. *citadel*: Strabo as a geographer uses the word Acropolis, the high
ground which was so often the fortified centre of an ancient city. There
could be temples, as on the Athenian Acropolis, but the word did not
in itself denote anything holy.

Strabo goes on to postulate law as a necessity for any society, law
resting on either religious or political foundations. He lists various
famous religious lawgivers of antiquity and finally:

¶ Such were Moses and his successors who after good beginnings
deteriorated.

Josephus, quoting Strabo's account of the Jews in Cyrene, repeats
the belief in Egyptian origins:

Josephus *Ant.* 14.7.2 (118)

¶ So the nation has gained strength in Egypt because the Jews were
originally Egyptians and those who left Egypt settled in neighbouring
territory.

CHAEREMON of Alexandria lived in the first century AD. He is
sometimes labelled as a Stoic philosopher, sometimes as an Egyptian
priest, and was a tutor of the young Nero (Emperor AD 54–68). Many
scholars have identified him as the Chaeremon who was one of the
Alexandrian spokesmen before Claudius in the dispute with the Jews
(p. 99). He wrote a *History of Egypt* surviving only in fragments, which
included an account of the Exodus. Josephus quotes this:

Josephus *Apion* 1.32.288–92

¶ After him [Manetho] I want to examine Chaeremon. He too professed
to compile a history of Egypt and gave the same names as Manetho
for king Amenophis[1] and his son Rameses. He says that: 'Isis appeared

to Amenophis in his sleep, reproaching him because her temple had
been destroyed in the war. Phritibautes, a sacred scribe, said that if he
purged Egypt of those tainted by pollution his fears would cease. So the
king picked out two hundred and fifty thousand of the diseased and
expelled them. Their leaders were scribes, Moses and Joseph, the latter
also a sacred scribe, and their Egyptian names were Tithisen for Moses
and Peteseph for Joseph. These reached Pelusium[2] and fell in with three
hundred and eighty thousand men left there by Amenophis, as he was
unwilling to let them into Egypt. They swore oaths of friendship with
them and launched an attack on Egypt. Amenophis did not dare to
await their onslaught, but fled to Ethiopia leaving his wife pregnant.
She hid herself in some caves and bore a son named Rameses. When
he came to manhood he chased away the Jews, about two hundred
thousand in number, to Syria and brought his father home again from
Ethiopia.'

1. *Amenophis*: see p. 41.
2. *Pelusium*: this was a city on the north coast, not far from the
eastern border of Egypt, preventing the entrance of nomadic tribes from
this quarter. Chaeremon does not identify the three hundred and eighty
thousand as Jews and the numbers he gives are inconsistent. It seems
as if Josephus abridged Chaeremon's account by piecing together a
number of fragmentary quotations.

A PION, first half of the first century AD, was a citizen of Alexandria,
who had a wide reputation for his scholarship and many literary works
written in Greek. He taught in Rome under Tiberius (Emperor
AD 14–37) and Claudius (Emperor AD 41–54) and also figured in
politics, representing the Alexandrians in their dispute against the Jews
before Gaius (Emperor AD 37–41). He nicknamed himself 'Multi-
victorious', but was dubbed 'The world's cymbal' (i.e. making a noise
everywhere) and 'Drum of his own reputation' by Tiberius. He wrote
a lost *Egyptian History* containing an account of the Exodus. Josephus,
trying to counter anti-Jewish prejudice, composed two books against
him, rebutting earlier false accounts of Judaism and quoting Apion's
own embroideries on these, referring expressly to the Exodus.

Josephus *Apion* 2.2.15, 20, 25

¶ As for the date at which he says that Moses led out the lepers and blind and cripples, in my opinion the accurate scholar [Apion] is in full agreement with his predecessors. ...He gives an amazing and plausible reason for the derivation of the name 'sabbath'. 'After marching six days', he says, 'they had tumours in the groin and when they had safely reached the country now called Judaea, they rested on the seventh day and called it "sabbaton", keeping the Egyptian word, for the Egyptians term pain in the groin "sabbatosis".' ...The amazing Apion after relating previously that they reached Judaea in six days, then says that Moses went up into the mountain called Sinai, which lies between Egypt and Arabia, and after concealing himself for forty days came down and gave the Jews their laws.

Apion had implied an Egyptian origin for the Jews by specifically naming Moses as an Egyptian priest, quoted by Josephus.

*Apion* 2.2.10–11

¶ 'Moses, as I heard from the Egyptian elders, was a citizen of Heliopolis, who conforming with the customs of his fathers erected prayer-houses open to the air in such areas as the city had available, all facing eastward. For this is also the orientation of the city of the Sun [Helios]. Instead of obelisks[1] he set up columns at the bottom of which was a bas-relief of a boat[2] and the shadow cast on this describes a circle which corresponds with the Sun's circuit in heaven.'

    1. *obelisks*: slender, tapering columns topped by a small gilded pyramid to catch the rays of the Sun were a feature of Heliopolis.
    2. *boat*: it was thought that the Sun traversed the heavens in a boat.

DIO CASSIUS, *c.* AD 150 to 235, born in Bithynia, son of the Roman governor of Cilicia, passed through the normal stages of a political career. He wrote in Greek a *History of Rome* from the beginning to AD 229 of which only books 36 to 54 (68 to 10 BC) survive in full, but other parts were summarized by later Byzantine scholars, giving the gist of his narrative.

Dio Cassius *History of Rome* 37.16–17

¶ Such were events in Palestine at that time [63 BC]. That is the ancient designation of the whole land extending from Phoenicia to Egypt alongside the inner sea. They have also acquired another name, for the land is called Judaea and the people Jews.

I do not know the origin of this name, but it is also applied to all those others who, though of a different race, emulate their customs. This people exists even among the Romans and although often reduced they multiplied so much that they achieved complete freedom for their beliefs. They differ from the rest of mankind in their whole way of life, generally speaking, and in particular in that they honour none of the other gods, but greatly revere one alone. Nor did they ever have any statue in Jerusalem, but considering him ineffable and invisible they outdo the rest of men in their cultic observances. They built for him a very large and beautiful temple, except in so far as it was open and uncovered, and consecrated the day called Saturn's.[1] On this day they pursue many very singular practices and engage in no serious business.

All that concerns that god, his nature and the origin of his cult and the passionate fervour which they feel for him, have been treated by many authors and have no relevance for this history.[2]

1. *Saturn's*: cp. p. 65.

2. *no relevance*: Dio writing a century or so after the fall of Jerusalem can take it for granted that the Jews are no longer a mysterious or potentially dangerous people. Plenty of information is available elsewhere for those who want it, but their origins and way of life are of little interest to him as a Roman historian.

## Moses

There are many references to Moses in those authors who wrote of Jewish origins (see above pp. 36–54). He is quite often described as an Egyptian priest. As a lawgiver he is depicted as wise and good or as the originator of pernicious and anti-social customs, according to the standpoint of individual authors. Incidental references class him as a magician, either of high standing or a mere charlatan. When more became known of his works under the later Empire he emerged as a literary figure, a philosophic thinker whose teaching merited serious discussion.

PLINY (the Elder), AD 23/24 to 79, was born at Comum in north Italy and probably educated at Rome. He spent twelve years in a military career, the following ten (perhaps because of dislike of Nero's regime) in rhetorical studies and returned to public life in 69 to serve under Vespasian. He was also a most industrious scholar and writer, though only the *Natural History* (*NH*), an encyclopaedic work in thirty-seven books, survives. His nephew, the Younger Pliny (p. 149) describes with admiration his unflagging devotion to study and, in a letter to Tacitus (p. 16), the circumstances of his death, indelibly linked with his name. He tells how his uncle's scientific curiosity about the great eruption of Vesuvius in AD 79 led him to sail too near the coast, so that he was overcome by the fumes and died (*Letters* 6.16).

Pliny treats of Judaea in the geographical part of his work. This is factual, but elsewhere there are some incidental references to Judaism.

### Pliny *NH* 32.11

❡ There is another branch of magic,[1] derived from Moses, Jannes,[2] Lotapes[3] and the Jews, but many thousands of years after Zarathustra.

    1. *magic*: this quotation is from a part of the *NH* containing a history of magic.

    2. *Jannes*: in Exod. 7:11 no names are given to the wise men and magicians at Pharaoh's court, but the names Jannes and Jambres are found in 2 Tim. 3:8 and in pagan literature (see below).

    3. *Lotapes*: the name is unknown.

APULEIUS, AD 123 to *c*. 185, was an African, educated at Carthage, Athens and Rome. He returned to Carthage and was highly renowned there as a poet, philosopher and rhetorician. Only prose works, written in Latin, have survived. The best known of these is the *Metamorphoses* (often called *The Golden Ass* in English), a delightful account of the adventures of a young man whose curiosity about witchcraft led to his being changed into an ass. After his restoration to human form by the goddess Isis the description of his initiation into the mysteries of Isis and Osiris may well contain some autobiographical features and is a valuable source of information (pp. 243ff.).

### Apuleius *Apologia* 90

Apuleius had married a rich widow, Pudentilla, considerably older than himself, and was prosecuted by her family on the charge of having won her affections by magic arts. His defence has survived.

¶ If the slightest reason can be found why I should have sought to marry Pudentilla for some personal advantage, rank me with the notorious Carimondas or Damigeron or Moses or Jannes or Apollonius or Dardanus or any other celebrated magician later than Zoroaster and Hostanes.[1]

1. *Carimondas* is unknown, *Damigeron* was reputed as the author of a magical treatise on precious stones, *Jannes* was an Egyptian magician at Pharaoh's court (see above), *Apollonius* the famous sage and miracle worker of the first century AD (p. 115), *Dardanus* a Phoenician, *Zoroaster* (Zarathustra) and *Hostanes* both Persians. Moses is thus included among magicians of the highest standing.

DIODORUS SICULUS *fl. c.* 60 BC (p. 46)

*World History* 1.94.1–2

¶ After a settled way of life had been established in Egypt in ancient times, in the legendary days of the gods and heroes, they say that Mneves first persuaded the masses to use written laws; he was a man not only of a noble soul but also in his life the most public-spirited of those commemorated. He claimed that Hermes had given him these laws to be the cause of great blessings. Among the Greeks the same is said of Minos in Crete and Lycurgus among the Spartans, for the former said he had received his laws from Zeus and the latter his from Apollo.

Among many other nations too this kind of idea traditionally existed and was the cause of many blessings to those who believed it. It is said that among the Arians[1] Zarathustra[2] claimed that the Good Spirit had given him the laws. Among the tribe called Getae,[3] who think themselves immortal, Zamolxis made the same claim about the communal Hestia;[4] among the Jews Moses made the same claim about the god whom he invoked as Iao.[5] Either they thought that the idea was marvellous and inspired and likely to benefit the mass of mankind or that the crowd considering the superiority and power of those claimed as inventors would be more inclined to accept and obey.

1. *Arians*: this was an ancient name for the Medes.
2. *Zarathustra* (Zoroaster): this reputed founder of Persian religion was well known for his doctrine of conflict between the Good Spirit

and the Evil. In hellenistic times a large number of works on multifarious subjects were ascribed to him.

3. *Getae*: these were a Thracian tribe, cp. Herodotus 4.92–4.

4. *Hestia*: they personified the Hearth (Greek *Hestia*) as a goddess, like the Roman Vesta.

5. *Iao*: the name is often found in magical papyri and amulets, but among pagan writers first occurs in Varro, 116–27 BC (p. 125).

LONGINUS, an author now generally recognized as anonymous, wrote in Greek a literary treatise, probably to be dated in the first century AD. This passage follows a quotation from Homer illustrating the purity and majesty of the divine nature. The author is noteworthy as quoting from the Bible before the spread of Christianity had roused interest in the Septuagint among pagan readers.

### On the Sublime 9

¶ So too the lawgiver of the Jews, no ordinary man, conceived and expressed the power of the Divinity as it deserved, when he wrote at the very beginning of his laws: 'God said – what? "Let there be light" and there was. "Let there be earth" and there was.'

JUVENAL, late first century AD (p. 32):

### Satires 5.14.102–4 (see p. 34 for full context)

¶ They [proselytes] learn and keep and revere whatever Jewish ordinances Moses handed down in a mysterious volume: not to show the way to any one who does not practise the same sacred rites, to bring only the circumcised to the spring which they are trying to find.

NUMENIUS of Apamea in Phrygia was a Pythagorean philosopher of the second century AD who exerted a considerable influence on later philosophers. Only fragments of his works, written in Greek, survive in quotations. He had some knowledge of both Judaism and Christianity. Eusebius, (the fourth century bishop of Caesarea and church historian) quotes from him.

### Eusebius *Preparation for the Gospel* (PE) 9.8.1–2

¶ In the third book[1] the same author refers to Moses as follows: 'Next lived Jannes and Jambres, Egyptian sacred scribes, ranked as magicians second to none at the time when the Jews were being expelled from Egypt. At any rate they were chosen by the Egyptian people to confront Musaeus, the Jewish leader, a man very powerful in prayer to God. They showed themselves capable of delivering Egypt from the worst of the disasters which Musaeus brought upon it.'

1. *third book*: Eusebius had just been citing Numenius' work *On the Good*.

Origen (p. 60) knew of Numenius' interest in Judaism, mentioned in a context where Origen is criticizing Celsus' objection to allegorizing scripture.

## Origen *C. Celsum* 4.51

¶ I know that even Numenius the Pythagorean, by far the best commentator on Plato and a leading exponent of Pythagorean teaching, in many places in his works quotes passages from Moses and the prophets and gives convincing allegorical interpretations, as for example in the one entitled *Epops*[1] and in his treatises *On Number* and *On Place*. In the third book *On the Good* he quotes even a story about Jesus, without mentioning his name, and interprets it allegorically; whether successfully or not, must be treated on another occasion. He also quotes the story about Moses and Jannes and Jambres.

1. *Epops*: the Greek word means the *Hoopoe* bird and throws no light on the contents.

Clement of Alexandria, the Christian scholar *c.* AD 150 to *c.* 215, credited Numenius with what has become a famous saying, inserting it in a context arguing for the dependence of Plato and Pythagoras on Hebrew thought and leading up to a disquisition on Moses:

## Clement *Stromateis* (*Miscellaneous Studies*) 1.22.150

¶ Numenius, the Pythagorean philosopher, writes outright: 'What is Plato but Moses talking Attic[1] Greek?'

1. *Attic*: Plato as a native of Athens naturally used the Attic dialect, which in scholarly circles came to be recognized as the best and purest form of Greek. Eusebius in *PE* 9.6.9 quotes this word for word and attributes it to Clement, but he also knew it as a current saying, *PE* 9.10.14. After a lengthy quotation from Numenius' second book *On the Good* he continues:

Eusebius *PE* 9.10.14

¶ So writes Numenius, expounding together the teaching of Plato and much earlier of Moses. Naturally then that current saying is referred to him, whereby he is reported to have said: 'What is Plato but Moses talking Attic Greek?'

Whether this saying can properly be attributed to Numenius has been doubted. Clement does not name the written source. Eusebius knew it both at secondhand from Clement and as a floating saying current in his own day.

APOLLONIUS MOLO, first century BC, was born in Caria and taught rhetoric in Rhodes, where Cicero and Caesar were among his pupils. He is reported to have written a special book about the Jews, in Greek, which according to Josephus showed a strongly anti-Jewish bias. The following quotation from Josephus shows how Moses could be seen as a charlatan rather than as a wise man skilled in magic:

Josephus *Apion* 2.14.145

¶ Apollonius Molo and Lysimachus[1] and some others, partly through ignorance but mainly through malevolence, have made statements about our lawgiver Moses and his laws which are neither just nor true, slandering the former as a charlatan and cheat and alleging that the laws have instructed us in vice and not in any virtue.

  1. *Lysimachus*: see above p. 45.

CELSUS, late second century AD, was a pagan philosopher who composed a reasoned and elaborate indictment of Christianity, *True Teaching* (about AD 178), the earliest literary attack of this kind of which we have detailed knowledge. The treatise itself has not survived, but in the following century (about 248/9) the great Alexandrian Christian scholar Origen wrote a reply, *c. Celsum* (*Against Celsus*), in which he quoted Celsus extensively and dealt with his arguments point by point. Celsus also inserted some incidental polemic against the Jews, including the following uncomplimentary reference to Moses (see also p. 116 below):

Origen *c. Celsum* 1.23

¶ Celsus says next that 'shepherds and goatherds following their leader

Moses were beguiled by gross deception into the belief that there was only one God.'

The most bizarre statement about Moses is attributed in *Suidas* (or *Suda*, not an author but the title, meaning *Fortress*, of a famous tenth century historical and literary encyclopaedia and lexicon) to:

ALEXANDER POLYHISTOR, a first century BC Greek from Miletus, who wrote among many other lost works a book *On the Jews*:

Quoted in *Suidas* A 1129

❡ He wrote innumerable works including five books on Rome; in these he says that there lived a Hebrew woman called Moso,[1] who was the author of the Law of the Hebrews.

1. *Moso*: Alexander, whom Eusebius quotes with respect, was probably mentioning one divergent view of Moses, not necessarily his own.

GALEN, AD 129 to 199, was born at Pergamum in Asia Minor, but from 162 spent most of his life in Rome, where he had close connections with the imperial court. He had a great reputation as a philosopher and a physician, but was not committed to any one school of philosophy nor was he an original philosophic thinker. In medicine however his knowledge was consistently valued. His works were translated into Arabic from Greek and some of them only survive in that translation. There are five incidental references to Jewish and/or Christian thought and one eulogy of Christian morality. These can be consulted most easily in R. Walzer's *Galen on Jews and Christians*. He gives passages in the original along with translation both of Greek and Arabic and discusses the context. The translations and page references given below are from his book.

Galen Reference 1 (p. 10)

❡ They compare those who practise medicine without scientific knowledge to Moses, who framed laws for the tribe of the Jews, since it is his method in his books to write without offering proofs, saying 'God commanded, God spake'.

Reference 2 (p. 11)
Galen uses the eyelash as an illustration:

¶ Did our demiurge[1] simply enjoin this hair to preserve its length always
equal[2] and does it strictly observe this order either from fear of its
master's command, or from reverence for the god who gave this order,
or is it because it itself believes it better to do this? Is not this Moses'
way of treating Nature and is it not superior to that of Epicurus?[3] The
best way, of course, is to follow neither of these but to maintain like
Moses the principle of the demiurge as the origin of every created thing,
while adding the material principle to it. For our demiurge created it
to preserve a constant length, because this was better. When he had
determined to make it so, he set under part of it a hard body as a kind
of cartilage, and under another part a hard skin attached to the cartilage
through the eyebrows. For it was certainly not sufficient merely to will
their becoming such: it would not have been possible for him to make
a man out of a stone in an instant, by simply wishing so.

It is precisely at this point in which our own opinion and that of
Plato and of the other Greeks who follow the right method in natural
science differs from the position taken up by Moses. For the latter it
seems enough to say that God simply willed the arrangement of matter
and it was presently arranged in due order; for he believes everything
to be possible with God, even should he wish to make a bull or a horse
out of ashes. We however do not hold this; we say that certain things
are impossible by nature and that God does not even attempt such things
at all but that he chooses the best out of the possibilities of becoming.
We say therefore that since it was better that the eyelashes should always
be equal in length and number, it was not that he just willed and they
were instantly there; for even if he should just will numberless times,
they would never come into being in this manner out of a soft skin;
and, in particular, it was altogether impossible for them to stand erect
unless fixed on something hard. We say thus that God is the cause both
of the choice of the best in the products of creation themselves and
of the selection of the matter. For since it was required, first that the
eyelashes should stand erect and secondly that they should be kept equal
in length and number, he planted them firmly in a cartilaginous body.

If he had planted them in a soft and fleshy substance he would have suffered a worse failure not only than Moses but also than a bad general who plants a wall or a camp in marshy ground.

1. *demiurge*: this originally meant any skilled craftsman. Plato, in the *Republic* and *Timaeus*, referred it to the creator of the world and it came to mean this in the language of philosophy and theology.

2. *hair*: Galen was discussing the unvarying length of the eyelashes.

3. *Epicurus*: according to the philosophy of Epicurus (341 to 270 BC) the universe arose from the random combinations of atoms in space, not from any divine action.

Reference 3 (p. 14)

❡ One might more easily teach novelties to the followers of Moses and Christ than to the physicians and philosophers who cling to their schools.

Reference 4 (p. 14)

❡ In order that one should not at the very beginning, as if one had come into the school of Moses and Christ, hear talk of undemonstrated laws, and that where it is least appropriate.

Reference 5 (p. 14)

❡ If I had in mind people who taught their pupils in the same way as the followers of Moses and Christ teach theirs – for they order them to accept everything on faith – I should not have given you a definition.

### Sabbath

Most references to the sabbath mark its essential observance as a day of rest. Some are brief in themselves, some are from longer passages quoted elsewhere in this book. Their interest lies in the different attitudes, periods and backgrounds of their authors. They have been divided into four sections:

    I   The sabbath denoting inactivity
   II  The sabbath regarded as a waste of valuable time
  III  Erroneous association of fasting with the sabbath
  IV  Knowledge, often garbled, of sabbath-observances

I

OVID (P. Ovidius Naso), 43 BC to AD 17/18, was one of the best
known of Roman poets. He was very prolific in his output, but today
is remembered chiefly for his love poems and that great treasure of
mythology, *The Metamorphoses*.

*Art of love* 1.75–6
Ovid is listing, for the would-be lover, places and occasions favourable
for picking up a girl.

⁋ Do not overlook Adonis¹ mourned by Venus nor the seventh day
held sacred by the Palestinian Syrian.²

    1. *Adonis*: this beautiful youth had been killed by a boar. His death
was celebrated annually, when the streets would be crowded with
worshippers and business forgotten.
    2. *Palestinian Syrian*: this was a synonym for a Jew as early as
Herodotus (p. 38), 2.104.2.

*Art of love* 1.413–16
Courtship may begin on days not used for business.

⁋ You may begin on the day when mournful Allia¹ was stained with
the blood of Latin wounds and on the day when every week the day
less fit for business returns, the festival celebrated by the Palestinian
Syrian.

    1. *Allia*: the anniversary of the Gauls' defeat of the Romans at the
river Allia in the fourth century was one of the unlucky days in the
Roman calendar, not propitious for business.

*Cures for love* 217–20
The lover who wishes to free himself must run away from his mistress,
however unsuitable the day for taking any action.

⁋ But the less you wish to go, the more you must be mindful of going.
Hold out; force your unwilling feet to run. Do not wish for rain nor
be delayed by foreign sabbath nor Allia well known for its disasters.

HORACE (Quintus Horatius Flaccus), 65 to 8 BC, son of a freedman, was born at Venusia in Apulia, received a liberal education and became one of the most celebrated poets of his day, an intimate friend of Maecenas, the great statesman and patron of literature. He wrote odes, satires and epistles. These two latter were written in verse, lightly criticizing and describing all aspects of the society in which he moved. The following extract describes how Horace is accosted by a bore and cannot shake him off. Here they meet a friend of Horace's, who mischievously refuses to help him out.

Horace *Satires* 1.9.67–72

¶ 'Didn't you say there was something you wanted to tell me in private?'

'I remember it well, but I'll tell you at a better time. Today is the thirtieth,[1] the sabbath. Do you want to insult the circumcised Jews?'

'I have no religious scruples,' said I.

'But I have: I'm rather weak, one of the crowd. Excuse me; I'll talk another time.'

1. *thirtieth*: scholars argue as to whether a specific Jewish festival may be meant or whether it is an invention of the speaker, a garbled reference to the well-known weekly sabbath.

TIBULLUS (Albius), second half of the first century BC, contemporary with Horace and Ovid, who refer to him, but not in the same court circles, best known for his slender output of love poems.

Tibullus *Book 1* 3.15–18

The poet lying sick in a foreign land remembers how, after comforting his mistress Delia, he had sought excuses to delay his departure.

¶ I myself, her comforter, when I had already given my commissions, was still anxious and sought lingering delays. I alleged either birds[1] or evil omens or that the day sacred to Saturn[2] had held me back.

1. *birds*: these were recognized as omens.
2. *Saturn*: division of the month into seven-day periods was becoming familiar even in the first century BC. Saturn's day had no religious significance, but coincided with the Jewish seventh-day sabbath, so the poet merges the two in one, as the sabbath would have inhibited all activity. This identification became widely current, just as today the Jewish sabbath is identified with Saturday.

APION, first half of first century AD, quoted by Josephus (see earlier, p. 53):

Josephus *Apion* 2.2.20

¶ 'After marching six days', he says 'they had tumours in the groin and when they had safely reached the country now called Judaea, they rested on the seventh day and called it "sabbaton", keeping the Egyptian word, for the Egyptians term pain in the groin "sabbatosis".'

TACITUS AD 56 to 112/113 (p. 16).

*Hist.* 4.11–18 (see p. 21 for full context and commentary):

¶ They [the Jews] say that a rest was instituted on the seventh day because that brought an end to their labours; then because of the pleasures of idleness the seventh year was also given to indolence. Others say that it is held in honour of Saturn, either because the Idaeans, traditionally banished with Saturn, and the founding fathers of the race, transmitted their religion; or because out of the seven stars by which mortals are ruled the star of Saturn moves in the highest orbit and is outstandingly powerful and most of the heavenly bodies complete their way and their course in periods of seven apiece.

DIO CASSIUS, *c.* AD 150 to 235 (p. 54).

*History of Rome* 37.17.3

¶ They built for him [God] a very large and beautiful temple, except in so far as it was open and uncovered, and consecrated the day called Saturn's. On this day they pursue many very singular practices and engage in no serious business.

II

SENECA (Lucius Annaeus, the Younger), 4 BC/AD 1 to AD 65, born of Italian stock at Corduba in Spain, author of short ethical and philosophical treatises (many in the form of letters), dramatist, Stoic philosopher, tutor and political adviser of the Emperor Nero in the first years of his reign, was finally forced by Nero to commit suicide. We find a quotation from *On Superstition* in Augustine (Saint, of Hippo, 354–430).

Augustine *City of God* 6.11

❡ Among other superstitions involving a national theology[1] he [Seneca] also condemns the religious observances of the Jews, especially the sabbath. He asserts that this is an unprofitable practice, because by the interruption of a weekly day of leisure they lose a seventh of their lives and suffer injury by leaving much pressing business undone.

  1. *national theology*: Seneca elsewhere censured the Egyptian cult of Isis (see p. 240) and the Phrygian cult of Cybele (see p. 229).

JUVENAL within AD 50 to 150 (see p. 32).

*Satire* 5.14.105–6 (see p. 34 for the full context)

❡ The father is to blame, who spent every seventh day in sloth without any contact with life.

AGATHARCHIDES, second century BC, native of Cnidus, resident in Alexandria, wrote a *History of Asia* and a *History of Europe* in Greek of which only fragments survive. One such fragment occurs in Josephus:

Josephus *Apion* 1.22.205–11

❡ After telling this story and ridiculing Stratonice's[1] superstition he gives as an example the story told about us and writes: 'The people called Jews inhabit a city which is of all cities the strongest, called by the natives Jerusalem. They have a custom of doing no work on every seventh day. At these times they neither bear arms nor till the fields nor busy themselves with any other public duty, but pray with outstretched hands in the Temple until evening. When Ptolemy,[2] the son of Lagus, entered the city with his army, instead of defending it the people persisted in their foolishness; the country received a cruel master and the law was exposed as imposing a useless custom. The event has taught all other men, with the exception of these, to have recourse to dreams and traditional ideas about law only when they are at their wits' end to find a way out of their difficulties by human reasoning.'

1. *Stratonice*: Agatharchides had just described how Stratonice, a Seleucid princess, after provoking a rebellion, could have escaped. In obedience to a dream she delayed her departure and was killed.

2. *Ptolemy I Soter* took Jerusalem in 320 or 312 BC. Cp. 1 Macc. 2:29–41 for a massacre arising from sabbath-observance in the Maccabaean period (cp. also 2 Macc. 6:11). As a result of this, Mattathias had declared that it should be lawful to take up arms against direct attack even on the sabbath, confirmed by Josephus in *Ant.* 12.6.2 (274–6). Cp. 2 Macc. 15:1–5 for an attack threatened on the sabbath on the assumption that the Jews would take no action.

STRABO, 64/3 BC to AD 21 (see p. 50), referring to Pompey's capture of the Temple in 63 BC.

### *Geographica* 16.2.41

¶ Pompey took the city, it is said, after watching for the day of fasting,[1] when the Jews were abstaining from all work; he filled in the ditch and threw ladders across it.

1. *day of fasting*: other chronological references rule out the Day of Atonement, which would have been a fast. Strabo was probably influenced by the popular misconception of the sabbath as a day of fasting, see section III below. Josephus (*Ant.* 14.4.2–3 (63–8)), possibly using Strabo as his source, also assigns the capture to the 'day of fasting'. After describing how the priests continued with their ritual in the Temple he goes on: 'All those who have related the exploits of Pompey bear witness that this was not simply a story of praise of imaginary piety; among them are Strabo, Nicolaus [see p. 47] and also Titus Livius [see p. 124], author of the History of Rome.' In *War* 1.7.3–4 (146–8), however, following some other source, he specifies only these siege operations as being carried out on the sabbath, 'when the Jews abstain from all work because of their cultic observances.... Only in self-defence do they resist even on the sabbath.' He then describes how the priests carried on with their 'normal daily ritual'.

PLUTARCH, *c.* AD 50 to 120 (see below, p. 72).

### *On Superstition* 8
After including sabbath rests among other squalid rites:

¶ The Homeric warrior prayed to God for success in battle, but the Jews sitting unwashed on the sabbath, when the enemy were putting ladders to the walls and capturing them, did not get up, but remained as if bound together in a single net by superstition.

FRONTINUS, *c.* AD 30 to 104, was a soldier, engineer and military expert.

*Art of Strategy* 2.1.17
Dealing with the choice of strategic occasions for attack:

¶ The late Emperor Vespasian[1] attacked and defeated the Jews on the day of Saturn, when it is sinful for them to undertake any business.

  1. *late Emperor*: not *Vespasian* (Emperor 69–79) but his son Titus took Jerusalem in AD 70.

DIO CASSIUS, *c.* AD 150 to 235 (see p. 54).

*History of Rome* 37.16.2–4
Referring to Pompey's capture of the city in 63 BC:

¶ If they had put up a similar resistance every day he [Pompey] would not have taken the Temple. As it was, they used to let pass the days called Saturn's without any action at all and so gave the Romans the opportunity of damaging the wall in these intervals. The latter, when they learnt of their fanaticism, did not engage actively at other times, but at the periodic return of those days they used to attack the ramparts with the utmost vigour. Thus the Temple was taken on the day of Saturn without any resistance and all its wealth looted.

*Epitome* 65.7.2
Referring to the capture of the Temple by Titus in AD 70:

¶ So perished Jerusalem on the very day of Saturn,[1] which the Jews even now revere more than any other day.

  1. *day of Saturn*: no specific day is mentioned by either Josephus or Tacitus.

### III

AUGUSTUS, first Roman Emperor 27 BC to AD 14 (born 63 BC). Suetonius (see p. 84) quotes a fragment of a letter from Augustus to his stepson.

Suetonius *Life of Augustus* 76

❡ Not even a Jew, my dear Tiberius, keeps the sabbath fast as rigorously as I have done today. At long last after the first hour of the night I ate two mouthfuls in the bath before I began to be anointed.

POMPEIUS TROGUS, 27 BC to AD 14 (see p. 48).

Quoted by Justinus *Epitome* 36.3.14

❡ When Moses with the people, wearied out by seven days of going without food, at last arrived there through the deserts of Arabia, they hallowed the seventh day, habitually called sabbath by that nation, by a fast for all time to come. This was because that day put an end to their fasting and wandering.

PETRONIUS, first century AD, was the writer of a fragmentary, picaresque novel, in prose interlarded with verse, relating the fortunes of three disreputable adventurers. Best known is the episode 'Trimalchio's feast', where they are entertained by a rich freedman. Whether the author was the famous 'Arbiter of Elegance' at Nero's court is debateable.

*Satyricon*, Fragment 37 (see p. 82 for the full context)

❡ the sabbath with its ordinance of fasting

MARTIAL, *c.* AD 40 to *c.* 104, born at Bilbilis in Spain, was educated in Spain, came to Rome in 64 and, though a poor man, was eventually acepted in literary circles. He wrote numerous epigrams, many of them satirical, some with a touch of obscenity.

*Epigrams* 4.4

Martial is attacking Bassa for her bad breath and among other stenches which would be preferable he lists:

❡ the stench of women keeping fast on the sabbath

## IV

MELEAGER, end of second to beginning of first century BC, born at Gadara, lived in Tyre and finally in the Greek island of Cos, and was celebrated as an erotic poet.

*Greek Anthology* 5.160

❡ White-cheeked Demo, someone delights in your embrace, but my heart now groans within me. If you are in love with a sabbatarian, no wonder! Love is aflame even on chilly[1] sabbaths.

    1. *chilly*: Jews were forbidden to light fires on the sabbath, as Meleager coming from Gadara would know. This is one of the earliest references to the sabbath in pagan literature and presupposes that Jewish practices would be known to his readers.

PERSIUS (Aulus Flaccus), AD 34 to 62, prosperous, well educated, moving in literary circles in Rome, was an ardent adherent of Stoicism. His satires, in form like those of Horace, contain some vivid sketches of contemporary society, but his main purpose was to recommend the Stoic way of life.

*Satires* 5.179–84

The man who thinks himself free may be a prey to superstitions, Jewish, Phrygian, Egyptian:

❡ But when the days of Herod[1] are come and the violet-wreathed lamps,[2] set in order in the greasy window, have poured a thick cloud of smoke and the tail of the tunny-fish curls round the red dish and is afloat, and the white jar is bursting with wine, then you move your lips without speaking and grow pale with fear before the sabbath of the circumcised.

    1. *days of Herod*: in view of what follows, this is more likely to refer to the sabbath kept by Herod personifying the Jewish people, than to Herod's birthday or accession.

    2. *lamps*: fish, ranked as a delicacy, and lamps marked the festive nature of the sabbath. Lamps crowned with violets also featured in the honours paid to the little Roman household god, the Lar (Juvenal 4.12.89–92). Josephus, *Apion* 2.39.282, listed the lighting of lamps as one of the religious observances which, he alleges, had been taken over from the Jews by other peoples.

SENECA (p. 66).

*Moral Letters* 95.47
Seneca is deprecating any ritual which might seem to belittle the transcendence of God, not expressly attacking Judaism.

¶ Instructions are usually given as to how the gods should be worshipped. Let us forbid lamps to be lit on the sabbath,[1] since the gods do not need light and men find no pleasure in soot. Let us ban morning salutations and crowding the doors of temples; human ambition is captivated by those observances. He who knows God worships him. Let us ban the bringing of towels and strigils to Jupiter, the offering of mirrors to Juno; God seeks no servants. Of course not; he himself does service to the human race and is at hand to help all men everywhere.

    1. *lamps*: Seneca, like his contemporary Persius, associates lamps with the sabbath, so this feature of keeping the sabbath must by now have become well known.

JUVENAL, late first century AD (p. 32), gave rein to fantasy in imagining sabbath-observance in its native land (cp. p. 33 for full context):

*Satires* 2.6.159
¶ the land [i.e. Judaea] where kings celebrate the sabbath bare-footed

PLUTARCH, born before AD 50, died after 120, came from Chaeronea in Greece. He was a travelled scholar, knew Athens and Rome well and had a large circle of influential friends. For the last thirty years of his life he was a priest at Delphi and combined the study of philosophy and antiquities with a sincere piety. His literary output was voluminous and much of it survives, including the famous *Lives*, short treatises on moral themes (under the general heading of *Moralia*) and nine volumes of learned table-talk (*Quaestiones Conviviales*, quoted as *Quaest. Conv.*).

*Quaest. Conv.* 4.6.2. (see pp. 126ff. for full context)
¶ I think that the sabbath festival too is not entirely without a Dionysiac

element. Even now many call Bacchic worshippers Sabi, and this is the cry they utter in their revelry in honour of the god. This can be confirmed of course by both Demosthenes and Menander and it would not be unreasonable to say that the name has arisen because of a kind of excitement [*sobesis*]¹ which possesses the Bacchanals. They themselves attest the theory, for whenever they celebrate sabbaths they challenge one another to drinking and drunkenness and, when some more important business prevents this, they make a habit of tasting at least a little neat wine.²

1. *sobesis*: this is an example of spurious learned etymology.
2. *neat wine*: wine was usually drunk mixed with water and, as such, was the normal drink. The association of drunkenness with the sabbath is pure fantasy.

OFFICIAL RECORDS often guarantee freedom to observe the sabbath, but the last word in sabbath observance is to be found in a statement, made without comment, in a description of the geography of Palestine by the ELDER PLINY (p. 56):

Pliny *NH* 31.24
❡ In Judaea there is a stream which dries up every sabbath.

### Food Laws

Abstention from pork is accepted as an essential feature of Judaism, odd and perhaps rather ridiculous, but not in itself reprehensible, except in so far as this deviation from the norm could be regarded as anti-social. Regulations on food were to be found in other cults too.

DIODORUS SICULUS, last half of first century BC (p. 46)

*World History* 34.1
Here the friends of Antiochus VII during the siege of Jerusalem 135/4 BC are recommending him to follow the example of his ancestor Antiochus IV Epiphanes in 167 BC:

❡ Antiochus himself detested this universal misanthropy and made it a point of honour to abolish their usages. He therefore sacrificed a large sow[1] before the statue[2] of the founder and the outdoor altar and poured the blood over them. He prepared the meat and gave orders that their sacred books containing the laws hostile to foreigners should be sprinkled with the broth from it and that the lamp which they call eternal and which burns continually in the Temple should be quenched. He also forced the high priest and the other Jews to partake of the meat.

1. *sow*: this is the first reference in pagan literature to the Jews' abstention from pork. In Jewish literature cp. 2 Macc. 6:18–31 for Eleazar's refusal and death; also Philo (p. 35), *Flacc.* 11.96, who describes how in the pogrom of AD 38 the Alexandrians forced Jewesses to eat pork in public.

2. *statue*: Antiochus was said to have found a statue of Moses in the temple (see p. 45).

CICERO, 100 to 43 BC (p. 117). Cicero on behalf of the Sicilians prosecuted the governor for extortion in a famous series of speeches, the Verrine Orations. The following anecdote is told only by Plutarch in his *Life of Cicero* and the pun does not come through so well in the Greek.

Quoted by Plutarch *Life of Cicero* 7.6

¶ Nevertheless many witticisms of his are reported in connection with this trial. The Romans call a castrated porker a 'verres'. So when a freedman called Caecilius,[1] who was suspected of Judaism, wanted to oust the Sicilians and prosecute Verres himself, Cicero said: 'What has a Jew to do with a porker [Verres]?'

1. *Caecilius*: Verres did have a quaestor called Caecilius who wanted to conduct the prosecution in order to hamper proceedings. It is unlikely that he was a freedman and Plutarch may have confused him with a later Caecilius, a Judaizing Greek historian in the time of Augustus (Emperor 27 BC to AD 14). Whatever his identity, the connection between Jews and abstention from pork is clearly taken for granted as a well-known fact even in Cicero's day. The trial took place in 70 BC.

**STRABO**, 64/3 BC to AD 21 (p. 50).

*Geographica* 16.2.37 (see p. 51 for full context)
¶ From superstition arose abstentions from foods, such as are customary even now.

**AUGUSTUS** (Emperor 27 BC to AD 14). This saying is quoted by Macrobius, a fifth century Latin author, who wrote a *Saturnalia* in seven books, an academic discussion on a great variety of topics.

Quoted by Macrobius *Saturnalia* 2.4.11
¶ When he heard that among the boys aged under two whom Herod, king of the Jews, had ordered to be put to death his own son had also been killed, he said:

'I would rather have been Herod's pig than his son.'[1]

1. *son*: no son of Herod's was killed in infancy. The author is clumsily combining a reminiscence of the Murder of the Innocents (Matt. 2:16) with a pagan anecdote about the bloodshed in Herod's own family, but the saying may well be genuine. The implication is, of course, that Herod would have refrained from killing a pig.

**GAIUS** (Emperor AD 37–41). In AD 40 an embassy from the Alexandrian Jews came to Rome to put their case before the Emperor (see p. 11). They had to follow him round some gardens and in the course of this survey he flung the following question at them, recorded by Philo:

Philo *Leg. Gaj.* 361
¶ 'Why do you refuse to eat pork?'

**APION**, first half of first century AD (p. 53). This reference comes from Josephus:

Josephus *Apion* 2.13.137
¶ He objects to our sacrificing domestic animals and not eating pork.

SENECA (the Younger), 4 BC/AD 1 to 65 (p. 66).

*Moral Letters* 108.98.22

¶ Under this incitement[1] I began to abstain from meat and by the end of a year the habit was not only easy but pleasant. I fancied that my mind was more active; today I could not affirm whether it was so or not. Do you ask how I gave it up? The period of my youth fell within the first part of the principate of Tiberius Caesar. At that time some foreign rites were being set on foot and among the marks of the cult was counted abstinence from eating certain animals. So at the request of my father, who did not fear a malicious prosecution,[2] but hated philosophy, I returned to my former habit and he persuaded me without difficulty to dine better.

    1. *incitement*: Seneca had attended the lectures of a certain Sextius, who followed Pythagoras in advocating vegetarianism.

    2. *prosecution*: this probably refers to the expulsion of Jews and worshippers of Isis in AD 19 (see p. 103), when Seneca might have been denounced for Jewish practices.

PLINY (the Elder), AD 22/24 to 79 (p. 56).

*NH* 31.95

¶ But another kind [of rich fish sauce] is used expressly for religious sexual abstinence and Jewish rites. This is made from fish without scales.[1]

    1. *scales*: actually the eating of fish without scales was forbidden, Lev. 11:12.

JUVENAL, within AD 50 to 150 (p. 32).

*Satires* 2.6.160 (see p. 33 for full context)

¶ [Judaea] where a long-established clemency spares pigs to grow old.

*Satires* 5.14.97–9 (see p. 34 for full context)

¶ Some who happen to have a father who stands in awe of the sabbath, worship nothing but clouds and the holy heaven and do not differentiate between human and pigs' flesh, from which their father abstained.

TACITUS, AD 56 to 112/113 (p. 16).

*Hist.* 5.4.7–9 (see p. 20 for full text and commentary)
¶ They abstain from eating pork, thanks to the disaster of their previous disfigurement by scabies to which that animal is subject. By frequent fasts they still bear witness to their long former famine and retain unleavened bread in token of the grain which they plundered.

PLUTARCH, *c.* AD 50 to 120 (p. 72).

*Quaest. Conv.* 4.4.4–5.3
¶ 'My grandfather', said Lamprias, 'always used to say in mockery of the Jews that it was the most proper kind of meat from which they abstained, but we shall assert that the most proper kind of food is what comes from the sea.'[1] [This leads to a discussion on the relative merits of meat and fish. Then reverting to Lamprias' grandfather's original statement:] 'I entirely agree', said Polycrates, 'but I also have another question to pose, whether it is in honour of pigs or because of aversion from the creature that they abstain from eating it. Their own accounts are like myths, unless after all they have some serious reasons which they do not disclose.'

   1. *What comes from the sea*: in the Graeco-Roman world, fish was considered a great delicacy.

¶ 'For my part', said Callistratus, 'I think that they hold it in some honour. Granted that the pig is ugly and muddy, he is no more odd in appearance or grosser by nature than a beetle or a crocodile or a cat, which various groups of Egyptian priests treat as most sacred. They say however that the pig is honoured for a good reason. With its projecting snout, as they say, it cut into the ground and was the first to make a furrow and lead on to the function of the ploughshare. It is for this reason, according to their account, that the implement was named after the pig.[1] Those Egyptians who farm the low-lying parts of the country, where the soil is soft, do not even need a plough at all. When the Nile overflows and soaks their fields, they follow it up by letting in their pigs. These by trampling and rooting soon turn up the soil in depth and cover the seed. So it is not surprising if, because of this, some people do not eat pork.'

    1. *named after the pig*: the Greek word for pig is *hus* (cp. Latin *sus*), and for a ploughshare *hunnis*. This etymological argument is not really applicable to Egyptians or Jews.

¶ [He then gives a long list of other creatures, honoured or abhorred by various peoples, some for quite illogical reasons, and goes on:] 'I fancy that the Jews too, if they abominated the pig, would kill it, as the magi[1] kill mice but, as it is, eating and slaughtering are prohibited alike. Perhaps it may be argued that just as they honour the ass[2] which showed them the spring of water, so also they honour the pig, which taught them how to sow and plough. Otherwise, of course, some one will say that their abstention from eating hare's flesh[3] is because they abominate it as a filthy and impure creature.'

    1. *magi*: this refers here to the Persian followers of Zoroaster.
    2. *ass*: see Tacitus (p. 20) who tells how a troop of wild asses returning from pasture disclosed water when the Jews were parched with thirst in the desert. Plutarch takes it for granted that his readers will grasp the allusion, which also presupposes that they will assume that the Jews came from Egypt.
    3. *hare's flesh*: the eating of this is prohibited in Lev. 11:6, immediately preceding the ban on pork.

¶ 'No, indeed', said Lamprias, taking him up, 'they abstain from eating the hare because of its very close resemblance to the ass, which they hold in the highest honour. For the hare is like an ass of less weight and size and there is an amazing resemblance in its colour and ears and the brightness of its eyes and its lustfulness. In fact there do not exist one thing so small and one thing so big which are so alike in appearance. Possibly of course they also take the Egyptian view[1] of characteristics and consider the animal's swiftness and the keenness of its senses something divine. Their eyes are untiring, for they even sleep with their eyes wide open. In sharpness of hearing it is reputed to excel, a trait so admired by the Egyptians that they use the hare's ear to represent hearing in their hieroglyphics.

    As for pork, the Jews apparently abominate it because barbarians[2] are particularly digusted by white scales and leprous diseases and think that such diseases ravage men by contact. We see that the underbelly of every pig is full of leprous scales and scurfy eruptions which apparently overrun the body, if it is in poor health and wasting away. Moreover the animal's filthy habits spoil the meat to some extent. We see nothing else so fond of mud and dirty and unclean places, leaving aside those born and bred in such a habitat. It is also said that pigs' eyes are so contorted and drawn down that they never notice anything above them nor look at the sky, unless they are carried upside down, when the eyes are unnaturally drawn upwards. That is why the animal, though given to excessive squealing, keeps quiet when carried in this way and is silent through amazement at the unaccustomed sight of the heavens and is restrained from making a noise through overpowering fear. If we are to bring in mythology, there is the story that Adonis[3] was killed by a boar, though some identify him with Dionysus.'

1. *Egyptian view*: this refers to the Egyptian representation of gods with animal features (see pp. 236ff.).

2. *barbarians*: for a Greek this often meant no more than a foreigner, though implying an inferior level of culture.

3. *Adonis*: he was the beautiful youth beloved by Venus, who was killed while out hunting. Here the identification with Dionysus (p. 196) serves as a clumsy link with the next question when the identification of Dionysus with the god of the Jews is discussed (see pp. 126ff.).

EPICTETUS, about AD 50 to 120, was born in Hierapolis in Phrygia and was for many years a slave. He was brought to Rome, received instruction in Stoicism and became a noted Stoic philosopher, though he had received no formal education. He wrote nothing, but his pupil, the historian and scholar Arrian, compiled collections of his sayings.

Epictetus 1.22.4
The author is maintaining that there are certain universally accepted preconceptions, e.g. that holiness is good, but the difficulty arises when men differ in specific cases in their definition of what is holy. The illustration about eating pork is quite dispassionate.

¶ This is the origin of men's conflict with one another. This is the conflict between Jews and Syrians and Egyptians and Romans, not whether holiness is to be preferred to everything else and pursued in every case, but whether this act of eating pork is holy or unholy.

SEXTUS EMPIRICUS, *c.* AD 200, was a Greek philosopher and physician.

*Outlines of Pyrrhonism* 3.24.223
In a catalogue of the differing beliefs and practices of different nations, we find:

❡ A Jew or an Egyptian priest would die rather than eat pork.

CELSUS, late second century AD (p. 60). This is quoted by Origen.

*c. Celsum* 5.43 (see p. 116 for full context)
❡ Moreover they are certainly no more holy than the rest of men... because they abstain from pork, for the Egyptians do this too and furthermore abstain from goats' meat, mutton, beef and fish, while Pythagoras[1] and his disciples abstain both from beans and from all living creatures.

    1. *Pythagoras*: this Greek philosopher and mathematician, late sixth century BC, believed in the transmigration of souls into men and animals – hence his vegetarianism.

### Circumcision

Circumcision is sometimes mentioned as a proof of the Egyptian origin of the Jewish people. For the ordinary man it was just one of those inexplicable practices which distinguished the Jews, a practice causing some instinctive revulsion. It was recognized as essential for proselytes who were fully converted to Judaism and therefore for them the practice was banned in the second century AD.

STRABO, 64/3 BC to AD 21 (p. 50).

*Geographica* 16.2.37 (see p. 51 for full context)
❡ From superstition arose...circumcisions and excisions.[1]

    1. *excisions*: operations on women, corresponding to circumcision

of males, though still current in some parts of Africa, were not practised
by the Jews.

## DIODORUS SICULUS, last half of first century BC (p. 46).

*World History* 1.55 (cp. p. 47)
⁋ Alleged as proof of the Egyptian origin of this people [the Colchians]
is the circumcision of males as in Egypt. This custom continues among
emigrants from Egypt, as for instance among the Jews.

## HORACE, 65–6 BC (p. 65).

*Satires* 1.9.68–70 (see p. 65 for full context)
Horace's friend is alleging sabbath-observance as an excuse for not
talking business:

⁋ 'I remember it well, but I'll tell you at a better time. Today is the
thirtieth, the sabbath. Do you want to insult the circumcised Jews?'

## PERSIUS, AD 34–62 (p. 71).

*Satires* 5.184 (see p. 71 for full context)
The superstitious man's reaction to Jewish sabbath-observances:

⁋ You...grow pale with fear before the sabbath of the circumcised.

## PETRONIUS, first century AD (p. 70).

*Satyricon* 68.8
A master is describing his slave, who has great natural talents:

⁋ 'Yet he has two blemishes; without these he would be incomparable.
He is circumcised and he snores.'

*Satyricon* 102.14
The trio of adventurers are trying to escape from their enemies and
one has suggested disguising themselves by blackening themselves so
as to look like negro slaves. Another takes up the suggestion ironically:

⁋ 'Why not? Circumcise us too so that we may seem to be Jews and
pierce our ears in imitation of Arabians.'

*Satyricon* Fragment 371

¶ Granted that a Jew worships the pig-god[1] and calls upon the highest ears of heaven, yet unless he also cuts back his foreskin with a knife he will leave the tribe and emigrate to Greek cities[2] and will not tremble at the sabbath with its ordinance of fasting.

> 1. *pig-god*: because the Jews did not eat pork they could be thought to worship a pig. There was a similar misconception that they worshipped an ass's head (pp. 106, 107).
> 2. *Greek cities*: there were many Jews of the Diaspora in the Greek cities of Asia Minor.

APION, first half of the first century AD (p. 53). This reference comes from Josephus.

Josephus *Apion* 2.13.137

¶ He ridicules our practice of circumcision.

MARTIAL, *c.* AD 40 to *c.* 104 (p. 70).

7.30.5

Caelia favours lovers of any nationality except Romans and among a list of foreigners:

¶ Nor do you shun the lovemaking of circumcised Jews.

11.94

¶ Your excessive envy and disparagement everywhere of my little books I pardon; circumcised poet, you are wise. This too I overlook, that while you cavil at my poems you pillage them; in this too, circumcised poet, you are wise. What does torment me is this, that though born actually in Solyma [Jerusalem] you, circumcised poet, attach yourself to my favourite boy. See! you deny it and swear to me by the Thunderer's temple.[1] I don't believe you; swear, circumcised one, by Anchialus.[2]

> 1. *Thunderer's temple*: an oath sworn by the temple of Jupiter on the Capitol at Rome would be a solemn guarantee for a Roman, but Martial disclaims its force for a Jew.

2. No convincing explanation for the name *Anchialus* has been found.

In three other poems Martial mentions circumcision in an obscene context.

JUVENAL, within AD 50 to 150 (see pp. 32 and 34).

*Satires* 5.14.96–106
Circumcision is an essential mark of the full proselyte:

¶ Some who happen to have a father who stands in awe of the sabbath, worship nothing but clouds and the holy heaven and do not differentiate between human and pigs' flesh, from which their father abstained; soon they also put aside their foreskins. Moreover as they are accustomed to despise Roman laws, they learn to keep and revere whatever Jewish ordinances Moses handed down in a mysterious volume: not to show the way to any one who does not practise the same sacred rites, not to guide any one to the spring he is seeking unless he is circumcised.

TACITUS, *c.* AD 56 to early second century (p. 16).

*Hist.* 5.5.8–9 (see p. 22 for full context)
Circumcision is included in other anti-social practices:

¶ They have instituted circumcision of the genitals in order to be recognized by the difference. Converts to their customs observe the same practice.

CELSUS, late second century AD (p. 60), quoted by Origen:

Origen *c. Celsum* 1.22
¶ Without blaming the Jewish practice of circumcision of the genitals he says that this custom has come to them from the Egyptians.

*c. Celsum* 5.43 (see p. 116 for full context)
¶ Moreover they are certainly no more holy than the rest of men because they are circumcised, for the Egyptians and Colchians practised this before them.

SUETONIUS (G. Tranquillus), *c.* AD 69 to after 121, born at Bedriacum in Cisalpine Gaul, wrote various biographies, including the famous 'Lives of the Emperors', from Julius Caesar to Domitian.

### *Life of Domitian* 12

¶ The Treasury department took its harshest measures[1] against the Jews in particular. Those were accused before it who were not professed Jews but followed the Jewish way of life and those who concealed their origin and had not paid the tribute[2] imposed on the nation. I remember being present as quite a young man when in a very crowded assembly an old man of ninety was examined by the procurator to see whether he was circumcised.

1. *harshest measures*: Suetonius had just listed various monstrous ways in which Domitian (Emperor 81–96) had tried to replenish his resources.

2. *tribute*: this refers to the diversion of the annual Temple tax to the upkeep of the temple of Jupiter Capitolinus at Rome, a measure taken by Vespasian after the campaign of AD 70 (cp. Dio Cassius p. 104: 'From that time a tax of two drachmas to be paid annually to Jupiter Capitolinus was imposed on those who cherished their national customs.').

SCRIPTORES HISTORIAE AUGUSTAE, a fourth century collection of imperial biographies, fictitious and often unreliable.

### *Hadrian* 14.2

¶ At that time the Jews also started a war,[1] because they were forbidden to mutilate their genitals.

1. *war*: this refers to the insurrection under Bar Kokhba, AD 132–5. Hadrian (Emperor 117–38) did tighten the law against castration, which he put on a level with murder (*Digest* 48.8.4.2). If this involved a universal ban on circumcision, then Antoninus (see below) pronounced a relaxation in favour of the Jews. Papyri show that Egyptian priests were also allowed circumcision as a religious observance. However circumcision and castration are clearly different and, if Hadrian did in fact ban the former, this is more likely to have happened after the suppression of the Jewish Revolt, as a deliberate attempt, like the foundation of Aelia Capitolina (see p. 9), to punish the Jews or simply to impose social conformity.

DIGEST, a sixth century codification of Roman law.

*Digest* 48.8.11.1

¶ By a rescript of the divine Antoninus[1] the Jews are allowed to circumcise only their own sons. If anyone performs the operation on a national of another race, he is liable to the same penalty as for castration.

1. *Antoninus*: this refers to Antoninus Pius, Emperor 138–61, the successor of Hadrian.

### Proselytism

It is clear that the Jews were well known for their proselytism and that the practice was discouraged by the authorities. Proselytes tended to be regarded with suspicion and dislike as renegades from traditional religion. Thorough-going proselytes, as against those who merely sympathized with Judaism, were to be recognized by circumcision, and after the fall of Jerusalem in AD 70 became liable, like the Jewish nationals, to payment of the Temple tax to Rome.

VALERIUS MAXIMUS, beginning of the first century AD, composed for the use of rhetoricians nine volumes of *Memorable Deeds and Sayings*. For the information given below he may have been dependent on the historian Livy (p. 124). Much of his work survives, but this passage is preserved only in two epitomes, the longer of which, given here, is that of Julius Paris, sixth century.

*Memorable Deeds and Sayings* 1.3.3 (Julius Paris *Epitome*)

¶ Cn. Cornelius Hispalus, praetor peregrinus[1] in the year of the consulate of P. Popilius Laenas and Lucius Calpurnius (139 BC.), ordered the Chaldaeans[2] by edict to depart from the city and Italy within ten days, because by their fallacious interpretation of the stars they confused light and foolish minds and made a profitable living by their lies. The same praetor compelled the Jews, who had tried to infect Roman customs with the cult of Jupiter Sabazius,[3] to return to their homes.

1. *praetor peregrinus*: the praetors were two senior magistrates elected annually, the praetor urbanus to dispense justice in suits between citizens, the praetor peregrinus in suits involving foreigners. He also

exercised a general supervision over foreigners resident in Rome. This is the first historical mention of resident Jews. Some scholars have thought that members of the deputation sent under Numenius by Simon Maccabaeus to confirm the former treaty of friendship with Rome (cp. 1 Macc. 14:16–24; 15:15–24) may have tried to proselytize. This embassy was sent at some time between 142 and 140, therefore just before the expulsion in 139.

2. *Chaldaeans*: because astrology originated in Babylon, the name came to be used as a general term for astrologers.

3. *Sabazius*: this was a minor Phrygian deity identified with Dionysus, as both had similar orgiastic rites. Similarity between *Sabazius* and *Sabaoth*, Lord of Hosts, may have led to confusion here. It has also been suggested that these Jews practised a syncretistic pagan cult, which would account for the otherwise inexplicable reference to altars. The Jewish god was later identified with Dionysus (cp. Tacitus p. 23, Plutarch p. 127).

The other epitome, otherwise noticeably shorter, adds:

¶ and cast out their private altars from public places.


HORACE, 65–8 BC (p. 65).


*Satires* 1.4.139–43
This light-hearted gibe is the first known reference to proselytism in Latin literature.

¶ When I have a moment to spare, I amuse myself with writing; this is one of those minor peccadilloes. If you don't excuse it, a big band of poets will come to my rescue; for we are much more numerous and like the Jews will compel you to join our gang.


JOSEPHUS (37–c. 100 AD), the Jewish historian (p. 35), is describing various outbreaks of hostility against the Jews at the beginning of the Jewish War.


*War* 2.2.20 (559–61)
¶ Meanwhile the Damascenes when they learnt of the destruction of the Romans[1] took steps to slay their own resident Jews. Acting on their suspicions[2] they had previously herded them together in the gymnasium, so they thought it an easy undertaking. However they were afraid of

their own wives who, all but a few, had adopted the Jewish cult. For this reason their greatest difficulty lay in acting without their knowledge. They attacked the Jews, numbering ten thousand five hundred[3] and all unarmed and, as they were in a narrow area, safely slaughtered them within one hour.

1. This refers to the disastrous attempt of the Roman commander, Cestius Gallus, to take Jerusalem in AD 66.

2. *suspicions*: the Damascenes had suspected that their own Jews might take part in the Jewish War and saw the Jewish military success as an encouragement to them. They now saw an opportunity to satisfy their rancour, probably exacerbated by the proselytism among their womenfolk, under the specious pretext of loyalty to Rome.

3. So large a number as ten thousand five hundred, massed in one gymnasium, is incredible but the cruelty of the massacre remains and is matched by accounts of similar atrocities in other Syrian cities.

In *Ant.*, Josephus represented the Empress Poppaea as sympathizing with the Jews. Agrippa had built a large dining-room, which had a lovely view over the city and also enabled him to see everything that was going on in the Temple. This offended the leading Jews, who built a high wall which obstructed not only the view from the palace but also from a Roman guard-point. Agrippa was indignant, as also the Roman governor Festus, who ordered them to pull it down. However, on the grounds that the destruction of any part of the Temple would be an intolerable religious affront, they obtained permission to send an embassy to Rome before Nero (Emperor 54–68).

*Ant.* 10.8.11 (186–96)

¶ He gave them a full hearing and not only consented to what they had done, but also allowed them to leave the building as it was. In this he was gratifying his wife Poppaea, for she was a worshipper of God and pleaded on behalf of the Jews.

Furthermore, according to *Life* 3.16 she showed marked favour to Josephus himself when he went on an embassy to Rome in 63. It is most unlikely however that Poppaea, a lady of unsavoury morals, was actually a proselyte or had any intention of becoming one. She had a Jewish favourite actor, called Aliturus, and may well have been superstitious enough to conciliate the God of the Jews.

SENECA (the Younger) 4 BC/AD I to AD 65 (p. 66).
A quotation from *On Superstition* is found in Augustine (see p. 67):

Augustine *City of God* 6.11

¶ Certainly it was of the Jews that he was speaking when he said: 'Meanwhile the practices of the villainous race have become so influential that they are now accepted throughout every land. The vanquished have given laws to their victors!' In saying this he showed his surprise, for he was unaware of God's providential action. He clearly appended a statement to show his opinion of their ceremonial system: 'They however know the reasons for their ritual; most people do not know why they are doing what they do.'

This distinction drawn in the last sentence is probably between Jews and adherents of other superstitions, rather than between Jewish priests and the people as a whole.

JUVENAL, within AD 50 and 150 (p. 32).

*Satires* 5.14.96–106
The first half of this satire deals with the corrupting influence of parental example. The father is a god-fearer, in that he observes the sabbath and abstains from pork; the son goes further and becomes a full Jew (see p. 34 for commentary):

¶ Some who happen to have a father who stands in awe of the sabbath, worship nothing but clouds and the holy heaven and do not differentiate between human and pigs' flesh, from which their father abstained; soon they also put aside their foreskins. Moreover as they are accustomed to despise Roman laws, they learn to keep and revere whatever Jewish ordinances Moses handed down in a mysterious volume: not to show the way to any one who does not practise the same sacred rites, not to guide anyone to the spring he is seeking unless he is circumcised. But the father is to blame, who spent every seventh day in sloth without any contact with life.

EPICTETUS, *c.* AD 50–120 (p. 79).

Epictetus 2.9.19–21

¶ Why then do you call yourself a Stoic, why do you deceive the multitude, why do you play-act the Jew, when you are a Greek? Don't you see how it is that individuals are called Jewish, Syrian, Egyptian? Whenever we see somebody facing both ways, we are in the habit of saying 'He is not a Jew, but playing a part.' But when he accepts the consequences of having been baptized and having made a choice, then he is a Jew both in fact and in name. So we too are counterfeit 'baptists', nominally Jews, but actually something else.

Epictetus is urging his disciples to live up to their profession. Some have thought, because of the emphasis on baptism, that he is confusing Jews with Christians, as real Christians were distinguished by consistency in faith and practice, while Peregrinus (pp. 187–9) was an example of a bogus Christian, who had joined only for what he could get out of it. Otherwise, the distinction is between the Gentiles on the fringe, who only play at being Jews, and the true proselyte who has deliberately chosen baptism with the obligations (circumcision and sacrificial offering) imposed to confirm his conversion to Judaism.

SUETONIUS, *c.* AD 69 to after 121 (p. 84).

*Life of Tiberius* 36

¶ He suppressed such foreign cults as Egyptian and Jewish rites and compelled the adherents of those superstitions to burn their priestly vestments along with all their cultic apparatus. On the pretext of military service he dispersed the Jews of fighting age among the more unhealthy provinces; the rest of the tribe and those who followed similar practices he banished from the city under penalty of perpetual enslavement if they disobeyed.

This expulsion took place in AD 19. Tacitus, *Ann.* 2.2.85 (see p. 103), gives further details, but does not refer so explicitly to proselytes.

*Life of Domitian* 12 (see p. 84 for fuller context and commentary)

¶ The Treasury department took its harshest measures against the Jews in particular. Those were accused before it who were not professed Jews[1] but followed the Jewish way of life and those who concealed their origin and had not paid the tribute imposed on the nation.

1. *professed Jews*: false accusations of being full proselytes were brought against those only on the fringe in order to make them liable to payment of the Temple tax, diverted to the Treasury after the fall of Jerusalem in AD 70. Domitian reigned from 81 to 96.

### Life of Domitian 15

¶ Finally on the slightest of suspicions, when his consulship had only just ended, he suddenly put to death his own cousin, Flavius Clemens, a man despised for his indolence, whose sons, while they were still small children, he had openly designated as his successors and changing their names had called one Vespasian and the other Domitian. By this act in particular he hastened his own destruction.

Cp. Dio Cassius (below) for his fuller account, and commentary.

## DIO CASSIUS, *c.* AD 150 to 235 (p. 54).

### History of Rome 57.18.52
A fragment quoted in a letter of John of Antioch, a fifth century bishop.

¶ Since many Jews had congregated in Rome and were converting large numbers of the inhabitants to their own way of life, he expelled most of them.

Editors insert this here, as it fits into the context of Dio's work after his statement that Tiberius had investigated the oracular books and found some of them spurious, dated in AD 19. Suetonius and Tacitus (see above) give more detailed accounts, but do not give proselytism as the main cause for the expulsion.

### Epitome of Xiphilinus 57.14.1−2

¶ In the same year[1] Domitian put many others to death, including the consul Flavius Clemens, although the latter was his cousin and had married Flavia Domitilla, who was his own kinswoman. Both were accused of atheism,[2] a charge under which many were condemned who had drifted into Jewish practices. Some were killed, others had their property confiscated. Domitilla was only banished to Pandateria.[3]

1. *same year*: A.D. 95.

2. *atheism*: refusal to acknowledge the divinity of the Emperor could be taken as atheistic and treasonable. Jews were excused the conventional acts of worship, but Clemens and his wife were probably on the fringe and the action against them was political, as Domitian jealously asserted his divine status. It is unlikely that they were Christians, as Clemens had just been consul. The tradition of Domitilla's Christianity is not found until the fourth century and archaeological evidence, formerly believed to point to an earlier date, has been discounted.

3. *Pandateria*: this was a small island off the west coast of Italy (see map 1).

DIGEST, a sixth century codification of Roman law.

48.8.11.1

¶ By a rescript of the divine Antoninus[1] the Jews are allowed to circumcise only their own sons. If anyone performs the operation on a national of another race, he is liable to the same penalty as for castration.

1. *Antoninus*: this refers to Antoninus Pius, Emperor 138–61, the successor of Hadrian. The latter, Emperor 117–38, had tightened the law against castration, which he put on a par with murder.

CELSUS, late second century AD (p. 60) in the course of a sustained criticism of Judaism shows his dislike of proselytes by an incidental reference, quoted in Origen.

Origen *c. Celsum* 5.41.4–6

¶ If it were on this basis [i.e. basis of tradition] that the Jews cherish their own law, they are not to be blamed, but rather those who forsake their own traditions and adopt those of the Jews.

## Governmental Attitudes

Every action taken by a government shows its policy and attitude towards those affected, but this book is not a history of the Jews, so a selection has been made in order to illustrate attitudes in different places and at different times.

I. First come some of the records quoted by Josephus in connection with the Jews in Asia Minor. There were long-established and prosperous Greek cities in Asia Minor with Jewish communities subject to the regulations of each municipality. In some places the Jews had to suffer irritating restraints or actual harassment, in others they were treated with consideration and might even enjoy special privileges. From the time of Julius Caesar (d. 44 B.C.) the Roman government issued decrees designed to safeguard Jewish rights. These may be summarized as commanding the Greek cities to guarantee for their Jewish inhabitants exemption from military service, freedom of sabbath-observance (when they were not to be summoned to attend the law courts), the right to assemble for religious meetings, to send their Jerusalem Temple tax without hindrance, and to settle internal legal disputes by their own authority. Furthermore their synagogues were not to be robbed of their funds or of their sacred books.

II. In Alexandria, where there was a large and vociferous Jewish community, there had long been friction between Greeks and Jews, culminating in the riots in the reign of Gaius (Emperor AD 37–41). The rescripts of his successor Claudius (Emperor 41–54) show his determination to maintain Jewish religious rights, while at the same time he was clearly irritated by what he saw as the Jews' turbulence and intransigence.

III. The same determined impartiality was shown in the case of Antioch, where there were much the same problems, and where the same policy was maintained by Vespasian (Emperor 69–79) even after the fall of Jerusalem in 70. Diversion of the Temple tax to Rome affected all Jews everywhere.

IV. In Rome local circumstances led to temporary decrees of banishment at various times. The Jews appear as undesirable proselytizers and instigators of riots. After the Jewish War and the risings under Hadrian (Emperor 177–38), which were rigorously suppressed, the Jews no longer presented a political threat, but there was some revulsion against their anti-social customs and the authorities attempted to prevent proselytism.

I

JOSEPHUS (37–c. 100 AD) quotes a number of official records to show the honour in which Julius Caesar and the senate had held the Jews, decrees observed by Roman officials in Asia Minor and the Greek cities there.

*Ant.* 14.10.8 (213)ff.

¶ '[Name uncertain] proconsul of the Romans to the magistrates, council and people of Parium,[1] greeting. The Jews in Delos[2] and some of the neighbouring Jews, in the presence of your own envoys too, have petitioned me and informed me that you were preventing them from observing their national customs and sacred rites. Now I object to the passing of such decrees against our friends and allies preventing them from living in accordance with their own customs and from contributing money to common meals and sacred rites, which even in Rome they are not forbidden to do. For Gaius Caesar, our consul, in the edict forbidding religious groups[3] to meet in the city exempted only these and did not forbid them either to collect contributions of money or to hold common meals. Similarly I too, while forbidding other religious groups, allow these alone to meet and feast in accordance with their native customs and rules.'

1. *Parium* lay on the coast, east of the Hellespont (see map 2).
2. *Delos*: now a small deserted island, was a bustling commercial port, centre of a flourishing slave market.
3. *religious groups*: ever since the scandal of the Bacchanalia in 187 BC (pp. 226–8) the Roman government had been acutely aware of the moral and political risks of religious societies, so this was a considerable concession to the Jews and marked it as a legally allowable religion (religio licita).

Another concession is mentioned in an edict from Julius Caesar in 47 BC included in certain financial regulations:

*Ant.* 14.10.6 (204)

¶ 'No one, whether magistrate or pro-magistrate, praetor or legate, is to raise auxiliary troops[1] in Jewish territory, nor are soldiers to be allowed to exact money from them either for winter quarters or on any other grounds, but they are to suffer no harassment of any kind.'

1. *auxiliary troops*: service in the legions was reserved for those who, whether from Italy or the provinces, held the privilege of Roman citizenship. Auxiliary troops were drawn, in general, from the provinces. The Jews, because of their sabbath-observance and food laws, were in any case unlikely to conform to military regulations.

In 47 BC the consul Lucius Lentulus had granted exemption from military service to Jews in Asia Minor and this is confirmed by records at Ephesus, Delos, Sardis and Cos, as preserved by Josephus. The two following quotations in which governors are shown as warning cities to respect Jewish traditions show how easily this rule could be infringed. The first is a reply from the magistrates of Laodicea acknowledging receipt of a letter from the governor in which he laid it down:

*Ant.* 14.10.20 (242–3)

¶ ‘ "that it should be lawful for the Jews to observe their sabbaths and carry out their other rites in accordance with their traditional laws and that no one should give orders to them, because they were our friends and allies, and no one should do them wrong in our province".[1]

When the people of Tralles objected, to your face, that they were dissatisfied with the decrees about them, you commanded that they should be put into practice. You added that you had been asked to write to us too in this connection. We therefore, following your instructions, have accepted the letter delivered to us and entered it among our public records and, as regards the rest of your instructions, we shall take care to give no grounds for complaint.'

1. *province*: this was the province of Phrygia in which Tralles lay some seventy-five miles west of Laodicea. This latter was a rich city, one of the most prosperous in Asia (cp. Rev. 3 : 17), and its citizens, while obliged to accept the Roman injunction, comply only sulkily.

In the second quotation it is again clear that the provincials had raised objections:

*Ant.* 14.10.21 (244–6)

¶ ‘Publius Servius Galba, son of Publius, proconsul, to the magistrates,

council and people of Miletus[1] greeting. Prytanis, son of Hermas, a
citizen of yours, came to me when I was holding court-sessions at
Tralles and disclosed to me that contrary to our ordinance you are
attacking the Jews and banning them from observing their sabbaths and
performing their native rites and handling their produce[2] in their
customary way and that he had published the decree in accordance with
your laws. I therefore would have you know that after hearing
arguments on both sides I have decided that you should not continue
to ban the Jews from following their customs.'[3]

1. *Miletus*: this rich trading port (see map 2), had no council of its
own under Roman rule until 46 BC, so this gives some indication of
date.

2. *produce*: probably refers to the annual sending of the Temple tax
to Jerusalem.

3. *customs*: the Jews were influenced by Greek customs instead, for
in the theatre there is an inscription from the imperial period marking
special seats as 'Reserved for practising Jews'.

The following show rather less grudging acceptance of the Jews.
Josephus quotes a directive from a Roman official, date unknown, to
the people of Sardis and also a decree, apparently later, of the Sardians
themselves, according some generous privileges.

*Ant.* 14.10.17 (235)

¶ 'Lucius Antonius, son of Marcus, proquaestor and propraetor to the
magistrates, council and people of Sardis,[1] greeting. Jewish citizens of
ours have come to me and informed me that from very early days they
have had a gathering of their own in accordance with their native laws
and a place of their own in which they determine their own affairs and
mutual disputes. At their request to do this, I have decided to maintain
it and grant them permission.'

1. *Sardis*: (cp. Rev. 3:1–6) was a rich and ancient city, not a Greek
colony (see map 2).

*Ant.* 14.10.24 (259–61)

¶ Decree of the people of Sardis. 'The following decree was passed by
the council and people of Sardis on a proposal of the magistrates. "The

Jewish citizens living in our city, who have always received many great kindnesses from the people, have now come before the council and people with the request that, as their laws and their freedom have been restored to them by the Roman senate and people, they may gather together according to their traditional customs and live as a community and judge suits among themselves, and that a place be assigned to them in which, with their wives and children, they may meet together and offer their traditional prayers and sacrifices[1] to God. Therefore the council and people have decreed that they should be allowed to gather on the days previously appointed and perform the requirements of their laws, and also that a place[2] should be set apart for them by the magistrates for them to build on and occupy, such as they may deem fit for this purpose, and that it should be incumbent on the market-officials of the city to see to importing suitable food for them."'

1. *sacrifices*: this is used in the general sense of offerings, not of sacrificial victims, which were found only in the Temple at Jerusalem.

2. *place*: this probably refers to a synagogue rather than a specifically Jewish quarter or ghetto. Remains of an exceptionally rich synagogue dating from the second century AD have been found as well as numerous inscriptions.

Josephus quotes a decree of unknown date from Halicarnassus:

*Ant.* 14.10.23 (256–8)

¶ Decree of the people of Halicarnassus.[1] 'In the priesthood of Memnon, son of Aristides and, by adoption, of Euonymus, in the month of Anthesterion,[2] the following decree was passed by the people on the proposal of Marcus Alexander. "At every time we have been deeply concerned with piety towards the Deity and holiness. Therefore in accordance with what the people of Rome, benefactors of all mankind, have written to our city regarding their friendship and alliance with the Jews, namely that their sacred services to God and customary festivals and gatherings should be maintained, we have also decreed that those Jews who wish, both men and women, may observe their sabbaths and perform their sacred rites in accordance with the Jewish laws and may build places of prayer[3] by the sea in accordance with their native custom. If any one, whether magistrate or private citizen, prevents them he is to be liable to the following fine and pay it to the city."'

1. *Halicarnassus*: this was an ancient Greek colony on the coast of Asia Minor (see map 1).

2. *Anthesterion*: this corresponded to February/March. In the original decree the day of the month would have been inserted.

3. *places of prayer*: the Greek could also be translated 'make their prayers', but 'place of prayer' was a recognized synonym for synagogue, cp. Acts 16:13.

General harassment of the Jews in Asia Minor kept on recurring under Augustus (Emperor 27 BC–AD 14), as shown by Josephus:

*Ant*. 16.1.3 (27–8)

¶ At that time,[1] when they were in Ionia, a great throng of Jewish inhabitants of the cities seized the opportunity to speak out freely and came and told them of the harassment they were suffering: they were not allowed to keep their own laws, were compelled to appear[2] in court on their holy days because of the intransigence of the examining magistrates, were deprived of the money sent as offering to Jerusalem, were compelled to take part in military service and civic burdens and spend their sacred money on these, although they had been exempt from these, because the Romans had always allowed them to live in accordance with their own laws.

1. *that time*: in 14 BC Marcus Agrippa, right-hand man of the Emperor Augustus, after a mission to Pontus, was travelling back through Asia Minor accompanied by Herod the Great. The latter persuaded him to listen to an eloquent plea on behalf of the Jews by Nicolaus (p. 47), and Agrippa confirmed the Jews' privileges.

2. *compelled*: non-appearance in court would mean that judgement would go against them by default.

Eventually Augustus himself issued a decree after receiving a complaint from the Jews in Asia and Cyrene about insulting treatment by Greeks and confiscation of their sacred funds. They petitioned for reinstatement of the equality of political rights granted by former rulers. His reply is given by Josephus:

*Ant.* 16.6.1 (162–5)

¶ 'Caesar Augustus, pontifex maximus,[1] with tribunician power, decrees: "Since the Jewish people and their high priest Hyrcanus[2] have been found well-disposed towards the Roman people not only at the present day but also previously and especially in the time of my father[3] Caesar, the Emperor, I therefore along with my council and by resolution of the Roman people have decided that it shall be guaranteed by oath that the Jews are to practise their own customs according to their traditional law as they practised when Hyrcanus was high priest of the Most High God; their sacred funds are to be inviolate and despatched to Jerusalem and paid to the Jerusalem treasurers; they are not to be put on bail to appear in court on the sabbath nor on the day of preparation[4] before this after the ninth hour. If anyone is caught stealing their sacred books or sacred funds from a synagogue or banqueting hall[5] he is to be held sacrilegious and his goods forfeited to the Roman state treasury. The resolution which they passed in my honour, regarding the piety which I practise towards all mankind, and in honour of Gaius Marcius Censorinus,[6] I order to be set up along with this edict in Ancyra[7] in the most conspicuous spot assigned to me by the federation of Asia. If anyone contravenes any of the above ordinances he shall suffer severe punishment."'

1. *pontifex maximus*: to translate this as high priest would be misleading. Under the Republic it had come to denote political power and the holder of the office had legal authority in the religious sphere. Augustus took over the office in 12 BC and from then on each emperor succeeded to the title, as he also took over *tribunician power* with its right of veto in the senate.

2. *Hyrcanus*: he was high priest from 63–40 BC and contemporary with Julius Caesar.

3. *father*: Augustus had been adopted by his great-uncle Caesar.

4. *day of preparation*: this is the word found in the Gospels for a Friday. The sabbath itself started at sunset on this day.

5. *banqueting hall*: it has been suggested that this was a corruption of a Hebrew word transliterated into Greek and therefore unfamiliar to Greek scribes, meaning 'ark' (of the Law).

6. *Censorinus*: he was proconsul of Asia in AD 2/3.

7. *Ancyra*: this was the modern Ankara and capital of Galatia (see map 1). There was a temple dedicated to 'Rome and Augustus', the remains of which are still to be seen, to which Augustus is referring here. This inscription, which has not survived, is not to be confused with the 'Monumentum Ancyranum' an inscription still extant on the wall of the temple recording the events of Augustus' reign.

## II

In Alexandria there was constant friction between the Jews and the Greeks whose ancestors had been settled there by Alexander the Great when he founded the city in 332 BC. After the troubles in the reign of Gaius, when Claudius succeeded him in AD 41 the Alexandrians hastened to try to win his favour by decreeing various statues and dedications in his honour. At the same time the Jews sent two separate delegations to state their own case. The Alexandrians had also asked for certain political privileges. Josephus, *Ant.* 19.5.2 (280–5), gives Claudius' reply. Fortunately Claudius' own words have been preserved in a papyrus (*Pap. Lond.* 1912), from which it is clear that Josephus, while recording the general tenor of the reply, has considerably modified the irritation which Claudius felt towards the factions continually disturbing the city.

First Claudius replied specifically to the twelve Alexandrian envoys, among whom are named Chaeremon (see p. 52) and Theon (see pp. 111, 113). He diplomatically accepted some of the honours decreed and, while granting some of the political requests, refused others. He then went on (in the words of the papyrus):

Claudius *Pap. Lond.* 1912.73–105

¶ As for the rioting and faction or rather, truth to tell, the war against the Jews, your envoys and Dionysius son of Theon in particular, showed great zeal in rebutting the charges. However I did not wish to examine in detail, although my anger remains implacable against those responsible for the recurrence. I simply proclaim that if you do not stop this destructive and stubborn fury against each other, I shall be forced to show you what a humane Emperor is like when instead he has become justly enraged. Therefore I even now also affirm that the Alexandrians are to deal gently and kindly with the Jews, who have for a long time inhabited the same city. They are not to violate any of their habitual rites of divine worship but are to allow them to practise the same customs as in the time of the late Augustus. These I have confirmed after hearing both parties.

The Jews I expressly command not to busy themselves with anything more than what they previously held and not in future to send out two embassies as if they dwelt in two cities, something without precedent. Nor are they to force their way into contests for magisterial or administrative offices,[1] but are to enjoy their own profits, reaping the advantage of an abundance of good things in a foreign city. Nor are they to bring in or welcome Jews who put in from Syria or Egypt, which will force me to entertain greater suspicions. If they do, I shall take all possible proceedings against them, on the grounds that they stir up trouble throughout the whole world.

If both of you abandon these ways and are willing to live gently and kindly with each other, I for my part will take the utmost care for the city with which I have a family friendship of long standing. I commend my friend Barbillus[2] who always promotes your interest with me and even now too has pleaded the case most zealously on your behalf, and my friend Tiberius Claudius Archibius. Farewell.[3]

1. *offices*: this bears on the vexed question of the Jews' political status in Alexandria. Claudius clearly views them as resident aliens, enjoying certain definable rights and privileges, but separate from the citizens proper.

2. *Barbillus*: he is probably to be identified with the Balbillus mentioned as an advocate for the Alexandrians in the Acts of Isidorus (p. 112). The tone of this pamphlet (probably AD 53) shows how justifiably Claudius was irritated by the Alexandrians.

3. For the Greek text in full, see *Documents Illustrating the Principates of Gaius, Claudius and Nero*, pp. 92–102.

After this edict to Alexandria, Claudius also issued an edict to safeguard the rights of the Jews at large throughout the Empire, quoted by Josephus.

Josephus *Ant.* 19.5.3 (287–91)

¶ 'Tiberius Claudius Caesar Augustus Germanicus, pontifex maximus, vested with tribunicial power, elected consul for the second time, decrees: "Since very dear friends of mine, Agrippa and Herod,[1] petitioned me to agree that the same rights should be safeguarded for the Jews throughout the Roman Empire as for the Jews in Alexandria, I consented with great pleasure, not only in order to gratify the petitioners, but also because I thought that those on whose behalf the request was made deserved it because of their loyalty and friendship towards the Romans. In particular, I deemed it right that not even a Greek city should lose these rights, since they had been guaranteed for them even in the time of the late Augustus. It is good therefore that the Jews in the whole world under our dominion should maintain the customs of their fathers without impediment. Them too I now command to make a more reasonable use of this kindness and not to set at nought the religious beliefs[2] of other peoples, but to keep their own laws. I desire the magistrates in the cities and colonies and municipalities both in and outside Italy, also kings and authorities through their own ambassadors, to have this edict of mine inscribed and posted up for not less than thirty days where it may easily be read from ground level."'

1. *Herod*: he was king of Chalcis; his younger brother, Agrippa I (the Herod of Acts 12), was king of Judaea and other minor territories. The latter's son, Agrippa II, is mentioned as Agrippa in Acts 25 and 26.

2. *religious beliefs*: this is a gentle reminder to the Jews that they should not flaunt their own religious separatism.

How easily trouble could arise even after this edict is shown by a minor incident at Dora in Phoenicia (see map 1), described by Josephus. Some young men, out of sheer devilment, set up a statue of Claudius in the local synagogue. King Agrippa at once complained to Petronius, the governor of Syria from 39 to 42, who took immediate action. He wrote to the magistrates, citing this edict and saying that as for the perpetrators:

*Ant.* 19.6.3 (300)ff.

¶ 'I have given orders that they are to be brought before me by Proclus Vitellius the centurion to give an account of their actions. To the chief magistrates I issue warning that unless they wish it thought that the offence took place with their connivance they must indicate to the centurion the persons responsible and allow no occasion to arise for strife or fighting, which seem to me to be the object of such actions. ...For the future therefore I command you to seek no pretext for sedition or riot, but that each should conduct their own religious rites.'

III

At Antioch too, the great and wealthy city on the Orontes in Syria (see map 1), where an obscure Jewish sect was first styled Christian (Acts 11:26), there was constant friction. On Claudius' accession the Antiochians like the Alexandrians had petitioned him against the Jews in their midst (Josephus *Ant.* 19.5.2 (279)ff.). Elsewhere Josephus contends that the Jews had enjoyed citizens' rights from the very beginning:

*Ant.* 12.3.1 (119–22)

¶ Seleucus Nicator[1] thought them worthy of citizenship in the cities which he founded in Asia and Lower Syria and in the capital Antioch itself and gave them equal privileges with the Greeks and Macedonians settled there, so that this citizenship remains even to the present time. A proof of this is the fact that he ordered that those Jews who did not wish to use foreign oil should receive a fixed sum from the authorities for the purchase of oil. When the people of Antioch in the present war proposed to abolish this, Mucianus[2] who was then governor of Syria maintained it. After this, when Vespasian and his son Titus became rulers of the world, the Alexandrians and Antiochians petitioned that the Jews should not continue to have the rights of citizenship and did not succeed.

Josephus introduces some fulsome flattery of the imperial clemency and concludes:

¶ They said that those who had taken up arms and fought against them had paid the penalty and they did not think proper to deprive those who had done no wrong of their existing rights.

1. *Seleucus Nicator* (i.e. the Victorious): he reigned from 262 to 247 BC. Whether the Jews were at this period given equal citizenship or whether Josephus, their partisan, is confusing this with guaranteed

freedom of worship, even to some extent publicly subsidized, is debateable. What is unmistakable is the hostile attitude of the Alexandrians and Antiochians and the impartiality of the Roman government.

2. *Mucianus*: he was governor of Syria when Vespasian was engaged in the Jewish War and became one of his principal supporters.

## IV

At Rome local circumstances had caused government action. As early as 139 BC Jews had been banished for proselytism (p. 85). Tiberius in AD 19 also banished them.

TACITUS, *c.* AD 56–115 (p. 16).

*Ann.* 2.2.85

¶ Action was also taken to expel Egyptian[1] and Jewish cults. The senate passed a decree that four thousand men of the rank of freedmen, infected with that superstition and of military age, should be transported to Sardinia to put down brigandage there; if they perished because of the unhealthy climate, little loss! The rest were to leave Italy, unless they renounced[2] their profane rites before a fixed date.

1. *Egyptian*: according to Josephus *Ant.* 18.3.4–5, this edict was related to a scandal in which priests of Isis had been bribed to procure a night's intercourse for a rejected and passionate lover with a noble and virtuous matron, a votary of Isis, under the pretext that the god Anubis wanted her to visit the temple as his own chosen love. When the plot was discovered Tiberius himself punished the culprits. He also took action in a somewhat similar case, when another noble Roman matron, this time a Jewish proselyte, was tricked by four Jewish scoundrels into giving them purple and gold for the Temple at Jerusalem, which they kept for themselves. He banished all Jews from Rome and the consuls drafted four thousand of them for service in Sardinia.

2. *renounced*: it is unlikely that Tiberius penalized a whole community because of the misdemeanour of four rogues. Probably this marks an attempt to check proselytism at Rome, since those who abjured Judaism (something unthinkable for any true Jew!) were to be allowed to remain. The accounts given by Suetonius and Dio Cassius (pp. 89–90) make more explicit mention of proselytes.

Claudius (Emperor AD 41–54) also banished Jews, but for political reasons.

SUETONIUS, *c.* AD 69 to after 121 (p. 84).

*Life of Claudius* 25

¶ The Jews, who were continually rioting at the instigation of Chrestus,[1] he banished from the city.

This decree, probably to be dated in 49, is mentioned in Acts 18:2 as the reason for the removal of Aquila and Priscilla to Corinth.

1. *Chrestus*: this was a common proper name and by now *e* and *i* had much the same pronunciation, so it might well have replaced the unfamiliar name *Christ*. In this case the reference is to troubles between Jews and Christians, not yet differentiated as separate sects. Jews must either have remained undetected or returned, for there were certainly Jews in Rome when Paul arrived (Acts 28:17–23).

DIO CASSIUS, *c.* 150–235 (p. 54), gives a rather different account, but emphasizes the risks of riots:

*History of Rome* 40.6.6

¶ As the Jews had multiplied again so that it would have been difficult to exclude them from the city without rioting by the mob, Claudius did not banish them, but ordered those who followed their traditional way of life not to assemble together.

The same author records a decree affecting all Jews alike throughout the Roman world after the destruction of the Temple in AD 70.

*History of Rome* 45.7.2

¶ From that time a tax of two drachmas to be paid annually to Jupiter Capitolinus[1] was imposed on those who cherished their national customs.

1. *Capitolinus*: there was a great temple of Jupiter on the Capitol at Rome. For the Jews no extra financial burden was involved, as they had already paid this sum every year for the maintenance of the Temple at Jerusalem, but it was a religious affront that this money should be diverted to the upkeep of a pagan temple.

Domitian (Emperor 81–96) had exacted this tax ruthlessly (see above p. 84), but Nerva (Emperor 96–8), as reported again by Dio Cassius, was more moderate:

*History of Rome* 48.1.2

¶ Nerva released those under trial for impiety[1] and recalled the exiles. . . . He allowed no accusations of impiety nor of a Jewish way of life.

1. *impiety*: the Greek word is used here technically for the disloyalty shown in refusing to acknowledge the divinity of the Emperor, a point on which Domitian had been sensitive. In his reign informers had proliferated and been encouraged to bring charges of treason. They could also levy blackmail by threatening to denounce proselytes for non-payment of the tax to which they were just as liable as Jewish nationals or could lay false information against those who might sympathize with Judaism but who were not actually proselytes. This point is illustrated by a coin issued by Nerva to commemorate the abolition of the abuse, although the tax itself was still levied. Four Latin words round the rim (*fisci Judaici calumnia sublata*) convey: 'Abolition of malicious prosecution in connection with the Jewish tax.'

*Miscellaneous Anecdotes, Aphorisms and Incidental Remarks*

These have been divided into three sections:

I   Greek writers opposed to Judaism. This section comprises writers, not necessarily Greek, but writing in Greek and with a Greek background, particularly those quoted by Josephus, who show a strong anti-Jewish bias. The Jews were said to worship an ass and practise anti-social customs, even as monstrous as murder and cannibalism. They were supposed to be dim-witted, had produced no inventions nor famous men and by their enslavement showed that they were fit for nothing else and certainly not favoured by heaven.

II  Latin writers prejudiced against Judaism. This prejudice was not politically motivated as in Alexandria. Jews could be seen in the streets of Rome all the time, often thought of as squalid nuisances, anti-social in their habits, but not competing for political privileges. The Jewish War embittered feelings and Tacitus, seeing the Jews simply as a fanatical and turbulent race, is probably typical of the conception of Judaism prevalent in his day.

III Greek and Latin authors showing respect for Judaism. From early days there had been some wonder among Greek writers and later among Latin authors too at Jewish monotheism and absence of images. This led to respect, even when based on some misconceptions, for Judaism as a religious system which deserved serious consideration.

I

MNASEAS from Patara in Asia Minor lived about 200 BC. He was a traveller and wrote treatises, now lost, of geographical and mythological interest. He is the first known authority for the allegation that the Jews worshipped an ass in the Temple. Josephus quotes him as Apion's source for the following story.

Josephus *Apion* 2.9.112–14

❡ Again Apion, in his role of the devotee, mocks us, adducing Mnaseas as authority for his story. For he says that the latter related that while the Jews were waging a long war against the Idumaeans, one of the inhabitants of the Idumaean town called Dorii,[1] a worshipper of Apollo and named (so he says) Zabidus, approached the Jews. Then he promised to hand over to them Apollo,[2] the god of his city, who would come to our Temple, if everybody left it. All the mass of the Jews believed him. Zabidus constructed a wooden frame to encircle his own body and fixed in it three rows of lights. When he walked it looked to bystanders at a distance as if stars were passing through the land. The Jews were overcome with amazement at the incredible sight, kept their distance and stayed quiet. Zabidus entered the sanctuary quite easily, tore off the golden head of the pack-ass[3] (as he flippantly called it) and returned to Dora with all speed.

　　1. *Dorii*: this is not Dora on the coast in Phoenicia (see map 1), but a town also called Adora and Dura in the south of Palestine.
　　2. *Apollo*: for Greeks he was to be identified with *Cos*, the national god of the Idumaeans. There is inscriptional evidence for a decree of the Idumaeans in the temple of Apollo at Memphis in Egypt. It was a common belief that a god conferred protection on his own temple and that this protection could be transferred if the god migrated elsewhere.
　　3. *pack-ass*: the word used here does not denote the ass as a species, but the everyday beast of burden.

POSIDONIUS, *c.* 135–51 BC (see p. 44) Josephus names Posidonius and Apollonius Molo (p. 60) as two sources for Apion's anti-Jewish propaganda. The following, quoted by Josephus in *Apion*, was probably taken from Posidonius' *Histories*:

Quoted by Josephus *Apion* 2.7.79–81

¶ I am surprised too at those who supplied him [Apion] with such
materials, namely Posidonius and Apollonius Molo. They accuse us
because we do not join with others in worshipping the same gods, yet
both alike tell lies and make up unseemly slanders about our Temple.
They do not consider themselves to be acting impiously, although it
is most disgraceful for high-minded men to tell lies on any grounds
whatever, much more so in reference to a Temple famed among all
mankind and of such mighty antiquity. In this sanctuary Apion has the
impudence to say that the Jews had set up an ass's head and that they
worshipped this and thought it worthy of the most reverential cult. He
affirms that this was disclosed when Antiochus Epiphanes[1] had looted
the Temple and that a head was found, made of gold and of very great
value.

    1. *Antiochus Epiphanes*: this notorious desecrator of the Temple lived
215–163 BC. Diodorus *fl. c.* 60 BC (p. 46), generally thought to be using
Posidonius for this period, says that the king found a stone statue of
a bearded man sitting on an ass and holding a book and assumed that
this represented Moses (see p. 45).

Josephus refutes the story of the ass and continues:

Josephus *Apion* 2.7.89–96

¶ In reference to the Greeks he added another story full of slanders against
us. On this point it will be enough to say that those who take it on
themselves to talk of piety ought to be aware that it is less profane to
pass through sacred precincts than to invent criminal slanders about the
priests. Those authors were more concerned to defend a sacrilegious
king than to give a right and true account of our history and the
Temple. In their desire to defend Antiochus and to conceal the perfidy
and sacrilege which he practised towards our people because of his want
of money, they told lies and made up the following story to our
discredit. Apion acting as a spokesman for others also related that
Antiochus found in the Temple a couch and a man reclining on it.
Beside it there was a small table loaded with dishes of sea-food, meat
and poultry. The man was lying in a daze, but when the king entered

he greeted him with adoration as if the king would bring him deliverance. Falling at the king's knees he stretched out his right hand and requested his freedom. The king commanded him to confide in him and tell him who he was, why he was living there and what was the meaning of the foods. Then the man lamenting with groans and tears described his plight. He said, according to Apion, that he was a Greek and that while he was travelling about the province to make a living he was suddenly kidnapped by foreigners, brought to the Temple, imprisoned there out of sight and gorged with abundant food of every kind. At first this unexpected kindness caused him pleasure, next suspicion, then stupefaction. Finally by questioning the servants who attended him he heard of the Jews' unspeakable law by reason of which he was being fed and that they did this every year at a certain fixed time. They seized a Greek stranger, fattened him for a year, brought him to a certain forest and killed him. The body they offered in sacrifice according to their ritual and tasted of its entrails. While sacrificing a Greek, they swore an oath of hostility against the Greeks and then threw the remains of the dead man into a pit. Then according to our author, he said that he had only a few days left and begged the king out of reverence for the gods of the Greeks to overcome the Jews' machinations against his life and deliver him from the evils which beset him.

DAMOCRITUS, known only from mention in *Suidas* (a tenth century encyclopaedia, see p. 61), probably lived in the first century AD and perpetuated the grisly story:

*Suidas* D 49

¶ Damocritus, historian. He wrote *Tactics* in two books and a work, *On the Jews*, in which he says that they used to worship an ass's head made of gold and that every seventh year they caught a foreigner and sacrificed him by shredding his flesh into small pieces and so killing him.

STRABO, 64/3 BC to AD 21 (p. 50), preserves Posidonius' only other known denigration of the Jews.

*Geographica* 16.2.43

In describing the extraction of asphalt from the Dead Sea:

¶ But Posidonius says that the men are charlatans and with a show of incantations they pour urine and other evil-smelling liquids over it, solidify and squeeze out the asphalt and cut it into pieces.

**APOLLONIUS MOLO**, first century BC (p. 60), was one of the most determined of the opponents of Judaism, according to Josephus.

Josephus *Apion* 2.14.145, 148

¶ Apollonius Molo and Lysimachus and some others, partly through ignorance but mainly through malevolence, have made statements about our lawgiver Moses and his laws which are neither just nor true, slandering the former as a charlatan and cheat and alleging that the laws have instructed us in vice and in no virtue.

Apollonius, unlike Apion, did not group his accusations in one block, but scattered them throughout his work. At one point he abuses us for being atheists and misanthropic, at another he reproaches us with cowardice, at another, on the contrary, accuses us of recklessness and frenzied folly. He also says that we are the most dim-witted of the barbarians and that for this reason we alone have contributed no invention to improve men's life-style.

**APION**, first half of the first century AD (p. 53) relied largely on quotations from other authors, but the following remarks are attributed to him personally by Josephus.

Josephus *Apion* 2.10.121; 11.125; 12.135; 13.137

¶ He also falsely alleges that we swear by the God who made sky and earth and sea that we will show goodwill to no foreigner, especially Greeks.

He says that it is a proof of our neither practising just laws nor worshipping God properly that ⟨we have no dominion⟩, but rather have been enslaved to different nations in succession and that our city has experienced disasters.

But [he says] we have not produced any remarkable men, such as inventors of crafts or illustrious sages.

He objects to our sacrificing ⟨domestic⟩ animals and not eating pork and ridicules our practice of circumcision.

ACTS OF THE PAGAN MARTYRS. The translation *Acts* tends to be misleading. In the New Testament and the Apocryphal New Testament it translates a Greek word meaning actions or doings, as in the Acts of the Apostles. A second meaning comes from the Latin technical term *acta*, used for the recorded proceedings of trials. Hence *Acts of the Christian Martyrs* (see p. 161), which are not biographies, but record their trials and deaths with differing degrees of historicity.

The collective name, *Acts of the Pagan Martyrs* (edited and translated by H. Musurillo) has been given to a number of Greek papyrus fragments found in Egypt, which purport to record trials of Alexandrians viewed as suffering martyrdom for their convictions. This was not a matter of religious faith, as with the Christians, but of political opposition to Roman rule. The literary theme of the brave individual, usually a philosopher, confronting the cruel tyrant had always been popular. So, although it is generally agreed that there was probably some historical basis, these Alexandrian pamphlets have embellishments and accretions designed to glorify. They are certainly anti-Jewish in tone, but it seems that their main purpose was not so much to attack the Jews as to extol heroic opposition to Rome.

*Acts of Isidorus.* Isidorus was a prominent Alexandrian demagogue, much involved in the troubles of AD 38 (p. 11) and in covert anti-government intrigues (cp. Philo in *Flacc.* and *Leg. Gaj.*). There are three recensions, the second of which supplements the gap after col. 2 of the first.

Recension A: col. 1.16ff.

¶ The Alexandrian envoys were summoned and the Emperor postponed their hearing until the following day. The fifth day of Pachon,[1] in the ⟨thirteenth?⟩[2] year of Claudius Caesar Augustus.

   1. *Pachon*: this was the name of an Egyptian month, April/May.
   2. *thirteenth*: from external evidence the most probable date is AD 53, so *thirteenth* is a plausible reconstruction, as Claudius reigned from 41 to 54.

Recension A: col. 2

¶ The sixth day of Pachon: the second day. Claudius Caesar hears the case of Isidorus, gymnasiarch[1] of Alexandria v. King Agrippa[2] in the...gardens. With him sat twenty senators [and in addition to these] sixteen men of consular rank, the women of the court also attending...Isidorus' trial.

Isidorus was the first to speak: 'My Lord Caesar, I beseech you to listen to my account of my native city's sufferings.'

The Emperor: 'I shall grant you this day.'

All the senators who were sitting as assessors agreed with this, knowing the kind of man Isidorus was.

Claudius Caesar: 'Say nothing...against my friend. You have already done away with two of my friends, Theon[3] the exegete[4] and...[supplemented from Recension B] Naevius,[5] prefect of Egypt and prefect of the praetorian guard at Rome; and now you prosecute this man.'

Isidorus: 'My Lord Caesar, what do you care for a twopenny-halfpenny Jew like Agrippa?'

Claudius Caesar: 'What? You are the most insolent of men to speak....'

1. *gymnasiarch*: Isidorus had held the highest office possible for an Alexandrian.

2. *Agrippa*: this suit against the son of Herod Agrippa I, whose relations with the Jews had been so troubled and which led up to the riots of AD 38, is not known from any other sources. Agrippa II had spent his youth at the court of Claudius, who gave him the principality of Chalcis 49/50. He proved himself a loyal supporter of Rome.

3. *Theon*: the name shows that he came from a well-known Egyptian family.

4. *exegete*: this is a technical term for one who expounds or interprets. Presumably he had been prosecuted by Isidorus and met his death.

5. *Naevius*: he is better known as Naevius Macro, a prominent adherent of the Emperor Gaius (37–41), but fell under suspicion and was forced to commit suicide. Perhaps the Alexandrian clique under Isidorus had contributed to Gaius' suspicions.

Recension A: col. 3

¶ Lampon[1] to Isidorus: 'I have looked upon death....'

Claudius Caesar: 'Isidorus, you have killed many friends of mine.'

Isidorus: 'I merely obeyed the orders of the Emperor at the time. So too I should be willing to denounce anyone *you* wish.'

Claudius Caesar: 'Isidorus, are you really the son of an actress?'

Isidorus: 'I am neither slave nor actress's son, but gymnasiarch of the glorious city of Alexandria. But you are the cast-off son of the Jewess Salome![2] And therefore....'

Lampon to Isidorus: 'We might as well give in to a crazy Emperor.'

Claudius Caesar: 'Those whom I told [to carry out] the execution[3] of Isidorus and Lampon....'

1. *Lampon*: he was coupled with Isidorus in the prosecution of Flaccus, governor of Egypt, in AD 38 (p. 11).

2. *Salome*: three ladies of the Herod family could qualify, see Musurillo pp. 128ff. for a detailed discussion.

3. *execution*: it is difficult to see why the prosecutors should have been executed, but it has been plausibly suggested that Claudius suspected them of bringing a false charge of treason, which would make them liable to being charged with this offence.

Recension C

¶ Isidorus: 'My Lord Augustus, with regard to your interests, Balbillus[1] indeed speaks well. But to you, Agrippa, I wish to retort in connection with the points you bring up about the Jews. I accuse them of wishing to stir up the entire world.... We must consider the entire mass. They are not of the same temperament as the Alexandrians, but live rather after the fashion of the Egyptians. Are they not on a level with those who pay the poll-tax?'[2]

Agrippa: 'The Egyptians have had taxes levied on them by their rulers.... But no one has levied taxes on the Jews.'

Balbillus: 'Look to what extremes of insolence either his god or....'

1. *Balbillus*: it is not necessary here to identify precisely this advocate for the Alexandrians.

2. *poll-tax*: for the question of Jewish payment of local taxes see pp. 92ff. for the position in the Empire at large.

*Acts of Hermaiscus.* The date and occasion of this hearing before Trajan (Emperor 98–117) are unknown. What does emerge is that the Alexandrians had sent a deputation to Rome with some complaint against the Jews, as the latter had immediately also sent a deputation of their own.

col. 1.3–18

¶ Dionysius, who had held many procuratorships, and Salvius, Julius Salvius, Timagenes, Pastor the gymnasiarch, Julius Phanian, Philoxenus the gymnasiarch-elect, Sotion the gymnasiarch, Theon, Athenodorus, and Paulus of Tyre, who offered his services as advocate for the Alexandrians. When the Jews learnt of this, they too elected envoys from their own group, and thus were chosen Simon, Glaucon, Theudes, Onias, Colon, Jacob, with Sopatros of Antioch as their advocate. They set sail, then, from the city, each party taking along their own gods,[1] the Alexandrians [a bust of Serapis, the Jews...].

col. 2.21–37

¶ He conversed with their companions; and when the winter was over they arrived at Rome. The Emperor learnt that the Jewish and Alexandrian envoys had arrived, and he appointed the day on which he would hear both parties. And Plotina[2] approached [?] the senators in order that they might oppose the Alexandrians and support the Jews. Now the Jews, who were the first to enter, greeted Emperor Trajan, and the Emperor returned their greeting most cordially, having already been won over by Plotina. After them the Alexandrian envoys entered and greeted the Emperor. He, however, did not go to meet them, but said:

'You say "hail" to me as though you deserved to receive a greeting – after what you have dared to do to the Jews!'

col. 3.40–55

¶ [Trajan:] 'You must be eager to die, having such contempt for death as to answer even me with insolence.'

Hermaiscus said: 'Why, it grieves us to see your privy council[3] filled with impious Jews.'

Caesar said: 'This is the second time I am telling you, Hermaiscus, you are answering me insolently, taking advantage of your birth.'

Hermaiscus said: 'What do you mean, I answer you insolently, greatest Emperor? Explain this to me.'

Caesar said: 'Pretending that my council is filled with Jews.'

Hermaiscus: 'So, then, the word "Jew" is offensive to you? In that case you rather ought to help your own people and not play the advocate for the impious[4] Jews.'

As Hermaiscus was saying this, the bust of Serapis that they carried suddenly broke into a sweat,[5] and Trajan was astounded when he saw it. And soon tumultuous crowds gathered in Rome and numerous shouts rang forth, and everyone began to flee to the highest parts of the hills.

1. *their own gods*: it is clear from what follows in col. 3 that the Alexandrians took with them a bust of Serapis. This Graeco-Egyptian god (p. 248) had a magnificent temple in Alexandria and was worshipped there with special reverence. It is inconceivable that the Jews should have had an image, but possibly they took with them the Roll of the Law, which the Alexandrians assumed to be a cult-emblem.

2. *Plotina*: there is no other evidence that Trajan's wife had Jewish sympathies. Probably this is sheer propaganda, just as Josephus, from the other side, could allege that the Empress Poppaea favoured the Jews (see p. 87).

3. *privy council*: at this date Jews were certainly not members of the senate. The sneer probably reflects popular explanation at Alexandria of what they saw as imperial favouritism of the Jews.

4. *impious*: this is a not uncommon charge. Tacitus (p. 22) and the Elder Pliny (p. 56) accused them of despising the gods (p. 120) and Apollonius Molo (p. 60) called them atheists (p. 109).

5. *sweat*: there are other instances of this miraculous phenomenon. Here it is adduced either to emphasize the power of Serapis as against that of Yahweh or to show the disastrous effect he could have on the Roman people at large if the Alexandrian envoys were scorned.

PHILOSTRATUS, AD *c.* 170–*c.* 245 was born in Lemnos. He studied at Athens and wrote, in Greek, *Lives of the Sophists* and also, at the instigation of the Empress Julia Domna a *Life of Apollonius of Tyana*, based on the memoirs of one of his disciples, an Assyrian called

Damis. Apollonius was an ascetic Neo-Pythagorean sage, travelling widely, even as far as India, teaching and working miracles. Some alleged letters, mainly aphorisms, survive. Although he was at odds with both Nero (Emperor 54–68) and Domitian (Emperor 81–96) he lived on into the time of Nerva (Emperor 96–8). Much of Philostratus' work is clearly fictitious, but there is no reason to doubt Apollonius' historicity and widespread reputation. Some scholars have thought that Philostratus was deliberately composing anti-Christian propaganda. Whether this is so or not, his *Life* provided material for comparison of Christ with Apollonius, to the former's disadvantage. In the fourth century a certain Hierocles of Nicomedia attacked Christianity on these lines and Eusebius (p. 58) thought it sufficiently important to rebut him by attacking Philosostratus' *Life* in some detail.

The following excerpt comes from a fictitious account of a conference between Vespasian, considering whether to make himself Emperor, Apollonius and two others. One of these, advocating re-establishment of the Republic, in a quite gratuitous attack on the Jews tells Vespasian that the forces which he had led against the Jews would have been more suitably employed in chastising Nero.

*Life of Apollonius of Tyana* 5.33

¶ For the Jews have long been in revolt not only against the Romans, but against all mankind too. Those who have devised an anti-social way of life, who do not share with the rest of men in table-fellowship or libations or prayers or sacrifices are more widely separated from us than Susa[1] or Bactra[2] or the Indians who lie beyond these. So it was inappropriate to punish them for revolting from us, when we would have done better not to acquire them at all.

1. *Susa* had been the winter residence of the kings of Persia.
2. *Bactra* (Balkh) was the capital of the ancient Persian province of Bactria (*Bokhara*).

LUCIAN, *c.* AD 120 to after 180 (p. 187) gives valuable information about Christians, but has only one explicit reference to Jews. In his *Tragedy of Gout*, a little parody of a tragic drama, the goddess Gout tells how her victims vainly resort to various drugs and quacks:

*Tragedy of Gout* 5.173

¶ Another fool is seized upon by a Jew who uses incantations.

CELSUS, late second century AD (p. 60) although he was mainly attacking Christianity, also included hostile remarks against the Jews. Origen quotes the following as a sustained attack:

Origen *c. Celsum* 5.41.1–28

¶ Let us see too what Celsus says next, where there is very little that refers to Christians and most of it to Jews. He says: 'If it were on this basis[1] that the Jews cherish their own law, they are not to be blamed, but rather those who forsake their own traditions and adopt those of the Jews. But if they pride themselves on the knowledge of some greater wisdom and shun the society of others as if these were not as pure as themselves, they have already been told that not even their doctrine about the sky is peculiar to them. To pass over all the other examples, it has long been the doctrine of the Persians, as Herodotus[2] too points out somewhere: "It is their custom", he says, "to go up to the highest mountain peaks and offer sacrifices to Zeus, giving the name of Zeus to the whole circuit of the sky." So I think there is no difference between the names of Highest[3] Zeus, Zen,[4] Adonai,[5] Sabaoth[6] or Amon, as with the Egyptians, or Papaeus, as with the Scythians.'

    1. *on this basis*: Celsus had been arguing that each nation had its own traditions.
    2. *Herodotus*: the fifth century Greek historian who wrote a history of the Great Persian War was also keenly interested in geography, anthropology and religion.
    3. *Highest*: this is a title of Yahweh in the Septuagint.
    4. *Zen*: this is the root found in the cases of Zeus other than the nominative and is sometimes found too as the nominative.
    5. *Adonai*: the Jews used this name as a reverential substitute for Yahweh.
    6. *Sabaoth*: an accidental resemblance between this Jewish 'of hosts' and the Phrygian god Sabazius had led to an equation of the two (see p. 128).

¶ 'Moreover they are certainly no more holy than the rest of men because they are circumcised, for the Egyptians and Colchians practised this before they did, nor because they abstain from pork, for the Egyptians do this too and furthermore abstain from goats' meat, mutton, beef and fish, while Pythagoras[1] and his disciples abstain both from beans and from all living creatures. Nor is it probable that the Jews enjoy God's favour and love to a greater extent than the rest and that angels are sent from heaven to them alone, as if they had been assigned a land of the blessed, for we see what fate they and their land have been judged to deserve.

So let this chorus take their leave after being penalized for their arrogance, since they do not know the great God, but were seduced and deceived by the sorcery of Moses and schooled in this to no good end.'

1. *Pythagoras*: this sixth century Greek philosopher believed in the transmigration of souls into men and animals (see earlier, p. 80).

## II

CICERO (Marcus Tullius) 106 to 43 BC, was a famous orator, philosopher, letter-writer and statesman. He does not mention the Jews in his philosophic works or in his letters. In his forensic speeches he naturally denigrates witnesses for the opposition and impugns their national character.

*Pro Flacco* 28.66–9
Cicero in 59 BC defended Flaccus, who as propraetor had governed the province of Asia (i.e. Asia Minor), against a prosecution for extortion brought by Laelius on behalf of the cities of Asia. One of the charges was that he had confiscated the Temple tax contributed annually by the Jews to be sent to Jerusalem for the upkeep of the Temple.

¶ Next comes that unpopular Jewish business. Of course that is the reason why this case is being pleaded not far from the Aurelian steps.[1] Because of this accusation, Laelius, you procured this place and that mob. You know how numerous[2] they are, how united, what weight they have in assemblies. So I will lower my voice in order that only the jurymen may hear. There are plenty who would incite them against me and against all good citizens. I shall not help them to do this more easily.

1. *Aurelian steps*: these were steps supporting a raised platform, apparently the scene of turbulent meetings.
2. *numerous*: this points to a large Jewish community in Rome, even before Pompey's capture of Jerusalem (63 BC) brought many Jewish slaves to Rome, who might later acquire their freedom.

¶ When it was usual for gold to be exported to Jerusalem from all the provinces annually by the agency of the Jews, Flaccus published an edict to ban its export from Asia. Who is there, gentlemen of the jury, who would not sincerely praise this? The senate often previously and also in my consulship [63 BC] issued a most weighty ban on the export of gold. To resist this barbarous superstition showed authority, to defy in the public interest the Jewish mob, often inflamed with passion in the assemblies, showed great strength of mind. 'But', somebody may say, 'Gnaeus Pompeius victorious over captured Jerusalem touched nothing from that shrine.' In this case, as in many others, he acted very wisely. In so suspicious and slanderous a state he left his detractors no grounds for talk. For I do not believe that illustrious general was deterred by the religious feelings of Jews and enemies, but by his sense of propriety. Where then is the charge? You make no accusation of theft, you approve the edict, you confess that judgement[1] was given, you do not deny that the gold was sought and brought out publicly. The very facts show that the business was transacted by men of the highest standing. At Apamea a little less than one hundred pounds of gold was seized openly and weighed in the forum in front of the praetor by Sextius Caesius, a Roman knight of the greatest honour and integrity, at Laodicea a little more than twenty pounds by Lucius Pedaecus, our juryman, at Adramyttium – by Gnaeus Domitius the commissioner, at Pergamum not much.

   1. *judgement*: it is probably implied that Flaccus had brought to court Jews disobeying the edict and obtained a verdict against them.

¶ The gold has been accounted for, the gold is in the treasury. There is no charge of theft, it is an attempt to discredit him. The plea is not directed to the jury, the speaker's voice aims to reach the encircling crowd and the mob. Each State has its own religion, Laelius, we have ours. Even while Jerusalem was standing and the Jews were at peace, their religious rites were alien to the splendour of this Empire, the weight of our name, the institutions of our ancestors. Now this is even more so, because that nation has disclosed under arms what it thought of our rule. How dear it was to the immortal gods it has shown by being vanquished, let out for taxes, enslaved.

*De provinciis consularibus* 5.10–12

Cicero speaking in 56 BC on the allotment of the provinces to the consuls for 55 BC proposed that Gabinius' government of Syria should not be extended. His main argument was that Gabinius had oppressed the Roman tax-farmers by introducing financial reforms with a bias in favour of the provincials.

❡ Also the wretched tax-farmers – how wretched too was I because of the miserable plight of those who deserved so well of me! – He enslaved them to Jews and Syrians, peoples born for slavery. From the beginning he made a rule and kept it, not to entertain a suit brought by a tax-farmer.

HORACE, 65–8 BC (p. 65), in a description of a journey with a party of friends from Rome down to Brundisium (see map 1) inserts a good-humoured gibe against Jewish superstition.

*Satires* 1.5.97–103

❡ Next Gnatia,[1] at whose building the water nymphs were angered, caused laughter and jest, trying to persuade men that on the threshold of the Temple incense melts without fire. Apella the Jew[2] may believe it, not I. For I have learnt that the gods spend their life free from care and that, if nature should produce some wonder, it is not gods out of humour[3] who send it down from the high abode of heaven.

    1. *Gnatia*: this town had a notoriously bad water-supply.

    2. *Apella*: this occurs frequently in inscriptions as a name of freedmen. There is nothing to show whether Horace was referring to a well-known Jew, who had masked his origins by taking a Gentile name, or is using the name for Jews in general.

    3. *gods out of humour*: Horace was writing as an Epicurean and may be mocking the Jewish belief of an angry Yahweh intervening in human affairs, but it is more likely that this is just general mockery of the ominous interpretation of thunderbolts and the like.

PLINY (the Elder) AD 22/24 to 79 (p. 56) has two contemptuous mentions of the Jews.

*NH* 12.113

¶ The Jews treated this[1] with the same savage wrath as they did their own lives.

    1. *this*: Pliny is here describing that rare and precious shrub balsam, peculiar to Judaea. The Jews had tried to deprive the Romans by destroying it as they had destroyed themselves. Pliny assumes that his readers will understand this reference to the Jewish Revolt.

*NH* 13.46

¶ This variety,[1] which we offer in divine worship, the Jews who are a people noted for their contempt of the gods call common.

    1. *this variety*: Pliny is writing of the varieties of dates grown in Judaea.

QUINTILIAN (M. Fabius Quintilianus), born *c.* AD 30/5 (date of death unknown) at Calagurris in Spain, was a celebrated rhetorician and teacher of rhetoric in Rome. He was the author of a famous textbook *Training of an Orator*. The following passage comes from a section instructing a speaker in ways of exciting prejudice against his opponent. It does not necessarily reflect the author's own opinion, but it does show how an appeal to anti-Jewish bias could be made in the law courts, not unnaturally in view of the recent Jewish Revolt.

*Training of an Orator* 3.7.21

¶ We also hate those who have fathered evil. Founders of cities incur disrepute if they have produced a people pernicious to others, as for example the originator[1] of the Jewish superstition.

    1. *originator*: he does not name Moses, perhaps did not know his name. For his purpose it was enough that it was common knowledge that the Jews looked back to a founder of their institutions.

SUETONIUS, c. AD 69 to after 121 (p. 84), in his *Life of Augustus*, after describing the Emperor's respect for dreams and omens goes on to say:

*Life of Augustus* 94.1–2

¶ As for foreign cults, he showed the greatest respect for those that were ancient and traditional, but an equal contempt for the rest. For having been initiated at Athens, when later he sat in court to decide a case concerning the privilege of the priests of Ceres[1] in Attica and certain rather secret issues were being propounded he dismissed the assembly and crowd of bystanders and himself alone heard the disputants. On the other hand, when travelling through Egypt, not only did he omit to turn a little out of his way in order to see Apis,[2] but he also commended his grandson Gaius because in passing by Judaea he did not offer prayers at Jerusalem.[3]

1. *Ceres* was the Italian fertility goddess identified with Demeter, in honour of whom and of her daughter Persephone the famous Eleusinian mysteries (p. 224) were celebrated.

2. Egyptian religion, represented here by the bull-god *Apis*, and Judaism, although also foreign, were just as traditional and ancient, more so in fact. Suetonius implies that a conventional gesture of respect might have been expected, in which he represents the viewpoint of the average pagan, but he is ascribing a motive to Augustus which was not necessarily the true one and may simply be his own view.

3. It is equally probable that *Gaius* was commended for political discretion because a special detour to Jerusalem (AD 1) would have been a mark of imperial support for Archelaus, then ethnarch but to be deposed for misgovernment five years later. Augustus (Emperor 27 BC to AD 14) had maintained the religious rights of the Jews (see p. 97) and even provided for a daily sacrifice of two lambs and a bull on behalf of his own well-being in the Temple at Jerusalem (Philo *Leg. Gaj.* 157, 317).

MARTIAL, *c.* AD 40–*c.* 104 (p. 70), like his friend Juvenal (p. 32), saw the Jew as part of the social scene. When asked why he so often leaves Rome to stay in the country he lists the noisy nuisances who crowd the streets, among them:

*Epigrams* 12.57.13

¶ the Jew taught to beg by his mother.

The following Latin authors set the Jews against a wider background:

FRONTO, *c.* AD 100–66, a celebrated orator, author of an address against the Christians, tutor and intimate friend of Marcus Aurelius

(Emperor 161–80), in a fragment from his *On the Parthian War*, addressed to the Emperor, underlined what must have been a popular reason for hatred of the Jews:

### On the Parthian War (section 2)

¶ In the reign of Hadrian[1] how many soldiers were killed by the Jews, how many by the Britons!

    1. *Hadrian*: in his reign (117–38) there had been Jewish troubles outside Judaea, 115–17, and the Second Jewish Revolt under Bar Kokhba, 132–5.

Perhaps also derived from Fronto is the incidental slur put in the mouth of the pagan Caecilius by Minucius Felix, the third century Christian apologist (p. 172).

### Quoted by Minucius Felix *Octavius* 10.4

¶ Only the wretched people of the Jews also worship one god, but they worshipped in public with temples, altars, victims and ritual and their god is so weak and powerless that he has been made captive to the Romans along with his own nation.

MARCUS AURELIUS (Emperor 161–80) is quoted by Ammianus Marcellinus, the fourth century Roman historian. The anecdote is purely incidental, as will appear from the context, and only the actual saying can be attributed to the Emperor:

### Quoted by Marcellinus *History* 22.5.4–5

¶ Often he [Julian, Emperor 361–3] used to say: 'Give ear to me to whom the Alamanni and the Franci[1] gave ear', fancying that he was copying a saying of the old Emperor Marcus, but he failed to realize that there was an immense difference. For the story goes that when Marcus was passing through Palestine on his way to Egypt he often grew weary of the stinking[2] and riotous Jews and sadly exclaimed: 'O Marcomanni, O Quadi, O Sarmatae,[3] at last I have found others more turbulent than you!'

    1. *Alamanni and Franci*: these were northern tribes whom Julian had faced in his Germanic campaigns.

2. *stinking*: this might seem strange in view of the Pharisaic emphasis on cleanliness, but Martial (p. 70) had noted 'the stench of women keeping fast on the sabbath' and in hot and dusty Palestinian streets crowds of Jews demonstrating or hordes of individual petitioners would generate their own smells.

3. *Marcomanni* etc.: the three tribes listed were from the Danube regions and Marcus Aurelius had found them difficult to subdue.

DIO CASSIUS, *c.* AD 150 to 235 (p. 54) gives a highly-coloured account of the Jewish revolt in Cyrene (115/116), suspiciously exaggerated in numbers and details which, whether deliberately or not, were likely to inflame feelings against the Jews. This survives only in the *Epitome of Xiphilinus*:

*Epitome of Xiphilinus* 48.32.1–3

¶ Meanwhile the Jews in Cyrene, under the leadership of a certain Andreas, were slaughtering both Greeks and Romans. They ate their flesh, made belts from their entrails, anointed themselves with their blood and clothed themselves in their skin. They also sawed many in half[1] from the head downwards. Others they gave to wild beasts and forced to engage in single combat, so that two hundred and twenty thousand perished in all. In Egypt they committed many similar acts and in Cyprus under the command of a certain Artemion; there too two hundred and forty thousand perished. For this reason no Jew is allowed to land there, but even if he is cast up under stress of storm he is put to death.

1. *sawed many in half*: this was one of the sufferings of Jewish martyrs listed in Heb. 11:37. Traditionally it was the fate of Isaiah under the wicked King Manasseh.

APULEIUS, AD 123–*c.* 185 (p. 56). In *Metamorphoses* he describes how the hero, the ass, had been bought by a miller, a decent man, henpecked by an awful wife who practised every vice under the sun. After a catalogue of these he goes on:

*Metamorphoses* 9.14

¶ Despising and scorning the divine gods for the sake of some religion[1] or other, in the false and blasphemous assumption that there was a god whom she called the one and only, she deceived everybody by her false and empty observances. She had given herself up to morning drinking and constant lechery.[2]

1. *religion*: in the story that follows of her adultery, discovery by her husband and her use of a witch to procure his murder, religion plays no part and seems to be dragged in here only to enhance her iniquities. Conversion to a monotheistic religion (the scene is set in Greece) points to Judaism or Christianity, but the former is the more likely if there were conspicuous outward observances.

2. *lechery*: Tacitus (p. 16) also thought the Jews a very lecherous people (see p. 22).

### III

The foregoing passages have all shown a poor opinion of the Jews, but the following show that the absence of images had impressed the Romans.

LIVY (Titus Livius), 59 BC to AD 12, born at Padua, was a celebrated Roman historian. Much of his history of Rome in one hundred and forty-two books has been lost, including his account of Pompey's Syrian campaign in which the capture of Jerusalem was probably prefaced by a description of the Jews. This is a quotation from an ancient commentator on Lucan (see below):

❡ Livy on the Jews: 'They do not state to which of the gods the Temple at Jerusalem belongs nor is there any image there, for they do not think that the God has any shape.'

LUCAN (M. Annaeus Lucanus), AD 39 to 65, born at Corduba in Spain, brought up in Rome, was a member of court circles under Nero and best known as author of an epic poem *Pharsalia* on the Civil War between Caesar and Pompey. In this Pompey lists the nations whom he has conquered:

*Pharsalia* 2.592–3

❡ The Cappadocians fear my standards and so too does Judaea devoted to the worship of an unknown god.

VARRO (Marcus Terentius), 116–27 BC, was a celebrated Roman scholar who produced many works on a great variety of subjects. Among these was a treatise on *Antiquities of Things Human and Things Divine*, now lost. Augustine (p. 67) quoted from it in two passages.

Augustine *City of God* 4.31

¶ Varro also says that for more than one hundred and seventy years the ancient Romans worshipped the gods without an image. 'If this had remained to our own day', he says, 'the worship of the gods would be purer.' To support this opinion of his he cites among others the example of the Jewish people. He does not hesitate to conclude the passage by saying that those who were the first to set up images of the gods for their peoples deprived their states of awe and added error, for he wisely judged that gods as insensate images could easily be despised.

Augustine *On The Agreement of the Gospel-Writers* 1.22.30

¶ Yet Varro, one of themselves [i.e. the Romans] and the greatest scholar to be found among them, identified[1] the god of the Jews with Jupiter, thinking it made no difference by what name he was called, provided that the same thing was understood. I fancy that he was frightened by his sublimity. The Romans are in the habit of worshipping nothing superior to Jupiter, to which the Capitol[2] bears sufficient and open witness, and they think him king of all the gods. So perceiving that the Jews worshipped the highest god, he could not suppose him to be anything other than Jupiter.

   1. *identified*: in the pagan world it was common practice to identify one god with another worshipped by a different race, provided that there was some similarity of function (p. 195).
   2. *Capitol*: on the Capitol hill in the heart of Rome stood the great temple of Jupiter Capitolinus.

   A third quotation comes from LYDUS, the sixth century compiler of a calendar.

Lydus *On the Months* 4.53

¶ The Roman Varro defining him [the Jewish god] says that in the Chaldaean mysteries he is called Iao.[1]

1. *Iao*: this name was very common in magical papyri and amulets. Cp. also Diodorus, *fl. c.* 60 BC (p. 57), who attributes its use to Moses.

Another passage does not mention the Jews by name, but Varro probably had them in mind. The absence of images would certainly fit them and, although sacrifices were offered in the Temple in Jerusalem, Varro would see none in Rome in the synagogues there. This is quoted by Arnobius, a Christian apologist under Diocletian (Emperor 284–305).

### Arnobius *Against the Pagans* 7.1

¶ 'What then', somebody will say, 'do you think that no sacrifices should be offered at all?' To reply to you, not voicing our own opinion but your own Varro's, 'None.' 'Because', he says, 'true gods neither desire nor demand them; much less do those made of bronze, pot, plaster or marble care for these things, for they cannot feel. No blame is contracted if you do not offer them nor, if you do, is any favour won.'

PLUTARCH, *c.* AD 50–120 (p. 72), whose discussion as to why the Jews abstain from pork has already been quoted (p. 77) goes straight on from that to the question 'Who is the God of the Jews', treating the subject as one worthy of academic discussion.

### *Quaest. Conviv.* 5.6.1

¶ Symmachus, in amazement at all that had been said, exclaimed: 'Do you, Lamprias, register and surreptitiously introduce among the secret rites of the Hebrews your national god Dionysus,[1] hailed with the cry "Euoe", exciter of women, glorying in ecstatic rites? Is there really an argument for identifying the one with the other?' Moiragenes interrupted: 'Let him be. For I am an Athenian and tell you in reply that they are one and the same. Most of the proofs of this can only be told and taught to those who are initiated among us at the Great Mysteries,[2] celebrated every two years. But I am ready to tell what there is no ban on telling in talk with friends, especially over the winecups, gifts of the god, if urged by those present.'

1. *Dionysus* was the god of wine, also known as Bacchus. His mother had been the Theban princess Semele, so Boeotians such as Lamprias and Plutarch himself could claim him as being of their nationality.

2. *Great Mysteries*: these were the famous Eleusinian mysteries celebrated at Eleusis near Athens in honour of Demeter, the fertility goddess, and her daughter Persephone. They were called 'Great' to distinguish them from the 'Lesser Mysteries', which were a preliminary stage of initiation occurring in the alternate intervening years (see p. 224). The ban of secrecy on the vital details of the ritual was rigorously imposed and kept.

¶ When everyone did beg and pray him, he said: 'In the first place the season and character of their greatest and most solemn festival is in keeping with Dionysus. They celebrate the so-called Fast[1] when the vintage is at its best and set out tables full of every kind of fruit in booths and huts made for the most part from vine twigs and ivy[2] intertwined. The first of the two days of the festival they call "Tabernacles". A few days later they celebrate another festival[3] in which Bacchus is named not by enigmatic allusions but openly. They also have a festival in which fig branches and wands are carried, in the course of which they enter the Temple carrying wands.[4] What they do after entering we do not know, but probably the ritual is a Bacchic revelry, for like the Argives at their Dionysiac festival they use little trumpets[5] to invoke the god and others proceed playing the harp; these they themselves call Levites, a name derived either from Lysias [Releaser] or Euios [hailed by the cry "Euoe"].'

1. *Fast*: the speaker seems to be confusing the fast of the Day of Atonement kept on the tenth day of the seventh month (Lev. 23:27) with the Feast of Tabernacles (Lev. 23:34).

2. *vine twigs and ivy*: neither of these is mentioned by Neh. 8:15 among the various kinds of branches used.

3. *another festival*: the allusion may be to the special ceremonies of the closing of the Feast of Tabernacles seven days later (Lev. 23:36; Num. 29:35; Neh. 8:18).

4. *wands*: the Greek word denotes a wand peculiar to Dionysiac worship, wreathed in vine leaves and ivy and with a fir cone on top. The Jews used palm branches processionally, but only at the Feast of Tabernacles.

5. *trumpets*: this would seem to point to the festival on the first day of the seventh month, which was announced by the blowing of trumpets (Lev. 23:24; Num. 29:1).

¶ 'I think that the sabbath festival too is not entirely without a Dionysiac element. Even now many call Bacchic worshippers Sabi,[1] and this is the cry they utter in their revelry in honour of the god. This can be confirmed of course by both Demosthenes[2] and Menander[3] and it would not be unreasonable to say that the name has arisen because of a kind of excitement [*sobesis*] which possesses the Bacchanals. They themselves attest the theory, for whenever they celebrate sabbaths they challenge one another to drink and drunkenness[4] and, when some more important business prevents this, they make a habit of tasting at least a little neat wine.'

1. *Sabi*: this presupposes identification of the Phrygian god Sabazius (p. 225) with Dionysus; both had an ecstatic form of worship. In 139 BC Jews had been expelled from Rome for trying to win converts to the worship of Jupiter Sabazius (p. 85). Tacitus too (p. 23) knew that some people thought that the Jews worshipped Bacchus, though he himself discounted this.

2. *Demosthenes*: the great orator and statesman, 384 to 322 BC, in a speech against his rival Aeschines (*De Corona* 260) had twitted him because as a boy he used to lead bands of initiates through the streets crying 'Euoe Saboe'. 'Euoe' was the recognized form of invocation of Dionysus, so 'Saboe' is used there to invoke Sabazius. Demosthenes' whole account is a parody of some vaguely Asiatic cult.

3. *Menander*: the works of the famous Athenian comic playwright only survive, mainly fragmentary, in quotation and on recently discovered papyri. The passage referred to here is unknown.

4. *challenge*: there is no foundation for this statement nor for the penalty of being deprived of wine mentioned below. The Jews did appreciate good wine (cp. Ps. 104:15 'wine to gladden men's hearts', also Judg. 9:13), but in the ancient world wine, generally mixed with water, was the everyday drink. Dinners were given on the sabbath (cp. Luke 14:1–6) and by the time of Augustine, AD 354–430, were proverbially luxurious. On the other hand cp. Lev. 10:8–9 'The LORD spoke to Aaron and said: You and your sons with you shall not drink wine or strong drink when you are to enter the Tent of the Presence, lest you die.'

¶ 'Now these arguments could be called probabilities, but their opponents are powerfully refuted in the first place by the fact that the high priest at festivals processes in a mitre and garbed in a gold-embroidered fawn skin,[1] wearing a robe, which reaches his feet, and buskins; many bells hang from his vestment which tinkle below him as he walks, as is usual with us too. Like us they celebrate nocturnal festivals noisily and call the god's nurses "bronze-rattlers".[2] There are also the wand which is displayed carved on the outside[3] of the Temple and the tambourines. Surely these are appropriate to no other god but Dionysus. Furthermore they do not offer honey[4] in their worship because it is thought to spoil wine if mixed with it and before the appearance of the vine was their libation and their drink. To this very day those barbarians who do not make wine have a drink made from honey, spicing its sweetness with wine-like bitter roots. The Greeks make the same "sober offerings"[5] and libations of honey, on the grounds that honey and wine are complete opposites. It is no light evidence for the Jews' practice of this that, although they have many punishments, one is held particularly odious, the punishment of deprivation of wine for as long a period as the judge determining the penalty assigns.'

    1. *fawn skin*: this was the traditional wear of Dionysus and his followers. The high priest's garb is described in Exod. 28 and by Josephus, *Ant.* 3.7.4, but the only points of similarity with the description given here are the long robe and the bells.

    2. *nurses*: these were nymphs, well-known in Greek mythology, who presumably used rattles to amuse the infant Dionysus. This is a particularly blatant example of the way in which Plutarch fills up a gap in his knowledge by formulating some fantastic theory of his own.

    3. *outside*: there is some textual corruption and such a carving is inexplicable.

    4. *honey*: Lev. 2 : 11 forbids offerings of honey, but not for the reason given here.

    5. *sober offerings*: this was a technical term for a mixture of water, milk and honey, offered to those grim goddesses, the Furies.

PLINY (the Elder), AD 22/24 to 79 (p. 56). The Essenes are mentioned with awe and respect by the Elder Pliny, who is otherwise so anti-Jewish in his incidental references, in his geography of Judaea.

*NH* 5.73.1–3

¶ On the west the Essenes[1] live removed far enough from its shores [the Dead Sea] to escape its harmful effects. They are a solitary people, marvellous above all others in the whole world, without any women, renouncing all love, without money,[2] finding companionship in palm trees. Every day the throng of refugees is renewed to an equal number whom, weary of life, the waves of fortune drive to adopt their customs. So through thousands of centuries – incredible to relate! – a race is eternal in which no one is born. So fruitful for them is other men's dissatisfaction with life. Below these was the town of Engada, second to Jerusalem[3] in its fertility and groves of palm trees, now another pile of ashes. Next is the fortress Masada[4] on a rock, itself not far from the Sea of Asphalt. This is the extent of Judaea.

1. *Essenes*: this ascetic Jewish sect was described in more detail by Philo and Josephus, but Pliny differs from them in locating the Essenes by the Dead Sea. He appears to be referring to the Qumran community (cp. Knibb, *The Qumran Community*, in this series).

2. *without money*: they needed no money because of their communal way of life.

3. *Jerusalem* could not be called famous for its fertility and palm trees, although destruction by fire does fit. Pliny may be carelessly confusing it with Jericho.

4. *Masada*: this was where the Zealots made their last stand in AD 74.

DIO CHRYSOSTOM, *c.* AD 40 to after 112, was a Greek orator and popular philosopher, born at Prusa in Bithynia and widely travelled. He seems at least to have recognized the existence of the Essenes, but there are no references to Jews or Judaism in his extant works and the following comes from the biography by the fourth century Synesius:

Dio Chrysostom *Testimonia* 1

¶ Moreover he praises the Essenes, a very blessed city, which lies near the Dead Sea in the interior of Palestine, hard by Sodom.

All these quotations have been taken from literary sources. The following, from a papyrus letter written in AD 41, by a Greek to another Greek who had money-troubles, though perhaps influenced by the tension between Greeks and Jews at that time in Alexandria, probably illustrates the attitude of the common man elsewhere.

Corpus Papyrorum Judaicorum (CPJ) 152.23–5

¶ As everybody else does, keep clear of the Jews.

# PART II

# Christianity

# Christianity

The members of the early church in Jerusalem were all Jews or proselytes, such as Nicolas of Antioch (Acts 6:5). They were found continually in the Temple (Acts 2:46; 5:42) and it was not until the persecution following the death of Stephen that they dispersed to take the message further afield. On the face of it they were, like the Essenes, just another sect within Judaism. As such, they came under the sheltering umbrella of the sanction accorded to Judaism as an official religion.

When Paul went abroad he won many converts among those who had been on the fringe and now eagerly embraced a cult which had all the attractive features of Judaism and which promised personal salvation without imposing circumcision and irksome food regulations. His success in promulgating teaching which many orthodox Jews must have thought downright blasphemy provoked jealousy and hostility. Such Jews were concerned to dissociate themselves and to prejudice the authorities against the Christians as dangerous revolutionaries. These Jews of the Diaspora in the regions of the eastern Mediterranean were numerous and prosperous, well-established communities within cities where they had been settled for generations. Their pagan neighbours accepted them and their odd habits as a fact of life, even if tensions sometimes arose.

The wonder is that the tiny Christian churches survived and increased. Jewish members might be tempted to relapse under the comforting shield of Judaism with its legal immunity, but pagan converts had no natural or national links with Jews. Although Jesus was a Jew and they saw themselves as a new Israel, the proper heirs of a new covenant with God, they did not identify themselves with the Jews but with their fellow-members in a faith which transcended race, sex and status (cp. Gal. 3:28). As non-Jews they could not rank in the eyes of the government as practising a legally authorized religion.

Their former friends and neighbours probably saw their conversion from paganism with amazement and horror. Obnoxious and anti-social practices were to be expected and could be tolerated among Jews, but these Christians had broken with the easy everyday intercourse of normal social life, which counts for so much in facilitating friendly relationships. They would no longer take part in festivals or attend the games or the theatre because they actually despised the very gods who had so long been the protectors of the nation. They did not even recognize the divinity of the Emperor as loyal subjects should. No good could come of this and some day the gods would vindicate themselves by sending some disaster. Some Christians would not even eat meat bought in the market, because it had been part of a sacrificial victim, much less accept an invitation to a friendly dinner party in a temple or attend the sociable club dinners of trading guilds also held in temples. As for cheerful sexual promiscuity, the ritual prostitution both male and female associated with certain fertility cults, jolly drinking bouts, all these had become anathema. The Christians were now kill-joys, skulking behind closed doors where it stood to reason that they indulged not only in the monstrous practices already attributed to Judaism, but other unmentionable crimes.

As early as 64 the Christians in Rome were a recognizable body, so numerous and unpopular that Nero (Emperor 54–68) felt he could safely make them scapegoats for the Great Fire of Rome and so divert the suspicion that he had caused it himself in order to put into effect his own architectural project for re-planning the city. There are some vague references to persecutions in the New Testament after Acts, but our first contemporary pagan reference is in the correspondence between Pliny, governor of Bithynia, and Trajan (Emperor 98–117) in 114, about the proper procedure in the trials of Christians. We also have some accounts of martyrdoms from the second century AD, which claim to be rescripts of trials and give valuable evidence about the charges brought and the attitude of the government and the populace in various places.

There are some incidental references in pagan authors to Christians, whose courage under persecution could be viewed as praiseworthy or as such contumacious obstinacy that it deserved punishment. Fronto, c. 100–66 (p. 121) directed a whole speech against them. Galen, 129–99, (p. 61) criticized them along with the Jews for their doctrine of divine revelation, but praised their virtues. Finally the philosopher Celsus, later second century (p. 60), thought them worth attacking in a closely reasoned treatise *Against the Christians*.

## New Testament Sources

Our earliest source-book for pagan attitudes towards Christianity must of course be the New Testament. In Jesus' lifetime he would appear simply as a healer, a worker of miracles. It was his healing power that the centurion requested for his sick servant (Luke 7 : 1–5 ; Matt. 8 : 5–13), but this centurion was already sympathetic towards Judaism. He had built a synagogue (according to Luke, but a detail omitted by Matthew) and was the stuff of which later converts were made. The Syro-Phoenician (or according to Matt. 15 :21 Canaanite) woman too wanted healing for her daughter (Mark 7:25–30).

The centurion at the crucifixion was impressed by Jesus' death:

Mark 15:39

¶ And when the centurion who was standing opposite saw how he died, he said, 'Truly this man was a son of God.'[1]

Matthew expands the Marcan version:

Matt. 27:54

¶ And when the centurion and his men who were keeping watch over Jesus saw the earthquake and all that was happening they were filled with awe, and they said: 'Truly this man was a son of God.'[1]

Luke 23:47 plays it down:

¶ The centurion saw it all and gave praise to God. 'Beyond all doubt', he said, 'this man was innocent.'

    1. *son of God*: this does not imply the Messiahship of Jesus. In the mouth of a pagan it means that the centurion recognized something superhuman in Jesus, the sort of thing familiar to him from many stories of Greek demi-gods. It may be because of this possible association that Luke avoids the phrase.

ACTS: For the development of the church, Acts must be our principal witness. (For the NEB text and commentary, see J. W. Packer, Cambridge Bible Commentary.) The date, authorship and venue remain debateable. It must also be remembered that Acts, while no doubt incorporating earlier material, is likely to reflect ideas and experiences contemporary with its author.

After the crucifixion, resurrection, ascension and Pentecost, the followers of Jesus developed a basic form of teaching and began to attract converts, but still remained within the main body of Judaism. As such they did not attract the attention of the Roman government and it was the conservative Jews who, seeing in them dangerous heretics, lynched Stephen and set on foot the persecution that dispersed them from Jerusalem (Acts 6 : 8–8 : 1). The author gives four examples of individual pagans who were predisposed to accept the missionaries' preaching:

8 : 27–31. The Ethiopian eunuch is a prototype of the intellectual convert, brought to the faith after previous study of Jewish scripture.

10 : 1–2. The centurion Cornelius, converted by Peter, is reminiscent of the centurion at Capernaum (Luke 7 : 1–5):

❡ He was a religious man, and he and his whole family joined in the worship of God. He gave generously to help the Jewish people, and was regular in his prayers to God.

13 : 6–7. The governor of Cyprus, Sergius Paulus, was sufficiently open-minded to keep a Jewish magician in his entourage and to send for Paul and Barnabas of his own accord.

16 : 12–14. Lydia at Philippi was one of the many women previously on the fringe.

It was in Antioch that there were the first mass-conversions from paganism and that the converts attracted a nickname differentiating them from the Jews.

## Acts 11 : 19–26

❡ Meanwhile those who had been scattered after the persecution that arose over Stephen made their way to Phoenicia, Cyprus, and Antioch, bringing the message to Jews only and to no others. But there were some natives of Cyprus and Cyrene among them, and these, when they arrived at Antioch, began to speak to Gentiles as well, telling them the good news of the LORD Jesus. The power of the LORD was with them, and a great many became believers, and turned to the LORD. . . . It was in Antioch that the disciples first got the name of Christians.

In his subsequent missionary journeys Paul used to go first to the synagogue, where he found Jews and proselytes and those sympathizers with Judaism who hovered on the fringe. It is alleged that actual opposition usually came from those Jews who refused to accept his message and these might use their influence to stir up the authorities against him. This was the case at Pisidian Antioch (13 : 42–50), where he was expelled from the city. At Iconium (14: 1–6) he was threatened with stoning, with the connivance of the authorities. At Thessalonica (17: 1–9) the mob accused them of political disaffection and they had to be smuggled away. From Beroea too (17: 10–14) Paul made a hasty escape to avoid similar trouble.

Lystra (14: 18–20) was rather different. After the healing of the lame man the simple country folk took Paul and Barnabas as gods in human form. When they were disabused of this notion they listened readily to Jews who had arrived from Antioch and Iconium; they stoned Paul and left him outside the city for dead. The whole story shows how hard it must have been to shake conservative pagans out of their entrenched beliefs.

At Philippi (16: 13–40) they were the victims of anti-Jewish prejudice. After some initial success Paul by exorcizing the slavegirl's oracular spirit antagonized her owners, as they had lost their source of profit.

## Acts 16 : 19–23

¶ When the girl's owners saw that their hope of gain had gone, they seized Paul and Silas and dragged them to the city authorities in the main square; and bringing them before the magistrates, they said, 'These men are causing a disturbance in our city; they are Jews, they are advocating customs which it is illegal for us Romans to adopt and follow.' The mob joined in the attack; and the magistrates tore off the prisoners' clothes and ordered them to be flogged. After giving them a severe beating they flung them into prison and ordered the jailer to keep them under close guard.

Vested financial interests and an appeal to national pride, for Philippi was a colony largely peopled by Roman veteran soldiers, had combined to stir up anti-Jewish feeling. Paul and Silas should have enjoyed the special privileges allowed to Jews to follow their own religious practices (cp. p. 92). Instead they had been flogged and imprisoned. After the episode of the earthquake and the jailer's conversion the magistrates sent word for their release. Paul however refused to be smuggled out. He complained that, although Roman citizens, they had been publicly flogged and imprisoned without trial. The magistrates acknowledged their fault by coming and apologizing, but requested them to leave.

It is noteworthy that the church at Philippi flourished and was especially dear to Paul.

At Athens he was faced with particular problems.

Acts 17:17–21; 32–33

¶ He argued in the synagogue with the Jews and Gentile worshippers, and also in the city square every day with casual passers-by. And some of the Epicurean and Stoic philosophers[1] joined issue with him. Some said, 'What can this charlatan be trying to say?'; others, 'He would appear to be a propagandist for foreign deities' – this because he was preaching about Jesus and resurrection. So they took him and brought him before the Court of the Areopagus[2] and said, 'May we know what this new doctrine is that you propound? You are introducing ideas that sound strange to us, and we should like to know what they mean.' (Now the Athenians and the foreigners there had no time for anything but talking or hearing about the latest novelty.)...

When they heard about the raising of the dead, some scoffed; and others said, 'We will hear you on this subject some other time.' And so Paul left the assembly. However, some men joined him and became believers, including Dionysius, a member of the Court of the Areopagus; also a woman named Damaris, and others beside.

    1. *philosophers*: Stoics and Epicureans are named, as being the two leading philosophic schools of the time (p. 200–1).

    2. *Court of the Areopagus*: this Court got its name from having originally met on the Areopagus, Hill of Ares (Mars). It was a small but powerful body, which among other functions had from very early times exercised control over religious matters. Paul, thought to be introducing a foreign cult, is politely asked to explain himself. His defence, adapted to such sophisticated hearers, was received with mockery or civil indifference; no measures were taken against him and he was dismissed as one of the many cranks frequenting Athens. This may be taken as typical of the pagan attitude to be expected in such a milieu in these early days.

At Corinth Paul had to confront a Roman governor, not local magistrates. After some initial opposition from the Jews he remained there for eighteen months, teaching.

Acts 18 : 12–18

¶ But when Gallio¹ was proconsul of Achaia, the Jews set upon Paul in
a body and brought him into court. 'This man', they said, 'is inducing
people to worship God in ways that are against the Law.' Paul was
just about to speak when Gallio said to them, 'If it had been a question
of crime or grave misdemeanour, I should, of course, have given you
Jews a patient hearing, but if it is some bickering about words and names
and your Jewish Law, you may see to it yourselves; I have no mind
to be a judge of these matters.' And he had them ejected from the court.
Then there was a general attack on Sosthenes,² who held office in the
synagogue, and they gave him a beating in full view of the bench. But
all this left Gallio quite unconcerned. Paul stayed on for some time.

    1. *Gallio*: he was the elder brother of Seneca (p. 66) the tutor and
adviser of Nero (Emperor 54–68) and had followed a political career,
culminating in the consulship. The exact date of his governorship is
unknown.
    2. *Sosthenes*: it is not clear whether he was a Christian convert now
attacked by the Jews or, more probably in the light of Gallio's rebuff,
a Jewish leader held responsible for their failure. According to some
less reliable MSS the beating was administered by 'all the Greeks', who
could have seen in Gallio's indifference an opportunity to indulge in
some anti-Jewish hostility. In any case Gallio's impartiality encouraged
Paul to prolong his stay in Corinth for a while instead of making a
hasty retreat.

    At Ephesus Paul had been working for two years and exercising
miraculous powers of healing. Then the episode of the discomfiture
of the seven Jewish exorcists made him well known. Many converts
confessed that they had been using magic spells and publicly burnt their
magic books to a total value of fifty thousand pieces of silver. This
public abjuration must have made a deep impression, especially the
economic consequences of giving up such a lucrative trade. At much
the same time economic and religious motives combined to rouse
feelings against Paul.

Acts 19 : 23 ff.

¶ Now about that time, the Christian movement gave rise to a serious
disturbance. There was a man named Demetrius, a silversmith who

made silver shrines of Diana and provided a great deal of employment
for the craftsmen. He called a meeting of these men and the workers
in allied trades, and addressed them. 'Men', he said, 'you know that
our high standard of living depends on this industry. And you see and
hear how this fellow Paul with his propaganda has perverted crowds
of people, not only in Ephesus but also in practically the whole of the
province of Asia. He is telling them that gods made by human hands
are not gods at all. There is danger for us here; it is not only that our
line of business will be discredited, but also that the sanctuary of the
great goddess Diana[1] will cease to command respect; and then it will
not be long before she who is worshipped by all Asia and the civilized
world is brought down from her divine pre-eminence.'

1. *Diana*: the goddess worshipped here, though equated with the
Greek Artemis (the Roman Diana), was not like them a huntress, but
an ancient fertility goddess. Her temple was of outstanding magnificence
and one of the seven wonders of the ancient world.

A great disturbance followed, which the town clerk finally quieted
by reminding them of the legal processes available, and ended:

Acts 19:40
¶ 'We certainly run the risk of being charged with riot for this day's
work. There is no justification for it, and if the issue is raised we shall
be unable to give any explanation of this uproar.' With that he
dismissed the assembly.

On his return to Jerusalem, because of allegations that he was
profaning the Temple, Paul was attacked by an angry mob. Eventually
he was arrested and was about to be flogged in order to discover the
reason for the rioting. (Flogging was a usual method of trying to elicit
truthful evidence from slaves and provincials.) He then protested.

Acts 22:25-9
¶ 'Can you legally flog a man who is a Roman citizen, and moreover
has not been found guilty?' When the centurion heard this, he went
and reported it to the commandant. 'What do you mean to do?' he
said. 'This man is a Roman citizen.' The commandant came to Paul.

'Tell me, are you a Roman citizen?' he asked. 'Yes', said he. The commandant rejoined, 'It cost me a large sum to acquire this citizenship.' Paul said, 'But it was mine by birth.' Then those who were about to examine him withdrew hastily, and the commandant himself was alarmed when he realized that Paul was a Roman citizen and that he had put him in irons.

When a hearing before the Council led to further disturbances Paul was taken into protective custody. The commandant, when he learnt of the intended assassination, sent him under protection of a strong escort to Caesarea, with a despatch.

Acts 23 : 26–33

¶ 'Claudius Lysias to His Excellency the Governor Felix.[1] Your Excellency: This man was seized by the Jews and was on the point of being murdered when I intervened with the troops and removed him, because I discovered that he was a Roman citizen. As I wished to ascertain the charge on which they were accusing him, I took him down to their Council. I found that the accusation had to do with controversial matters in their law, but there was no charge against him meriting death or imprisonment. However, I have now been informed of an attempt to be made on the man's life, so I am sending him to you at once, and have also instructed his accusers to state their case against him before you.'...

1. *Felix*: he was governor of Judaea from 52 to 60 (p. 8). By referring the case to him Lysias was acting very diplomatically. He had safeguarded the prisoner by sending such a strong escort, yet was conciliating the Jews by allowing them to re-open the case. Personally he found nothing criminal in Paul's stance, which for Christians was an important point.

Jews arrived from Jerusalem to press their case and after hearing both sides:

Acts 24 : 22–7

¶ Felix, who happened to be well informed about the Christian movement,[1] adjourned the hearing. 'When Lysias the commanding officer comes down', he said, 'I will go into your case.' He gave orders to the centurion to keep Paul under open arrest and not to prevent any of his friends from making themselves useful to him.

Some days later Felix came with his wife Drusilla, who was a Jewess, and sending for Paul he let him talk to him about faith in Christ Jesus. But when the discourse turned to questions of morals, self-control, and the coming judgement, Felix became alarmed and exclaimed, 'That will do for the present; when I find it convenient I will send for you again.' At the same time he had hopes of a bribe from Paul; and for this reason he sent for him very often and talked with him. When two years had passed, Felix was succeeded by Porcius Festus. Wishing to curry favour with the Jews, Felix left Paul in custody.

1. *Christian movement*: the Greek phrase so translated in the NEB has no hint of any possible political interpretation. It was natural that Felix, especially as he had a Jewish wife, should have heard of this dissident Jewish sect. Whether he expected a bribe or not (what we know of his character is in keeping), it was not uncommon for prisoners to be kept in custody because of a backlog of cases. The conditions of his imprisonment show that he was not regarded as a dangerous criminal. Felix's enjoyment of his conversation shows that in Paul he found a very intelligent exponent. At the same time Paul was undeniably a potential cause of trouble with the Jews, so Felix played safe.

When Festus arrived the Jews once more pressed unsubstantiated charges. Festus then asked Paul if he was willing to go to Jerusalem to stand trial there, whereupon Paul affirmed his innocence of any capital offence and appealed for trial before the Emperor at Rome. (This citizen right was later maintained by Pliny, who sent accused Christians to Rome (p. 150). In the persecution at Lyons too (p. 169) the Emperor was consulted about the punishment proper for Roman citizens.) So to Rome Paul went, although a hearing before Festus and king Herod Agrippa II left them convinced of his innocence. In Rome he lived under house arrest at his own expense (28:16ff.), with open access for all who cared to visit him and hear his teaching, for two years.

In a tendentious work such as Acts, addressed to a high-ranking official, it was natural that the Roman authorities, distinct from local magistrates, should be represented as just and impartial in their treatment of Christians. Obviously the latter in their early days were still regarded merely as a dissident sect within Judaism. They therefore had a right to the religious privileges of the Jews, but could also be the victims of local anti-Jewish prejudice.

Paul himself prescribed respect for the authorities, in a way which suggests that he had found them fair in carrying out their divinely appointed duties.

Rom. 13:1–6

¶ Every person must submit to the supreme authorities. There is no authority but by act of God, and the existing authorities are instituted by him; consequently anyone who rebels against authority is resisting a divine institution, and those who so resist have themselves to thank for the punishment they will receive. For government, a terror to crime, has no terrors for good behaviour. You wish to have no fear of the authorities? Then continue to do right and you will have their approval, for they are God's agents working for your good. But if you are doing wrong, then you will have cause to fear them; it is not for nothing that they hold the power of the sword for they are God's agents of punishment, for retribution on the offender. That is why you are obliged to submit. It is an obligation imposed not merely by fear of retribution but by conscience. That is also why you pay taxes. The authorities are in God's service and to these duties they devote their energies.

Similar injunctions are to be found in 1 Tim. 2:1; Titus 3:1; 1 Pet. 3:13–17.

In one trenchant phrase Paul summed up his own estimate of Jewish and pagan attitudes towards his preaching:

1 Cor. 1:22–4

¶ Jews call for miracles, Greeks look for wisdom; but we proclaim Christ – yes, Christ nailed to the cross; and though this is a stumbling-block to Jews and folly to Greeks, yet to those who have heard his call, Jews and Greeks alike, he is the power of God and the wisdom of God.

Leaving aside the vexed questions of dating and venue, 1 Peter, Hebrews and Revelation give evidence for persecution.

1 Pet. 4:12–16

Members of the Diaspora in Pontus, Galatia, Cappadocia, Asia and Bithynia are suffering for the fact that they are Christians, but whether this refers to action by the government, as in Bithynia in AD 112 (p. 149), or to general harassment by their pagan neighbours or fellow-Jews is left vague:

¶ My dear friends, do not be bewildered by the fiery ordeal that is upon you, as though it were something extraordinary. It gives you a share in Christ's sufferings, and that is cause for joy; and when his glory is revealed, your joy will be triumphant. If Christ's name is flung in your teeth as an insult, count yourselves happy, because then that glorious Spirit which is the Spirit of God is resting upon you. If you suffer, it must not be for murder, theft, or sorcery, nor for infringing the rights of others. But if anyone suffers as a Christian, he should feel it no disgrace, but confess that name to the honour of God.

Heb. 10.32–4

¶ Remember the days gone by, when newly enlightened, you met the challenge of great sufferings and held firm. Some of you were abused and tormented to make a public show, while others stood loyally by those who were so treated. For indeed you shared the sufferings of the prisoners,[1] and you cheerfully accepted the seizure of your possessions, knowing that you possessed something better and more lasting.

1. *prisoners*: this points to official action, but looting could have been an accompaniment of riot. This could not have been persecution designed to exterminate, for the readers still survive.

REVELATION: the dominating theme of the book is an attack on Rome for its persecution of Christians. In the Epistles to the Seven Churches there are obscure allusions to sporadic and local persecutions, with specific reference to one martyr in the church at Pergamum:

Rev. 2:13

¶ You did not deny your faith in me even at the time when Antipas, my faithful witness, was killed in your city, the home of Satan.

For pagan converts abstention from meat offered to idols must have been a great difficulty. It was normal practice that those parts of the victim which were not actually offered should be on sale in the meat market, the source of supply for city-dwellers. The Jews had their own butchers in order to preserve their ritual food laws. When Christianity broke with Judaism, Jewish and pagan converts alike were faced with this problem. The former with their inbred revulsion against anything smacking of idolatry perhaps found it easier to abstain from meat altogether (cp. the vegetarianism mentioned in Rom. 14:1–6). Some Greeks argued that heathen gods did not exist (with the logical consequence that they could not pollute) and Paul recognizes the force of their argument (1 Cor. 8:1–6), but goes on to qualify his assent:

1 Cor. 8:7–13

¶ But not everyone knows this. There are some who have been so accustomed to idolatry that even now they eat this food with a sense of its heathen consecration, and their conscience, being weak, is polluted by the eating. Certainly food will not bring us into God's presence: if we do not eat, we are none the worse, and if we eat, we are none the better. But be careful that this liberty of yours does not become a pitfall for the weak. If a weak character sees you sitting down to a meal in a heathen temple[1] – you, who 'have knowledge' – will not his conscience be emboldened to eat food consecrated to the heathen deity? This 'knowledge' of yours is utter disaster to the weak, the brother for whom Christ died. In thus sinning against your brothers and wounding their conscience, you sin against Christ. And therefore, if food be the downfall of my brother, I will never eat meat any more, for I will not be the cause of my brother's downfall.

1. *heathen temple*: this was often the venue for a happy social gathering among friends or business associates. Pagans might well look askance at those who completely broke such ties.

The Council of Jerusalem, Acts 15, among other prohibitions explicitly forbade the eating of such meat. The author of Revelation too saw in accommodation to pagan practice a dangerous heresy in his own day. He writes to Pergamum:

Rev. 2:14–15

¶ But I have a few matters to bring against you: you have in Pergamum some that hold to the teaching of Balaam,[1] who taught Balak to put temptation in the way of the Israelites. He encouraged them to eat food sacrificed to idols and to commit fornication,[2] and in the same way you also have some who hold the doctrine of the Nicolaitans.[3] So repent!

1. *Balaam*: cp. Num. 22:1; 31:16; 25:1–9; 2 Pet. 2:15; Jude 11; CBC *Letters of Peter and Jude* (ed. A. R. C. Leaney, p. 92).

2. *fornication*: this was linked with idolatry in Acts 15:20; 29 (Council of Jerusalem) and 1 Cor. 5–6, as often in the Old Testament. The word combines both a literal and a metaphorical meaning.

3. *Nicolaitans*: the name is found in the New Testament only here and in verse 6 of John's letter to Ephesus: 'You hate the practices of the Nicolaitans as I do.' There was a later Gnostic sect of this name. Here in Pergamum with its great temples and Emperor cult (pp. 212ff.) the pagan environment would exert a particularly strong influence.

A similar warning was given to the church at Thyatira (see map 2), an affluent, commercial centre where, as we know from inscriptions, there were a large number of trading guilds.

Rev. 2:20

¶ Yet I have this against you: you tolerate that Jezebel,[1] the woman who claims to be a prophetess, who by her teaching lures my servants into fornication and into eating food sacrificed to idols.

1. *Jezebel*: cp. 2 Kings 9:22; 1 Kings 16:31ff. for her 'fornication' and propagation of the cult of Baal.

### Pagan Sources

We have seen (p. 104) that Suetonius (p. 84) speaks of rioting under 'Chrestus' as early as the time of Claudius (Emperor 41–54).

TACITUS, born *c.* 56, date of death unknown (p. 16), writes of a lady who was arraigned before the senate in 57, perhaps as a Christian, and who lived on until his own day.

Tacitus *Ann.* 13.32.3–5

¶ Pomponia Graecina, a lady of noble family, wife of Aulus Plautius,[1] whose ovation[2] after the British campaign I have recorded, was accused of practising a foreign religion[3] and handed over to her husband's jurisdiction. In accordance with ancient tradition he held an enquiry in the presence of a family council in a case involving the status and reputation of his wife and pronounced her innocent. This Pomponia had a long life, spent in unbroken gloom. For after Julia,[4] daughter of Drusus, met her death through Messalina's[5] intrigues [AD 43] she spent forty years always wearing mourning, always melancholy. In the reign of Claudius this passed unpunished[6] and later it redounded to her glory.

1. *Aulus Plautius*: he was commander-in-chief of the force which invaded Britain in AD 43.

2. *ovation*: this was a minor kind of triumphal procession, the latter having become the monopoly of the imperial family.

3. *foreign religion*: practice of a foreign religion was not in itself an offence, but if it entailed disgusting or subversive actions it could be brought to the notice of the senate (cp. Bacchanalia p. 226). Pomponia might have adopted Judaism or the worship of Isis, both attractive to women, but there is a strong possibility that she was a Christian, as her gloomy habits were such as pagans associated with the Christians' withdrawal from society. In catacombs of the second century tombs have been found of Pomponius Bassus and Pomponius Graecinus.

4. *Julia*: she was the grand-daughter of Tiberius (Emperor AD 14 to 37). The charge on which she was convicted is unknown.

5. *Messalina*: this was the notoriously wanton wife of Claudius (Emperor 41–54).

6. *unpunished*: Pomponia must have shown considerable courage in inviting punishment by this implicit criticism of governmental action.

Tacitus is also our chief authority for the persecution of Christians after the Great Fire of Rome. In 64 a fire broke out, cause unknown. Fires were common enough in Rome, but this one, fanned by a strong wind, raged for six days and brought immense destruction of life and property. Of the fourteen wards of the city only four remained intact; three were razed to the ground and in the remaining seven the surviving buildings were half-burnt and damaged. Nero immediately took relief measures. He also set about rebuilding the city on modern lines to replace the warren of narrow streets. For himself he took a most desirable and central site to build a magnificent palace (his 'golden house') with a great surrounding park. At the same time the prescribed rituals of expiation were carried out to appease any divine anger which might have caused the fire.

The people however wanted a scapegoat. A story was rumoured that, while the city was burning, Nero had sung, accompanying himself on the lyre, a composition describing the destruction by fire of the city of Troy. There were ugly rumours that he had deliberately started the fire, so that his new architectural projects might have scope. Nero therefore took action as follows, according to Tacitus:

*Ann.* 15.44.2–8

¶ But not by human aid, not by distributions from the Emperor nor by appeasement of the gods could the slur be removed, but it was believed that the fire had been started by order. Therefore to abolish the rumour Nero substituted culprits and inflicted most extreme punishments on those, hateful by reason of their abominations, who were commonly called Christians. Christus, the originator of that name, had been executed by the procurator Pontius Pilate. The pernicious superstition, checked for the moment, was bursting out again not only throughout Judaea, the birthplace of the plague, but also throughout the city into which all that is horrible and shameful streams from every quarter and is constantly practised. Therefore first those who confessed[1] were arrested, then on their information a huge throng was convicted not so much on a charge of arson as because of their hatred of the human race. Mockery was added as they perished, so that they died either covered by the skins of wild beasts and torn to pieces by hounds or were nailed on crosses to be set on fire and when daylight failed were burnt to give illumination by night. Nero had offered his own gardens for the spectacle and produced a show like that of the games, mingling with the common people in the dress of a charioteer or driving his chariot. As a result compassion began to spring up, although it was for those who were guilty and deserved the most exemplary punishment, as if they were being destroyed not for the public good but to satisfy the cruelty of one man.

1. *confessed*: i.e. confessed to being Christians. Tacitus implies that the charge of arson was trumped up, but that the Christians' anti-social

habits had made them so unpopular that they could be thought capable of such an abominable act.

SUETONIUS, late first century AD (p. 84), corroborates Tacitus' account , but simply lists this in a catalogue of measures taken by Nero, in his *Life of Nero*:

*Life of Nero* 16

¶ The Christians, a kind of men given to a new and mischievous superstition, he tortured and put to death.

In Rome Christians had been charged with the specific crime of arson. The same charge could not be brought against Christians elsewhere, although the proceedings at Rome could no doubt have led to further prejudice against them. We have no evidence of any general directive from central government. There was a Christian tradition of persecution under Domitian and it is likely that he, with his jealous maintenance of his divine status, viewed any negation of this as high treason (cp. p. 209). Certainly by the time that the Younger Pliny (see below) was governor of Bithynia, *c.* 110–12, Christians could be brought into court simply for their faith, as their obstinate refusal to comply with even the most elementary requirements of Emperor worship marked them out as disruptive and disloyal subjects. In Bithynia there had been recantations as much as twenty years earlier, but Pliny knew little or nothing about Christians and the procedure to be followed in dealing with them. Our scanty evidence during the second century is of sporadic and local persecutions instigated by pagan neighbours and depending on the temper of the provincial governor or city magistrates. The pattern is much the same as that recorded in the New Testament, except that now there could be proper legal charges, not just mob violence. The following accounts are given in chronological order.

PLINY (Gaius Caecilius, the Younger) *c.* AD 61–112, a wealthy provincial born at Comum, had a successful career as a man of letters, a pleader in the law courts, and in various governmental posts. He was a nephew of the learned Elder Pliny (see p. 56) and had many aristocratic friends, including the historian Tacitus (see p. 16). His voluminous correspondence includes letters to the Emperor Trajan when Pliny was governor of Bithynia, *c.* 110–*c.* 112.

*Letter* 10.96.1–10

¶ It is usual, Sire, for me to refer to you all matters on which I have doubts. For who can better either direct me when I hesitate or instruct me when I am ignorant? I have never taken part in any examinations[1] of Christians, so I do not known what is the object of the investigation or the degree of the punishment.

I have had grave doubts whether there should be any distinction of ages or whether the young, however tender their years, should be in no way differentiated from the stronger; whether pardon should be granted to recantation or whether one who had been a complete Christian should have no benefit from having given it up; whether the name[2] itself, if free from crime or abominations[3] attached to the name, should be punished. Meanwhile I followed this method in dealing with those against whom information[4] was laid.

I asked them whether they were Christians. If they confessed it, I asked a second and a third time and threatened punishment; if they persisted, I ordered their execution. For I had no doubt that, whatever it was to which they confessed, their pertinacity and inflexible obstinacy ought certainly to be punished. There were others equally mad, whom I listed to be sent to Rome, because they were Roman citizens.[5]

1. *examinations*: trial in a magistrate's court is implied, as opposed to a formal prosecution before a jury. Pliny implies that trials of Christians were not unknown.

2. *name*: this was equivalent to the profession of being a Christian.

3. *abominations*: this referred to the allegations of infanticide and the like, popularly associated with Christianity (pp. 166, 174). Certain religious cults were regarded as actively anti-social, hence the wholesale execution of participants in the Bacchanalia (p. 226) and the abolition of the Druids by the Emperors Tiberius and Claudius because of human sacrifices. Nero's persecution, when he wanted scapegoats for the Great Fire of Rome in AD 64, seems to have been based on suspicion of unspecified crimes alleged against Christians in general. Rome tolerated foreign cults, for it was recognized that foreigners should have a right to seek the protection of their own national gods, provided that they in their turn respected the gods of their host country. Christianity however was not a national cult, being now sharply differentiated from Judaism, and it denounced as false all gods but God revealed in Christ.

4. *information*: individuals could either bring a case themselves or give information to the authorities so as to set on foot a public prosecution.

5. *Roman citizens*: these had the right of appeal to the Emperor, so the governor's authority to execute was limited, cp. Paul's appeal, Acts 25:11.

¶ Presently, as proceedings were under way, the charge spread in a variety of forms. An anonymous pamphlet was published containing the names of many. If they denied that they were or had been Christians, when, saying after me, they called upon the gods and with offerings of wine and incense prayed to your statue, which for this reason I had ordered to be brought along with the images of the gods, if moreover they cursed Christ, none of which, it is said, can those who are truly Christians be forced to do, I thought that they should be let go.[1]

Others named by an informer presently denied it, saying that they had indeed been Christians, but had stopped, some three years before, some several years before, a few even twenty years before.[2] These also worshipped both your statue and the images of the gods and cursed Christ.

Moreover they asserted that this had been the sum total of their guilt or error, namely that on a fixed day it was their custom to meet before dawn,[3] to sing a hymn by turns [i.e. antiphonally] to Christ as God, and to bind themselves by oath, not to some crime, but not to commit theft or banditry or adultery, not to betray a trust, not to refuse return of a deposit if requested. After doing this they were in the habit of parting and coming together again for a meal, but food[4] common and harmless; they had stopped doing this after my edict, by which according to your instructions I had banned clubs.

I therefore thought it the more necessary to discover what truth there was in this by also putting to torture two slavegirls,[5] who were called ministrants.[6] I found nothing but a degrading and extravagant superstition.

1. In all the provinces there were official cults of the state gods and of the Emperor, but atheism was not in itself a crime. Later such a religious test was universally applied as a test of loyalty to the Emperor, under Decius in 250, but here Pliny is using it to differentiate the true Christian.

2. *twenty years*: this earlier apostasy is some evidence for the Christian tradition of persecutions under Domitian (cp. p. 144).

3. *before dawn*: the working day normally started at dawn.

4. *food*: it is not clear whether this refers to the Agape (the communal meal), or the Eucharist and whether it was the apostates who had stopped or the whole Christian community.

5. *slavegirls*: in both Greek and Roman courts it was usual for the evidence of slaves to be elicited by torture.

6. *ministrants*: to Pliny this would be the usual Latin term for a female assistant in worship, e.g. a Vestal Virgin. It corresponds to the Greek *deaconess*, cp. Phoebe, Rom. 16:1.

¶ I therefore postponed the examination and hastened to consult you. I thought the matter fit for consultation, chiefly because of the number of those endangered. For many of every age, of every rank, of both sexes too are being cited and will be cited to face the danger. The contagion of that superstition had spread not only through cities, but also through villages and the countryside; it seems that it can be checked and corrected.

Certainly it is pretty well agreed that temples by now almost deserted have begun to be thronged and sacred rites long neglected are being resumed and on every side the flesh of sacrificial victims is being sold, which up till now very rarely found a purchaser.[1] From this it is easy to imagine what a host of people can be reclaimed if there is opportunity for recantation.

1. The economic effects are similar to those experienced by the silversmiths at Ephesus, Acts 19:24–7. Christian abstention from meat offered to idols had been an issue at Corinth, 1 Cor. 8:7–10 and p. 145.

*Letter* 10.97
Reply from the Emperor Trajan (98–117):

¶ My dear Secundus, you have acted as you ought in investigating the cases of those who had been denounced to you as Christians. No general rule can be laid down in fixed terms. They must not be sought out. Should they be denounced and convicted, they must be punished, with the reservation that one who says he is not a Christian and demonstrates in actual fact, i.e. by worshipping our gods, although suspect in the past, may obtain pardon by recanting. Certainly accusations published anonymously should not be entertained on any charge. For they both set a very bad precedent and are alien to the spirit of our age.

The early Christian fathers claimed this as an edict of toleration, but it is clear that Trajan was authorizing the punishment of convicted Christians, with much discretion left to individual governors. The great benefit for the Christians was that they were no longer at the mercy of anonymous informers, so they could remain unmolested unless a specific accuser brought a charge.

### Early Christian Sources

IGNATIUS, bishop of Antioch in Syria, was martyred sometime before the death of Trajan in 117. The circumstances of his trial are not known, but he was sent with two others to Rome overland through Asia. En route some time was spent in Smyrna, where he was welcomed by its bishop, Polycarp, and delegations from neighbouring churches. Letters are extant which he wrote to these and also to the church at Rome before his arrival there. He expected to be thrown to the beasts in the arena and welcomed this prospect of winning a martyr's crown. Desiring this exemplary and spectacular penalty, he probably provoked the authorities by showing to an extreme degree that contumacious obstinacy which Pliny found so deplorable. Of his treatment on his journey he wrote in his *Letter to the Romans*:

*Letter to the Romans* 5.1

⁋ From Syria as far as Rome I have been fighting with wild beasts by land and sea, being chained to ten leopards, my military escort. When they are kindly treated they become worse.[1]

   1. *worse*: it has been plausibly suggested that the soldiers received bribes from Ignatius' friends and handled him more roughly in order to exact more money. This could be expected in their behaviour towards any condemned criminal and does not necessarily reflect a particularly anti-Christian attitude. Ignatius was allowed visitors without hindrance and, though they were patently Christians, they were not molested on this account (see also Peregrinus p. 188).

MARTYRDOM OF POLYCARP: Polycarp, *c.* 69–155, was
bishop of Smyrna and a much respected figure in the church of Asia.
An account of his martyrdom was sent from the church at Smyrna to
Philomelium, at the request of the church there, to be passed on also
to other neighbouring churches. The passages quoted below have been
chosen to illustrate the attitude of the authorities and populace, the
procedure and the punishments. Pious reflections added by the writer
have been omitted.

*Martyrdom of Polycarp* 1–19

❡ We are writing to you, brothers, about the martyrs and the blessed
Polycarp, who put the seal, so to speak, on the persecution[1] by his
martyrdom and brought it to an end....

Some were lacerated by lashes[2] so that the bodily structure as far
as the veins and arteries inside was made visible. They endured so that
even the bystanders pitied and lamented.... The fire of the inhuman
torturers was cold for them.... In the same way too those who were
condemned to the beasts[3] endured terrible punishments and were forced
to lie upon trumpet-shells[4] and suffer other kinds of variegated tortures,
so that the tyrant might, if possible, by continuous tormenting bring
them to recant.

1. *persecution*: the Greek word is the one used in the Beatitudes,
Matt. 5 : 10: 'How blest are those who have suffered persecution.'
2. *lashes*: the Roman scourge was made of leather, heavily weighted
with pieces of metal.
3. *beasts*: clearly this was no random lynching, but the Christians
had been condemned as criminals and were being thrown to the beasts
as part of the show at some public festival.
4. *trumpet-shells*: these shells end with a sharp point and look rather
like a small trumpet.

❡ For the devil used many devices against them, but (thanks to God!)
he did not prevail against all. The noble Germanicus strengthened their
weakness by his own endurance. After he had distinguished himself in
fighting against the beasts the proconsul[1] wanted to persuade him and
bade him take pity on his youthfulness. But he drew the beast upon
himself by force, desiring a speedier release from their wicked and
lawless life. As a result all the crowd, amazed at the nobility of the

pious and godfearing race of the Christians, cried out: 'Down with the atheists![2] Hunt out Polycarp.'

But one, called Quintus, a Phrygian just arrived from Phrygia, when he saw the beasts, was afraid. He was the one who had forced himself and some others to come forward voluntarily. Him the proconsul after many entreaties persuaded to take the oath and offer sacrifice. So for this reason, brothers, we do not commend those who come forward voluntarily, for that is not the teaching of the Gospel.

The admirable Polycarp when he first heard was not disturbed but wanted to remain in town. However the majority tried to persuade him to slip away and he slipped away to a little farmstead not far from the city. There he remained with a few companions, doing nothing bur praying for all men and the churches throughout the world, as was his custom. As he prayed, he had a vision two days before his arrest and saw his pillow aflame with fire. He turned to his companions and said: 'I must be burnt alive.'

1. *proconsul*: presumably he was there for the festival, as his seat of government was at Pergamum, but he assumes over-riding authority, the Christians having already been condemned to the beasts.

2. *atheists*: this was a charge often brought against Christians (cp. p. 166).

¶ As the search for him persisted, he removed to another farmstead. Immediately his pursuers were hard on his heels. As they did not find him, they arrested two slaveboys, one of whom confessed when put to the torture.[1] For he could not remain hidden, as those who betrayed him were of his own household. The chief of police, who had the same name as Herod,[2] made haste to bring him into the arena, so that Polycarp might fulfil his own destiny, sharing in Christ's passion, while those who had betrayed him might suffer the same punishment as Judas.

1. *torture*: it was usual for slaves to be tortured, cp. Pliny p. 151.

2. *Herod*: the reference is to the Herod to whom Jesus was sent for examination, Luke 23:7ff. All through, the writer is trying to trace parallels between the death of Polycarp and Christ's passion.

¶ So with the slaveboy, pursuers and cavalry with their usual weapons set out on the Friday about supper time,[1] speeding as if they were in pursuit of a bandit. They arrived late in the day and found him in bed in a small attic. From there too he could have removed to another spot, but refused, saying: 'God's will be done.' When he heard of their arrival he came down and spoke to them. Those who were there were amazed at his age and his calmness and at the haste made to arrest an old man like him. At once he ordered that they should be given as much as they wanted to eat and drink, even at that hour, but requested them to grant him one hour to pray unmolested. When they gave permission, he stood and prayed, being full of God's grace, so that for two hours he could not stop. His hearers were amazed and many repented of having come against such a godly old man.

1. *Friday*: the word actually used is 'Preparation-day' (that is, the day before the sabbath), as in Mark 15:42.

¶ When he had finally stopped praying after remembering all who had ever encountered him, both great and small, notable and obscure, and the whole catholic church throughout the world, the time came to go. They seated him on a donkey and led him to the city, where it was high sabbath. The chief of police, Herod, and his father Nicetas met him and transferred him into the carriage, sat beside him and tried to persuade him, saying: 'What harm is there in saying that Caesar is Lord and in sacrificing and all the rest of it and in saving yourself?' At first he made no answer, but when they persisted he said: 'I am not going to do as you advise.' When they failed to persuade him, they used awful language and pulled him down so hastily that in getting out of the carriage he grazed his shin. He took no notice and as if he had suffered nothing went on his way quickly and eagerly. While he was being brought into the arena, there was such an uproar in the arena that nobody could be heard.

As Polycarp was entering the arena there came a voice from heaven: 'Be strong Polycarp and play the man.' No one saw the speaker, but those of our folk who were present heard the voice. Afterwards when he was brought forward, there was a great uproar when they heard that Polycarp had been arrested. When he was brought forward, the proconsul asked whether he was Polycarp. He assented and the proconsul tried to persuade him to recant, saying: 'Have respect for your age', and more to the same effect, the usual formula: 'Swear by Caesar's Fortune,[1] recant, say: "Down with the atheists."' Polycarp with a grave face eyed all the crowd of impious pagans[2] in the arena, gestured to them, groaned and looking up into heaven said: 'Down with the atheists.' The proconsul pressed him hard and said: 'Swear and I will release you. Revile Christ.' Polycarp said: 'Eighty-six years have I served him and he has done me no wrong. How can I blaspheme the king who saved me?'

1. *Fortune*: the Greek word is used here in the sense of an individual's fortune, good or bad, equivalent to the Latin formula of swearing by the Emperor's 'genius'. A man's genius was a kind of attendant spirit, which accompanied him and his fortunes throughout his life. In the Roman domestic cult particular respect was shown to the genius of the father of the family; slaves venerated their master's genius. So it was an easy step for the Emperor's subjects at large to show their veneration and loyalty in this way, as he was the father of the state.

2. *pagans*: this is the Greek word used by the Jews for the Gentiles (literally: *nations*) and by the Christians for non-Christians.

¶ When he persisted again and said: 'Swear by Caesar's Fortune', he replied: 'If you imagine that I shall swear by Caesar's Fortune, if you pretend ignorance of what I am, hear me affirm boldly that I am a Christian. If you want instruction in the teaching of Christianity, appoint a day and give me a hearing.' The proconsul said: 'Persuade the people,' and Polycarp said: 'You I thought worth instruction, for we have been taught to render to rulers and authorities the honour[1] that is their due, if it is not to our hurt, but them I do not consider fit to hear our defence.'

The proconsul said: 'I have wild beasts and will throw you to them, if you do not recant', but he said: 'Call them. I cannot possibly change from the better to the worse, but it is a good thing to change from what is mischievous to what is right.' He said to him again: 'I will have you burnt to death, if you despise the beasts, unless you recant.' Polycarp said: 'You threaten me with the fire which burns for a while and after a little time is quenched, for you are ignorant of the fire of the judgement to come and the eternal punishment of fire in store for the impious. But why do you delay? Produce what you like.'

1. *honour*: cp. Romans 13 :7; 1 Pet. 2 : 13ff. (p. 143–4).

¶ He said much more, being filled with confidence and joy, and his face
was full of grace. Not only did he not collapse through fear of what
was said to him, but on the contrary the proconsul was amazed and
sent his own herald to proclaim three times in the middle of the arena:
'Polycarp has confessed that he is a Christian.' After the herald's
proclamation all the throng of the native and Jewish inhabitants of
Smyrna cried out loudly and in unrestrained anger: 'This is the teacher
of Asia, the father of the Christians, the destroyer of our gods, teaching
many not to offer sacrifice or worship.' With such cries they demanded
that Philip, the Asiarch,¹ should let loose a lion on Polycarp. He said
that he could not, as the animal-fighting was now over. Then they
decided to shout out all together that Polycarp should be burnt
alive....

   1. *Asiarch*: this was the title of the priest of the imperial cult. The
name Philip shows that he was a Greek, who probably held his
priesthood by virtue of being the chief magistrate of the province.

¶ This happened quicker than words can tell. Straightway the mob
collected wood and kindling from the workshops and baths and the
Jews, as usual, were specially keen to offer their services. When the pyre
was ready, he took off all his clothes and untied his girdle. He also tried
to undo his shoes, but was not used to doing so, because the faithful
had always competed to touch his person. For even before his
martyrdom he had been reverenced with every honour because of his
good way of life. Immediately then they began to rig him out with
the usual apparatus of the pyre, but when they were going to nail him
to it he said: 'Leave me as I am. He who has granted me to endure
the fire will also grant me to remain on the pyre unscathed without
the security of your nails.'

   They did not nail him, but tied him to it, binding his hands behind
his back....

   When he had finished his prayer the men in charge of the pyre
kindled it. A great flame shone forth and we, to whom the sight was
granted, saw a great wonder and were preserved to tell the rest what

happened. For the fire, taking the shape of an arch, like a sail filled by wind, encircled the martyr's body. Within, it was not like burning flesh, but bread being baked or like gold or silver being fired in the furnace. Moreover we had a whiff of fragrance[1] like the breath of incense or some other precious spice.

1. *fragrance*: it has been plausibly suggested that wood from the baths might be scented by the bath-essences used there and that such wood could be damp and therefore be slow to burn.

¶ Finally when the sinners saw that his body could not be consumed by the fire they ordered the *confector*[1] to come and insert his dagger. When he did this, so much blood gushed out round the point that it extinguished the fire and all the crowd marvelled that there should be such a difference between the unbelieving and the elect....

The evil one...made it his business to prevent our taking even his poor body, although many desired to do this and to have a share in his holy flesh. So Nicetas, father of Herod and brother of Alce, was suborned to entreat the magistrate not to give up the body, 'Lest', he said, 'they abandon the crucified one and begin to worship this one.' The Jews also, who kept watch too, when we were going to take the body from the fire, strongly urged this.[2]...

So when the centurion saw that the Jews were making an issue of it, he put the body on view and burnt it,[3] as is their custom. Later we took up his bones, more costly than precious stones and more valuable than gold and laid them in a fitting place. There, in so far as is possible,[4] we shall gather with joy and exultation and the LORD will grant us to celebrate the anniversary of his martyrdom, in memory of those who have already contended and to train and prepare future contestants.

Such is the story of the blessed Polycarp, who along with those from Philadelphia was one of the twelve martyred in Smyrna, but he alone is more specially and universally commemorated, so that even among the pagans there is talk of him everywhere.

1. *confector*: this is a Latin technical term (literally: *despatcher*) for the man detailed to give the death-stroke in the arena.

2. *Jews*: cp. Matt. 27:62ff. for similar Jewish importunity that Jesus' corpse should be guarded.

3. *burnt*: a similar concern was shown by the authorities at Lyons, but there the ashes were actually swept into the river (p. 171).

4. *possible*: the number martyred was relatively small, but the Christians were under no illusions about the likelihood of further persecution.

JUSTIN MARTYR, *c.* 100–65, was born in Samaria of pagan parents. He studied philosophy, became a Christian about 130, taught in Ephesus and later opened a school in Rome. He and some of his followers were martyred (p. 161). He wrote an *Apology* (i.e. Defence of Christianity) addressed to the Emperor Antoninus Pius and the Emperor's two adopted sons, Marcus Aurelius and Lucius Verus, about 155, and a second addressed to the Roman senate, about 161. He also published the *Dialogue with Trypho*, a disputation held with a Jew in Ephesus.

Justin took as the occasion for his *Second Apology* the recent execution of some Christians in Rome, as an illustration of the unreasonable attitude of the authorities. A woman convert, unable to divert her husband from his licentious way of life in which she herself had previously shared, obtained a divorce while he was away in Alexandria. On his return he was angry and denounced her as a Christian. She appealed to the Emperor for time to regulate her affairs before coming to trial and this was granted. Now read on:

*Apology 2.9–20*

¶ Her former husband, thwarted of charging her for the moment, turned upon a certain Ptolemaeus, who had given his wife Christian teaching and had received a sentence from Urbicus.[1] He persuaded a centurion, a friend of his, who had put Ptolemaeus in prison, to get hold of him and ask him this one question, whether he was a Christian. Ptolemaeus confessed, since he was honest and no cheat or liar at heart, that he was a Christian. The centurion imprisoned him and by way of punishment kept him in jail for a long time. Finally when the man was brought before Urbicus, in the same way he was asked this one question, whether he was a Christian. Again he confessed.... Urbicus ordered him to be led to execution. A certain Lucius,[2] who was himself also a Christian, seeing how unreasonable the sentence was, said to Urbicus: 'What is your reason for punishing this man, who is convicted neither as an adulterer nor a fornicator nor a murderer nor a thief nor a robber nor of committing any crime at all, but confesses to being called a Christian? Your judgement, Urbicus, is not worthy of the Emperor Pius[3] nor the philosopher, the Emperor's son, nor the sacred senate.' Without any other answer he said to Lucius: 'You too seem to me to be such a one.' When Lucius said: 'Certainly', he commanded his execution also. But Lucius even professed thanks, knowing that he had been set free from such wicked masters and was on his way to the father and king of heaven. A third man came forward and he too was sentenced to be punished.

    1. *Urbicus*: Q. Lollius Urbicus after a distinguished administrative career had become urban prefect, i.e. the high-ranking official responsible for maintaining law and order in Rome.

    2. *Lucius*: his intervention is like that of Vettius at Lyons (p. 165).

    3. *Pius*: this refers to Antoninus Pius (Emperor 138–61) and the Philosopher was his (adopted) son, Marcus Aurelius (Emperor 161–80).

    The account is rather confused. No charge is specified for Urbicus' previous conviction of Ptolemaeus, but presumably he was not then charged with being a Christian. Imprisonment was not in itself a punishment, but the accused might be kept in prison for a long time awaiting trial under unpleasant conditions. Most likely the centurion had arrested and imprisoned Ptolemaeus to face the previous charge. He could therefore identify him and arrest him to stand this second trial. This was no case of a systematic persecution, but arose from a purely private feud. The populace is never mentioned, there are no exaggerated accusations and no torture. The accused had that execution by beheading which was granted to Roman citizens (cp. at Lyons p. 170).

    The two preceding descriptions of martyrdom were literary. The next is the first of a long succession of *Acts of Christian Martyrs* which like the *Acts of the Pagan Martyrs* (p. 110) purported to be transcripts of the trials without extraneous details of background and subsequent events.

ACTS OF JUSTIN AND COMPANIONS (there are three recensions of which the one given below is the shortest):

*The Martyrdom of Saints Justin, Chariton, Charito, Euelpistus, Hierax,*
*Paeon, Liberianus and their company*

¶ At the time of the wicked decrees of idolatry the saints recorded
above were brought before Rusticus,[1] prefect of Rome.

When they were brought in the prefect said to Justin:[2] 'What life
do you live?'

Justin said: 'A life blameless and irreproachable in the eyes of all
men.'

The prefect Rusticus said: 'What kind of doctrines do you practise?'

Justin said: 'I have tried to gain knowledge of all doctrines, but gave
my assent to the true doctrines of the Christians, even if they are
unacceptable to those who hold false opinions.'

Rusticus said: 'Are those doctrines acceptable to you then?'

Justin said: 'Yes, because I follow and put my belief in them.'

Rusticus said: 'What sort of belief?'

Justin said: 'We have a pious belief in the God of the Christians,
whom we consider the sole and original creator of the whole world,
and in God's son Jesus Christ, who by the earlier proclamation of the
prophets was to come to proclaim salvation to mankind and to give
good teaching. I say little of his divinity, for I acknowledge the power
of prophecy, in that there had already been proclamation of him whom
I said just now to be the son of God. Know that in earlier times the
prophets foretold his coming among men.'

The prefect Rusticus said: 'Where do you meet?'

Justin said: 'To suit the individual's choice and convenience. In any
case do you think it possible for us all to meet in the same place?'

Rusticus said: 'Tell me, where do you meet and in what place?'

Justin said: 'I have lived over the bathhouse of Myrtinus all the time
of this my second stay in Rome. This is the only meeting place I know.
If any one wanted to visit me I used to impart to him the words of
truth.'

Rusticus said: 'Finally, are you then a Christian?'

Justin said: 'Yes, I am a Christian.'

1. *Rusticus*: Q. Iunius Rusticus, himself a Stoic, is known to have
influenced the young Marcus Aurelius (Emperor 161–80). He twice
held a consulship and was urban prefect between 163 and 168. It was

natural that he should be interested in the Christian way of life and beliefs.

2. *Justin*: (see p. 160) the circumstances of his prosecution are unknown, but he had been involved in bitter debate with a Cynic called Crescens (*Apol.* 2.3), and Tatian, one of Justin's disciples (p. 182) mentioned Crescens as trying to bring about his death (*Address to the Greeks* 19.1).

¶ The prefect Rusticus said to Chariton: 'Chariton, are you a Christian too?'

Chariton said: 'I am a Christian by God's command.'

The prefect Rusticus said to Charito:[1] 'What do you say, Charito?'

Charito said: 'I am a Christian by God's gift.'

The prefect Rusticus said to Euelpistus:[2] 'What are you, Euelpistus?'

Euelpistus said: 'I too am a Christian and share in the same hope.'

The prefect Rusticus said to Hierax: 'Are you a Christian?'

Hierax said: 'Yes, I am a Christian and worship the same God.'

The prefect Rusticus said: 'Did Justin make you Christians?'

Hierax said: 'I have been a Christian for a long time.'

Paeon took the stand and said: 'I too am a Christian.'

Rusticus said: 'Who taught you?'

Paeon said: 'We have received it from our parents.'[3]

Euelpistus said: 'I used to enjoy listening to Justin's teaching, but it was from my parents that I have received my Christianity.'

Rusticus said: 'Where are your parents?'

Euelpistus said: 'In Cappadocia.'

The prefect Rusticus said to Hierax: 'Where are your parents?'

Hierax said: 'They are dead. It is a long time since I was dragged away from Phrygia.'

The prefect Rusticus said to Liberianus: 'Surely you are not a Christian too?'

Liberianus said: 'I too am a devout Christian.'

1. *Charito*: this is a female name and she is the only woman in the group.

2. *Euelpistus*: a pun is involved, because the name means *Hopeful*. The other recensions add the detail that he was an imperial slave.

3. *parents*: the change to the first person plural may show that this was a group of second generation Christians, not dependent on Justin for their conversion.

¶ The prefect said to Justin: 'If you are scourged and beheaded, do you believe that you are going to ascend into heaven?'

Justin said: 'I hope so, if I endure with patience. I know that the divine gift waits for those who have lived righteously up to the conflagration.'[1]

The prefect Rusticus said: 'You imagine then that you will ascend?'

Justin said: 'I do not imagine, but am thoroughly convinced.'

The prefect Rusticus said: 'If you [plural] do not obey, you will be punished.'

Justin said: 'We have faith that if we are punished we shall be saved.'

The prefect Rusticus published his decision: 'Those who have refused to sacrifice to the gods are to be scourged and led to execution in accordance with the laws.'

The holy martyrs went out to the usual spot[2] glorifying God and fulfilled their testimony by witnessing to their belief in our saviour, to whom is glory and power with the Father and the Holy Spirit for evermore. Amen.

    1. *conflagration*: to Justin this meant the fire of the Last Judgement, to Rusticus since he was a Stoic it would mean the conflagration which periodically destroyed the present world and was the start of a new cycle.

    2. *usual spot*: it is clear that at Rome by now there was a more or less routine procedure against Christians, ending with capital punishment.

It is worth noting that, although the trial in Rome would be conducted in Latin, this rescript is in Greek and the names of the accused, with the exception of Liberianus, are not Latin. It is well known that the common language of the early church was Greek, that *Koine* (p. 14) which had spread over the Mediterranean world.

LETTER OF THE GALLICAN CHURCHES: Eusebius, *c.* 260–340, bishop of Caesarea, in the preface to Book 5 of his *Church History* records that in 177 under Marcus Aurelius (Emperor 161–80) there was a great persecution of Christians in various parts of the world. To illustrate this he gives verbatim the following letter sent from the Gallican churches to the churches in Asia. It is a long letter, so parts of the narrative have been condensed and enclosed in square brackets, while ellipses mark the omission of the many pious reflections:

Eusebius *Church History* 5.1.3–63

¶ The servants of Christ who dwell in Vienne[1] and Lyons[2] in Gaul to the brothers in Asia and Phrygia....

    1. *Vienne* (Vienna), an ancient Gallic town, was a neighbour of Lyons, and, like it, a Christian centre. The letter was written in Greek, although Latin would be the language of administration and of the ordinary citizen.

    2. *Lyons* (Lugdunum): this had been founded as a Roman colony in 43 BC and had become the capital of the Augustan province of Lugdunensis. It was thoroughly Romanized and in 12 BC had become the centre of the imperial cult for the Gallic provinces; here every year delegates came from the whole of Gaul to take part in a great festival and to renew their oath of allegiance to the reigning Emperor. As a rich trading city, it was also cosmopolitan and had commercial links with Asia Minor at the other end of the Mediterranean. The churches too had ties of friendship, for Irenaeus (*c.* 130–*c.* 200), saint and scholar, had come from Asia to Gaul and later succeeded Pothinus (see below p. 168) as bishop of Lyons. He was absent in Rome at the time of the persecution.

¶ [The devil had already been training his followers] against the servants of God so that not only were we debarred from houses and baths and market,[1] but had been banned from appearing at all in any place whatever....

    [Under persecution steadfast Christians] in the first place nobly endured all that was heaped on them by the whole throng of the populace, hostile shouts and blows and violence and looting and stone-throwing and imprisonment and all the usual behaviour of a savage mob towards those thought to be enemies personal and public. They were brought into the forum and examined by the commandant and the civic authorities before the whole mob. When they confessed, they were confined in prison until the governor's arrival.

    1. *market*: this Greek word means both *market* or *market square* and the open square which was the centre of public life, the Roman *forum*.

¶ Then they were brought before the governor. When he treated them with all the cruelty usual towards us, Vettius Epagathus,[1] one of the brothers... very zealous for God and fervent in spirit, could not endure this unreasonable condemnation of us, but was indignant on behalf of the brothers and claimed a hearing in our defence, saying that among us there was no atheism or impiety. Those round the judgement seat shouted him down, for he was indeed a distinguished man, and the governor would not suffer his just claim, but only enquired whether he too was himself a Christian. He confessed it in a loud clear voice and he too was taken up to receive the martyrs' lot.

[Arrests continued daily and ten recanted. This blunted the first enthusiastic fervour to confess their faith, for fear of further recantations. Eventually however all the strongest supporters of both churches had been gathered in.]

Some pagan slaves of ours were also arrested, since the governor had ordered a public search for us all. Entrapped by Satan and fearing the tortures which they saw the saints suffering, egged on by the soldiers they told false stories against us of Thyestean[2] feasts and Oedipean[3] intercourse and things which for us are unspeakable and unthinkable; it is even incredible that any such thing ever did happen among mankind.

1. *Vettius*: cp. the similar behaviour of Lucius before the urban prefect, Urbicus, at Rome (p. 161).

2. *Thyestean*: Thyestes unknowingly ate the flesh of his own children which was served up to him by his brother Atreus at a pretended feast of reconciliation.

3. *Oedipean*: Oedipus, unaware of his parentage, killed his father and married his mother. Both these stories were favourite subjects of Greek tragedy and the names had become bywords. These charges of devouring babies and of incest were commonly brought against Christians (cp. Minucius Felix quoting from Fronto p. 174) and the Christian apologists were at pains to rebut them.

¶ Because of these slanders all were enraged against us and any who because of friendship had previously been moderate were greatly angered...Then the holy martyrs endured tortures beyond all description, since Satan was striving to obtain through them too some slanderous utterance. In particular all the anger of the crowd and the governor and the soldiers fell upon Sanctus, the deacon from Vienne, and Maturus, newly converted but a doughty champion, and Attalus

a Pergamene[1] by birth, who had always been a pillar and support of
the church there and Blandina [a slavegirl whose frail physique had led
the rest to fear that she would be unable to hold out] ...Blandina was
filled with such strength that those who by relays were applying every
kind of torture from dawn to dusk fainted and gave up. They
themselves confessed that they had been beaten, for they had nothing
left to do to her and were amazed that she remained alive, since her
whole body had been broken and torn open and they testified that one
kind of racking was enough to kill, let alone tortures so varied and so
numerous. But the blessed girl like a true athlete was rejuvenated by
her confession and found recovery and refreshment and insensibility
to her pains in saying: 'I am a Christian and among us nothing wrong
takes place.'

1. *Pergamene*: Pergamum (map 1) was a rich and prosperous city
of Asia Minor (cp. Rev. 2:12–17). Attalus' presence in Gaul and
affiliation with the local church shows the strong links between them.

¶ Sanctus, too, nobly put up an exceptional and superhuman endurance
of suffering inflicted by men, when the impious hoped that because
of the great and persistent tortures they would hear from him of some
wrongdoing. He withstood them so resolutely that he would not even
tell his own name, nor race nor city of origin, nor whether he was
slave or free, but to all the questions replied in Latin: 'I am a Christian.'
As a result the governor and the torturers tried their hardest against
him and when there was nothing left for them still to do to him, finally
they fixed red-hot plates of bronze to the most tender parts of his
anatomy. These were burning, but he endured inflexible and unyielding,
firm in his confession. ...His body bore witness to his treatment, for
it was wounded and bruised all over and shrivelled and had lost the
semblance of human shape. ...Some days later the torturers again
racked the martyr, thinking that when he could not bear even to be
touched, if they applied the same tortures as when bodies are swollen
and inflamed, they would overcome him or by dying under torture
he would inspire fear among the rest. Not only was there no such result
but against all human expectation in the tortures that followed he
revived and straightened himself and recovered his own form and the

use of his limbs so that by the grace of Christ the second racking was not a punishment but healing. [A girl called Belies who had recanted, when tortured again to obtain criminal accusations, withdrew her recantation and was martyred.]

When the tyrannical punishments were frustrated by Christ through the endurance of the martyrs, the devil thought up other devices, confinement in darkness and the most cruel dungeon[1] and the stretching of the feet in the stocks, where they were extended as far as the fifth notch,[2] and the rest of the sufferings which angry jailers, and this full of the devil, usually inflict on prisoners, so that the majority perished in prison. ...The blessed Pothinus,[3] who had been entrusted with the ministry of bishop in Lyons, over ninety years old and very infirm, breathing with difficulty because of his physical weakness, but strengthened with spiritual zeal because of his urgent desire to bear his witness, was also dragged to the judgement seat. ...The governor asked him who the Christians' God was and he said: 'If you are worthy, you shall know.' At this he was jostled unmercifully and suffered a variety of blows, for those nearby battered him in every way with fists and feet and had no reverence even for his age, while those at a distance hurled at him whatever came to hand. All thought that they were greatly at fault and impious if any failed in brutality against him, and that in this way they would vindicate their own gods. Scarcely breathing he was thrown into prison and died two days later.

1. *dungeon*: nominally they were remanded to prison to await the execution of sentence, but imprisonment under such conditions could be as good as a death sentence.

2. *notch*: the further the legs were stretched apart in the stocks, the greater would be the pain.

3. *Pothinus*: there are some similarities between him and Polycarp, the aged bishop of Smyrna (p. 154).

¶ Those who at the time of the first arrest recanted were also kept in prison and shared in the dangers and in this crisis their denial brought them no advantage. Those who confessed what they were, were imprisoned as Christians and no other charge was brought against them, but the others were then confined as murderers and abominable wretches and punished twice as much as the rest, [because the martyrs went to their death joyfully, but the renegades looked mean and downcast, execrated as murderers]. Maturus and Sanctus and Blandina and Attalus were publicly brought to the beasts as a spectacle for the savage and impious populace, for the day for the beast-fights[1] was granted on purpose for our folk. Maturus and Sanctus again went through every torture in the amphitheatre as if they had previously suffered nothing at all. . . . They again endured the lashings that are usual there and the violence of the beasts and all that the frenzied mob shouted for and urged from every side, above all the iron chair on which their bodies were broiled and exhaled a sacrificial odour. Not even so did they cease, but were all the more maddened, wanting to overcome their endurance. Yet even so they heard nothing from Sanctus but the words with which he had habitually confessed from the beginning. So these, though their souls long endured through a great conflict, were finally sacrificed in the course of that day and instead of all the variety of single combats[2] were in themselves a spectacle to the world. Blandina was hung upon a cross and exposed as prey to the onslaught of beasts. . . . At that time none of the beasts touched her, so she was taken down from the cross and returned to the prison, kept for other games. . . . Attalus too was greatly in demand by the crowd, for he was a man of note . . . He was led round the amphitheatre and a placard preceded him on which was written in Latin: 'This is Attalus the Christian.' Though the people were inflamed with anger against him, the governor on learning that he was a Roman[3] ordered him to be taken back along with the rest of those in prison about whom he had sent a despatch to Caesar[4] and was awaiting his decision. . . .

1. *beast-fights*: normally murderers and the like were condemned to the beasts to provide entertainment. Here a day has been set aside specially for the Christians.

2. *single combats*: this refers to gladiators, who like matadors were highly trained professionals and exhibited their skill for the pleasure of the spectators.

3. *Roman*: like Paul, Attalus probably held Roman citizenship, for Attalus is a Pergamene name.

4. *Caesar*: this is often used to denote the reigning Emperor, in this case Marcus Aurelius, who reigned from 161 to 180.

¶ [In the interval many who had recanted recovered their faith.] Caesar
sent word that they were to be beheaded, but any who recanted were
to be released. The great festival[1] here (this is well attended, as it is
a gathering of the pagan tribes) was just starting and the governor
brought the blessed martyrs to the judgement seat, making a public
show and procession for the crowds. So he examined them and
beheaded all those who were deemed to hold Roman citizenship and
sent the rest to the beasts. ...During the examination a certain
Alexander, a Phrygian by birth and a doctor by profession,[2] who had
lived for many years in the Gallic provinces and was known to almost
everyone because of his love of God and outspoken preaching of the
word (for he was not without a tincture of apostolic charisma), stood
by the judgement seat and by nodding encouraged them to confess.
It was clear to those who stood around the judgement seat that he was
in deep distress. The crowds were vexed that those who had previously
recanted were confessing again and cried out against Alexander for
doing this. The governor stood over him and asked him who he was
and, when he said that he was a Christian, he was angry and condemned
him to the beasts. Next day he went in along with Attalus too, for
the governor to gratify the mob gave up the latter to the beasts again.
[Both died bravely after suffering all manner of tortures, including the
iron chair.] After all these on the last remaining day of the single
combats Blandina was brought in again with Ponticus, a boy of about
fifteen. They had been brought in every day to see the punishment of
the rest and in an attempt to make them swear by idols. Because they
remained firm and made nothing of it, the people were enraged against
them, so that they neither pitied the boy's years nor respected the
woman. They subjected them to every suffering and put them through
the whole round of torture, trying one after another to make them
swear, but without success. For Ponticus was urged on by his sister,[3]
so that even the pagans saw that it was she who was encouraging and
supporting him. After nobly enduring every torture he expired. ... The
blessed Blandina after the lashing, after the beasts, after the broiling
was put in a net and thrown to a bull and after being tossed several
times she too was sacrificed. Even the pagans themselves agreed that

never among them had a woman undergone sufferings so varied and so numerous.

    1. *festival*: this was the festival instituted as part of the imperial cult and to foster the loyalty of the Gallic tribes.

    2. *doctor*: he was probably itinerant, wandering all through Gaul.

    3. *sister*: in the Christian sense, not the physical.

¶ But not even so were their frenzy and their savagery against the saints satisfied. Wild and barbarous[1] tribes, their feelings stirred up by a wild beast,[2] could not be easily checked and their violence began in another way of their own against the bodies. ...They used to throw to the dogs those who had died in prison and they kept careful watch by night and day lest any should receive proper burial from us. Then they also displayed what was left from the beasts and the fire, some mangled, some burnt to a cinder, and the heads of the rest with their severed bodies and in the same way kept them unburied under military guard for several days. Some were enraged and gnashed their teeth at them, seeking to exact some further punishment from them; others mocked and taunted, at the same time extolling their own idols and attributing to them the vengeance that had befallen these. The more moderate, who were thought to sympathize to some extent, were full of reproaches, saying 'Where is their God and how did the religion avail them which they chose even in preference to their own life?' Such were their different attitudes. On our part there was great grief because we could not bury the bodies. Night did not help us in this nor could money bribe nor entreaties win over, for they kept watch in every way, as if it would be a great gain if they did not obtain burial. ...The bodies of the martyrs were put on show in every way and exposed to the open air for six days. Then they were burnt and reduced to ashes[3] by the impious and swept down into the river Rhône which flows past close by, so that not even a relic of them might still appear above ground. They did this as if they had the power to overcome God and deprive them of resurrection, in order that, as they said, 'they may not have even a hope of resurrection, trusting in which they introduce to us a new and foreign religion and despise sufferings, coming to death readily and with joy. Now let us see whether they will rise again and whether their God can help them and deliver them out of our hands.'

    1. *barbarous*: to civilized Greeks the Gauls ranked as barbarians.

    2. *wild beast*: it is not clear whether this refers to the blood lust excited by the games or is a synonym for the Devil.

    3. *ashes*: cp. the similar action taken at Smyrna (p. 159).

This account cannot be taken as typical, although the cruelty of the tortures had parallels in later martyrdoms. Both Lyons and Vienne had mixed populations and the former in particular, as a Roman colony and provincial seat of the imperial cult, was concerned to display its loyalty. No Jews are mentioned as fomenting ill-will, but a segregated Greek-speaking community, probably including many immigrants from Asia Minor, could be seen as undesirable aliens and these were subjected to earlier harassment. A first wave of persecution followed and in the trials the governor showed himself hostile to the Christians. There was then a second spate of arrests, which included all the most prominent members. False accusations of practising monstrous abominations enraged the crowd and led to an intensification of tortures in the hope of eliciting more such slanders. Sanctus' refusal to answer any questions and the obstinate courage of others angered them still more. Many died from cruel treatment in prison, others in the arena. The governor sent to Rome to ask the Emperor how Roman citizens should be treated. The reply was that they were to be executed by the sword, but those who recanted were to be released. The great imperial festival had now arrived, so crowds of Gauls had swarmed into the city. The governor gratified the frenzy of the mob by torturing Attalus again, although he had Roman citizenship. The culmination was the death of Blandina after suffering the most horrible tortures that could be devised. The pagans put the martyrs' remains on public show, burnt them so that the Christians might not obtain relics and swept them into the Rhône. In so doing some felt their bloodlust was still unsatisfied, others that they were vindicating their own gods and showing their gods' powers of vengeance, while the more moderate felt that the Christians' God had shown himself impotent to save them.

The kind of obscene slanders which stimulated persecutions are illustrated by MINUCIUS FELIX, first half of the third century. Little is known of him, but he was clearly well educated in literature and rhetoric and he says himself that he was converted to Christianity late in life. He wrote in Latin a dialogue called *Octavius*, a conversation between himself, a dearly loved Christian friend Octavius (now dead) and a pagan called Caecilius, in defence of Christianity. There are good grounds (9.6) for believing that Caecilius reproduces the arguments of the teacher and intimate friend of Marcus Aurelius, Fronto (p. 121), so the following passage is given below as representative of scurrilous popular beliefs about Christians already current in the second century at the time of the persecution in Gaul in 177.

*Octavius* 8.3–5
The pagan Caecilius is speaking:

¶ Is it not deplorable that men of an illegal sect, a sect beyond hope or cure, should attack the gods? From the lowest dregs[1] they collect the ignoramuses, and also credulous women, gullible because of their sex, and form the common herd of an impious conspiracy,[2] whose members are linked together by nocturnal meetings and solemn fasts and inhuman foods, not by any sacred rite but by crime. They are a tribe that seeks secrecy and shuns the light, mute in public, talkative in corners. They despise temples as tombs, abominate the gods, ridicule sacred rites and though pitiable themselves express pity, if one may say so, for the priests. They despise honours and purple robes,[3] though themselves half-naked. O amazing foolishness and unbelievable audacity! They spurn present torments while they fear torments that are uncertain and in the future[4] and, while they are afraid of dying after death, meanwhile have no fear of dying. Their treacherous hope so soothes their fears by the consolation of a life to come.

    1. *dregs*: this criticism of the composition of the Christian community was common, found in Celsus (p. 182) and rebutted by Christian apologists.
    2. *conspiracy*: ever since the suppression of the Bacchanalia (p. 228) in 186 BC the authorities had been suspicious and afraid of possible conspiracies arising from the meetings of religious sects.
    3. *purple robes*: these were worn by kings and magistrates.
    4. *future*: this refers to fear of the Last Judgement and death in the torments of Hell.

*Octavius* 9.1–6
¶ Now, as evil is quicker to breed, their vicious habits are daily spreading abroad throughout the world and those most foul sanctuaries where

they hold their impious meetings are on the increase. This abominable conspiracy must be utterly destroyed. They recognize one another by secret marks and signs and love one another almost before making acquaintance. Moreover this is combined with a kind of religious sexuality and they call themselves promiscuously *brothers* and *sisters*, so that not uncommonly by warranty of the sacred name there is incestuous lewdness. Thus their vain and demented superstition glories in its crimes. If there were not a basis of truth shrewd Rumour would not spread most abominable and insulting reports about them. I am told that under some foolish persuasion they worship the consecrated head of a filthy animal.[1] Worthy is the religion born of such practices! Others say that they revere the genitals of high priest and priest and in a manner of speaking adore the natural make-up of their own father: perhaps false, but suspicion certainly attends secret rites performed at night. The story that their ritual centres on a man who suffered capital punishment for crime, the fatal wood of the cross, assigns fitting altars to the abandoned criminals, so that they worship what they deserve.

1. *filthy animal*: the current slander that the Jews worshipped an ass's head (cp. pp. 78, 106, 107) had been extended to the Christians, cp. the well known graffito found on the Palatine at Rome which shows a worshipper of a crucified man with an ass's head and a rude scrawl 'Alexamenos worships his god.'

¶ Next there is the story of their initiation of novices, as horrible as it is well known. A baby covered with pastry, so as to deceive the unwary, is set before the initiate in their rites. The novice is encouraged by the pastry crust to give it seemingly harmless jabs and the baby is killed by the unseen and hidden wounds. Thirstily – O for shame! – they lick up his blood, compete in sharing out his limbs, league themselves together by this victim, pledge themselves to mutual silence by this complicity in crime. These rites are fouler than any sacrilege. The details of their feasting are well known also. They are common talk everywhere and a speech of our countryman from Cirta[1] attests them. On a fixed day they assemble for a feast, both sexes and of every age, along with all the children, sisters and mothers. There after much feasting, when the company has warmed up and the drunken heat of incestuous lust has been set ablaze, a dog chained to a candlestick is teased, by having a gobbet of meat thrown towards it, into rushing and leaping beyond the length of its confining chain. When the light, which would have borne witness, has thus been overturned and extinguished, in the shameless darkness they entwine in unnatural lust according to the vagaries of chance. Not all commit the act, but all are equally privy to the lewdness, since whatever can happen in commission by individuals is the object of universal desire.

1. *Cirta*: this was an African city (map 3). Caecilius may have been an actual person, for inscriptions bear witness to the name and there was a local magistrate called Caecilius in 210. Fronto was also a native of Cirta and had composed a speech *Against the Christians*, now lost. Later (see below 31.1–2) he was mentioned by name.

*Octavius* 10.1–4

¶ There is much that I pass over on purpose. Even the above is more than enough and the secrecy of the impious religion proclaims by itself that all or most of this is true. Why do they make great efforts to hide and conceal whatever it is that they worship, when honourable deeds always rejoice in being made public, while crimes are kept secret? Why do they have no altars, no temples, no well-known images, never talk openly, never gather freely, unless what they worship in concealment is either criminal or shameful? Whence or who or where is the one God, solitary, abandoned, whom no free people, no kingdoms, not even Roman superstition[1] recognize? Only the wretched people of the Jews also worship one God, but they worshipped in public with temples, altars, victims, and their God is so weak and powerless that he has been made captive to the Romans along with his own nation.

1. *Roman superstition*: by now along with traditional Roman religion the State had adopted and given official support to such foreign cults as those of Cybele (p. 229) and Isis (p. 241).

*Octavius* 31.1–2
The Christian Octavius replies:

¶ The tall story about incestuous feasting was a lie against us[1] arising from a demonic conspiracy, in order to besmirch our reputation for chastity[2] by casting infamous aspersions, so that before enquiring into the truth men might be turned away from us, terrorized by a monstrous fancy. Thus your own Fronto did not bring evidence in confirmation, but like a speech-maker spattered invective.

1. *us*: Octavius the Christian has now taken up the argument against Caecilius, the previous speaker, who was a fellow-countryman of Fronto.

2. *chastity*: this was recognized as a Christian characteristic by Galen, AD 129–99 (p. 186).

At the time of the persecutions under Marcus Aurelius it is relevant to mention his own opinion of the Christians.

MARCUS AURELIUS (Emperor 161–80) was a Stoic philosopher and the author of a famous book of *Meditations* (literally: 'To himself'), written in Greek. As a good Stoic (p. 201), he commended suicide if undertaken for the right motives, but not if it was the result of contumacy or exhibitionism as with the Christians.

*Meditations* 11.3

¶ How admirable is the soul which is ready, if by now it must be freed from the body, to be extinguished or dispersed or to continue. This readiness must proceed from one's own decision, not from mere opposition as with the Christians, but with due consideration and dignity, so as to have a convincing effect on others without theatricality.

ACTS OF THE SCILLITAN MARTYRS: At Scillium in North Africa in AD 180 seven men and five women were martyred. The brief Latin transcript of the trial survives and is the first documentary evidence for Christianity in North Africa.

¶ When Praesens and Claudian were consuls, the former for the second time, on 17 July at Carthage Speratus, Natzalus, Cittinus, Donata, Secunda and Vestia were brought to trial.

Saturninus the proconsul said: 'You can earn the pardon of our Lord the Emperor,[1] if you return to a sound mind.'

Speratus said: 'We have never done wrong, we have committed no crime. We have never uttered curses, but when ill-treated we have given thanks. For this reason we revere our Emperor.'

Saturninus the proconsul said: 'We too are religious and our religion is simple and we swear by the genius of our Lord the Emperor and pray for his well-being, which you also ought to do.'

Speratus said: 'If you will give me a quiet hearing I will tell you the mystery of simplicity.'[2]

Saturninus said: 'I will not give you a hearing if you initiate evil teaching about our rites; rather, do you swear by the genius of our Lord the Emperor.'

Speratus said: 'I do not recognize the kingdom of this world, but rather I serve that God whom no man has seen nor can see with these eyes. I have not committed theft, but if I buy anything I pay the sales-tax, because I recognize my Lord, King of Kings and Emperor of all peoples.'

Saturninus the proconsul said to the rest: 'Give up being of this persuasion.'

Speratus said: 'It is an evil persuasion[3] to commit murder, to bear false witness.'

Saturninus the proconsul said: 'Do not share in this madness.'

Cittinus said: 'We have none to fear except the LORD our God, who is in heaven.'

Donata said: 'Honour to Caesar as Caesar, but fear to God.'[4]

Vestia said: 'I am a Christian.'

Secunda said: 'What I am I wish to be.'

Saturninus the proconsul said to Speratus: 'Do you persist in being a Christian?'

Speratus said: 'I am a Christian.'

All agreed with him.

Saturninus the proconsul said: 'Do you want any time to consider?'

Speratus said: 'In so just a case there is no consideration.'

Saturninus the proconsul said: 'What are the things in your satchel?'

Speratus said: 'Books and the letters of Paul,[5] an upright man.'

Saturninus the proconsul said: 'Have a delay of thirty days and think things over.'

Speratus said again: 'I am a Christian.'

All agreed with him.

Saturninus the proconsul read out his verdict from the tablet: 'It is our decision that Speratus, Natzalus, Cittinus, Donata, Vestia, Secunda and the others who have confessed that they live according to Christian religious usage be executed by the sword.'

Speratus said: 'We give thanks to God.'

Natzalus said: 'Today we are martyrs in heaven. Thanks be to God.'

Saturninus the proconsul ordered proclamation by the herald: 'I have ordered Speratus, Natzalus, Cittinus, Veturius, Felix, Aquilinus, Lactantius, Januaria, Generosa, Vestia, Donata and Secunda to be led to execution.'

One and all said: 'Thanks be to God.'

So they all at the same time were crowned with martyrdom and reign with the Father, Son and Holy Spirit throughout all ages. Amen.

1. *Emperor*: under Marcus Aurelius (see p. 176) there had been the great persecution in Lyons in Gaul in 177 (p. 164).

2. *simplicity*: i.e. the secret of what is truly a simple religion.

3. *evil persuasion*: the implication is that false witness had been borne against them and their death will be murder.

4. Cp. Mark 12:17, 'Pay Caesar what is due to Caesar, and pay God what is due to God.'

5. *Paul*: this is valuable evidence for knowledge of the Pauline epistles here at this time and recognition of Paul's importance.

Apart from the obviously Christian postscript this reads like a genuine transcript of a regular judicial procedure. There is no hint of mob pressure, the charge is solely that of being a Christian; proof of loyalty to the Emperor shown by taking the oath (in itself for the Christian involving recantation) will bring immediate pardon. Torture is not threatened nor even flogging before execution. The proconsul clearly regards the accused as demented rather than criminal and does his best to persuade them to reconsider.

CELSUS, late second century AD (p. 60), had composed an elaborate indictment of the Christians, extensively quoted by Origen in his refutation, *Against Celsus* (*c. Celsum*), from which all the following passages are taken.

Origen *c. Celsum* 1.9
The irrationality of Christianity:

¶ After this Celsus urges men to follow reason and to accept doctrines under a reasonable guide, for without this stipulation there are some which certainly cannot be accepted without error. He compares irrational believers to begging priests of Cybele[1] and soothsayers, devotees of Mithras[2] and Sabazius,[3] whatever one might come across, apparitions of Hecate or any other daemon or daemons.[4] For just as among them rogues often take advantage of the ignorance of the gullible and lead them as they please, so also, he says, this happens among Christians. He says too that some who are unwilling even to give or receive a reason for their beliefs use the sayings:[5] 'Do not question, but believe' and 'Thy faith will save thee' and he quotes them as saying 'Wisdom in the world is a bad thing and foolishness a good thing.'

1. *Cybele*: she was the Anatolian fertility goddess, the Great Mother (p. 229), whose fanatical worship was now widespread.
2. *Mithras*: it is hard to see why Celsus should have coupled the devotees of this originally Persian god (p. 249) with those of *Sabazius*, for Mithraism had its own doctrines, as Celsus himself (cp. p. 256), was aware.
3. *Sabazius*: this Phrygian god (p. 86) with his enthusiastic and noisy rabble could not be expected to appeal to a philosopher.
4. *Hecate*: this grim goddess of magic and incantations, worshipped by night at crossroads, was not a *demon*, but a *daemon*. The two words have the same root, but the Christian demon is always evil, while *daemon* covers a wide range, from a minor divinity either beneficent or malignant to a hero such as Oedipus, who after death received cult-worship and was credited with some vague supernatural power.
5. *sayings*: the first two are reminiscent of such Gospel texts as Mark 5:36; 9:23 and parallels, Luke 17:19; 18:42, but these are all set in a context of miraculous healing; for the third, cp. 1 Cor. 1:18ff.

*c. Celsum* 1.28
Alleged Jewish taunts against Jesus, such as were actually made by the Jews and are to be found in the Talmud:

¶ After this Celsus stages an imaginary dialogue between a Jew and Jesus himself, convicting him on many charges, as he thinks, first for having made up the story of the virgin birth. He also taunts him with having come from a Jewish village and from a poor countrywoman who made her living by spinning. He says that she had been driven out by her husband, a carpenter[1] by trade, because she was found guilty of adultery. Next he states that after being expelled by her husband she became a shameful vagabond and gave birth to Jesus in secret. And he says that the latter because of poverty hired himself out in Egypt and there became acquainted with certain magical powers on which the Egyptians pride themselves. He returned pluming himself on these powers and because of them proclaimed himself God.

    1. *carpenter*: cp. Matt. 13:55, 'Is he not the carpenter's son?'

*c. Celsum 2.55*
Comparison of Jesus with others said to have risen from the dead:

¶ After this the Jew says to his fellow-countrymen who believe in Jesus: 'Come now, let us accept[1] that he did say this to you. How many others tell such marvellous tales in order to persuade their simple hearers and take advantage from deceiving them! This was the case, they say, with Zamolxis,[2] Pythagoras' slave, among the Scythians and Pythagoras[3] himself in Italy and Rhampsinitus[4] in Egypt who even dined with Demeter in Hades and obtained from her and carried off as a gift a golden napkin. There were also Orpheus[5] among the Odrysae and Protesilaus[6] in Thessaly and Heracles at Taenarum[7] and Theseus.[8] But what we must consider is whether anyone who had really died ever rose again body and all.'

    1. *accept*: i.e. that Jesus foretold his death and resurrection.
    2. *Zamolxis*: there was a story (Herodotus 4.95) that he deceived the Scythians by hiding in an underground chamber for three years from which he emerged as if from the dead.
    3. *Pythagoras*: this sixth century BC philosopher and mathematician claimed to be a reincarnation of the Trojan Euphorbus.
    4. *Rhampsinitus*: Herodotus, 2.121, says that he won by playing dice with the goddess Demeter.
    5. *Orpheus*: this Thracian (Odrysian) musician went down to Hades to recover his wife, Eurydice. By his playing of the lyre he persuaded

Pluto, king of the underworld, to allow his wife to return, on condition that he should not look back. She followed him, but he did look back and so lost her and returned alone to the upperworld.

6. *Protesilaus*: he was a Thessalian leader, the first Greek to be killed at Troy, immediately on disembarkation. At his wife's entreaties he was allowed to return from Hades to visit her for three hours, presumably as a ghost.

7. *Taenarum*: on this headland in southern Greece Heracles was said to have emerged from a cavern dragging with him from Hades the watchdog Cerberus.

8. *Theseus*: this Athenian hero with his friend Peirithous went down to Hades to abduct Pluto's wife, Persephone, but was caught. He was rescued by Heracles when the latter came to carry off Cerberus. With the exception of Protesilaus these legendary figures were supposed to have gone down to Hades alive and of their own free will.

¶ Do you consider that the stories of the others really are legends as they are thought to be, but that you have discovered a denouement of the drama which is noble or plausible, the cry on the cross when he was expiring and the earthquake and the darkness? As for your story that, when alive, he did not defend himself, but when dead rose again and displayed the marks of his punishment and how his hands had been pierced, who saw this? A hysterical woman,[1] as you say, and any other under the same spell or in such a state that he had a dream and in his disordered fancy was subject to hallucination inspired by his own wishful thinking, which has happened to countless others before now; or, more likely, he wanted to astound the rest by this marvellous tale and through such a fiction provide material for other charlatans.

1. *hysterical woman*: this is presumably a reference to Mary Magdalene, John 20: 11ff.

*c. Celsum* 3.12
Criticism of the existence of sects among the Christians:

¶ Then, as if bringing a charge against the Gospel, Celsus reproaches us with the existence of sects[1] in Christianity, saying: 'Since they have spread to become a multitude they split and separate and want each to have his own faction.' He says that: 'Because of their numbers they are divided again and criticize one another. There is one thing they still have in common, so to speak, if indeed they do, and that is the name. This alone however they are ashamed to abandon. Otherwise they are ranged in different parties.'

1. *sects*: such an acute and intellectual pagan observer as Celsus could not but be aware of the proliferation of heresies in the second century.

*c. Celsum* 3.55
Charges of illiteracy and proselytizing the gullible and the young:

¶ Celsus says: 'We see too in private houses wool-workers and cobblers and launderers and the most illiterate[1] and loutish clod-hoppers who dare not say a word in front of masters who are older and wiser. But when they get hold of their children privately and along with them some weak and foolish women they make some amazing assertions, saying that they ought to put their belief in them and pay no attention to their father and tutors. These latter, they say, talk stupid nonsense and neither know what is really good nor are able to accomplish it, being preoccupied with idle chatter, but they alone know the proper way to live and the children, if they believe them, will be blessed and make their home happy. While they are speaking, if they see one of the tutors coming or somebody with more wit or even the father himself, the more cautious of them scatter in fear, but the more reckless egg on the children to revolt. They whisper to them that in the presence of the father and tutors they themselves will be reluctant and unwilling to explain anything good to the children, as they are put off by the former's ignorance and crass stupidity; these are utterly corrupt, far gone in vice and punish them. The children, if they wish, ought to leave both father and tutors and go with the womenfolk and their little playmates into the wooldresser's or the cobbler's or the launderer's in order to learn perfection. It is by such sayings that they persuade.'

1. *illiterate*: charges of this kind were familiar to Tatian, the Assyrian second century Christian apologist (*Address to the Greeks* 32).

*c. Celsum* 5.14
Criticism of doctrine of Last Judgement and resurrection of the dead:

¶ Celsus says: 'It is also foolish of them to think that when God, like a cook, applies fire, all the rest of mankind will be baked through and through, but they alone will survive, not only the living but also those long dead, rising up from the earth in the very same flesh. This is simply the hope of worms. What sort of human soul would still long for a putrefied body? The fact that this doctrine is not held by some of you[1] and by some of the Christians shows how extremely repugnant it is, both abominable and impossible. What kind of body, when completely rotted, could return to its original nature and the very same constitution that it had before being dissolved? As they have nothing to say in reply, they take refuge in a most absurd retreat,[2] that "To God everything is possible." However, God cannot do anything shameful nor does he will anything unnatural. If you in your depravity have some loathsome desire, God will be unable to execute it and you must not believe that it will straightway come to pass. God is the author not of sinful desire or disorderly licence but of a natural order that is right and just. To the soul[3] it would be in his power to grant eternal life, but "Corpses", says Heraclitus,[4] "are to be thrown out, more so than dung." Flesh then, full of things which it is not decent even to mention, God will be neither willing nor able to make immortal contrary to all reason. For he is himself the reason[5] of all that exists. Therefore he is unable to do anything contrary to reason or contrary to himself.'

1. *some of you*: i.e. the Jews. The Sadducees did not accept the idea of a bodily resurrection nor, in Celsus' time, did the Gnostic sects. Paul had difficulty in convincing the Corinthians, see 1 Cor. 15:12ff.
2. *retreat*: cp. Mark 10:27; Matt. 19:26; Luke 18:27, in the context of the possibility of the salvation of the rich.
3. *soul*: Celsus concedes the doctrine of the immortality of the soul, so important for Plato, as a possibility.
4. *Heraclitus*: he was a Greek philosopher from Ephesus. Only fragments of his work, written about 500 BC, survive, but he had a great reputation in antiquity.
5. *reason*: this is good Stoic doctrine (p. 201).

*c. Celsum* 7.9
Celsus' travesty of Christian prophetic preaching:

¶ Since Celsus also promises to describe the method of divination in Phoenicia and Palestine as if he had firsthand experience and knowledge, let us examine this too. In the first place, he says that there are many kinds of prophecies, but does not detail them, for he could not, for he was making false professions. Let us look at the one which he says is the most fully developed among the men of this region. 'There are many nameless men', he says, 'who with the greatest ease and for any slight reason both in temples and outside temples, some too going about begging[1] in cities or camps, become excited forsooth as if uttering an oracle. The formula that usually springs to their lips is: "I am God or Son of God or Holy Spirit. I have come, for the world is perishing and you, O men, are destroyed because of your sins. But I wish to save you and you shall see me again returning with heavenly power. Happy is he who has embraced my cult now, but on all other men and cities and countries I will hurl eternal fire. Men who do not know the punishment that is theirs will repent and groan in vain, but those who have believed me I will keep safe for ever." They then follow up these threats with sayings that are so unintelligible, frenzied and completely obscure that no rational man could discover their drift; but because they are dark and meaningless any fool or charlatan on any occasion has the opportunity to appropriate them in any sense he pleases.'

1. *begging*: the begging priests of Atargatis, the Great Syrian Goddess (p. 260), were a familiar sight in the Middle East; they were of the dancing dervish type (p. 261).

### c. Celsum 8.24
The illogicality of refusing to eat meat offered to idols:

¶ Let us see what arguments Celsus uses in urging us to eat meats offered to idols and public sacrifices offered at public festivals. They are as follows: 'If these idols are nothing, what risk is there in sharing in the high festival? If they are some sort of daemons,[1] it is clear that these too belong to God and that we ought to believe in them and offer sacrifices according to law and prayers in order to win their goodwill.'

1. *daemons*: Greek daemons were not necessarily malignant, but could use their powers for good or ill, so it was always wise to placate them.

*c. Celsum* 8.67–9

The necessity for maintaining Emperor worship:

¶ 'Even if someone orders you to swear by the Emperor, this too is not dreadful. Earthly things have been given to him and whatever you receive in life you receive from him.' ...

Next Celsus says: 'One ought not to disbelieve an ancient author who said long ago: "Let there be one king[1] to whom the son of crafty Kronos[2] has granted power."' He adds: 'If you deny this doctrine, naturally the Emperor will punish you. If all were to act like you, nothing will prevent him from being left deserted and abandoned, while earthly things fall into the hands of the most savage and lawless barbarians[3] and nothing more is heard among men either of your cult or of true wisdom.'[4]

1. *one king*: educated men would recognize this as a well-known tag from Homer, with all the authority of Homeric sanction behind it. The line comes from *Iliad* 2.205, where Odysseus is trying to reunite the Greek host to follow Agamemnon.

2. *Kronos*: he was the father of Zeus, greatest of the gods.

3. *barbarians*: Marcus Aurelius (Emperor 161–80) already had to repel barbarian tribes on the Danube. Later, as the threats of barbarian invasion became more imminent, this accusation against the Christians was more of a danger to them.

4. *true wisdom*: Celsus' own treatise was entitled *True Teaching*.

¶ Surely you will not say this, that if the Romans under persuasion from you neglect their usual observances in regard to both gods and men and invoke your Most High, or whatever you like to call him, he will come down and fight for them and no other aid will be needed. Previously the same God promised, as you yourselves say, this and much more to his devotees and you see how much help he gave both to them and to you. The former,[1] far from being masters of the whole world, are left with not so much as a clod or a hearthstone. As for you, if any one of you does still wander about undetected, yet he is sought out to be sentenced to death.

1. *the former*: Celsus refers to the Jews and the destruction of Jerusalem.

GALEN, AD 129–99, the famous Greek physician, also criticized Christianity for basing its teaching on divine revelation, coupling it with Judaism (see above pp. 61–3 for relevant passages). However he did recognize Christian bravery in the face of death, and their moral standards. (From R. Walzer's translation (see p. 61); he puts in square brackets variants among the Arabic translations. The Greek is not extant.)

Reference 6 (p. 15)

§ Most people are unable to follow any demonstrative argument consecutively; hence they need parables,[1] and benefit from them – and he [Galen] understands by parables tales of rewards and punishments in a future life – just as now we see the people called Christians drawing their faith from parables [and miracles], and yet sometimes acting in the same way [as those who philosophize]. For their contempt of death [and of its sequel] is patent to us every day, and likewise their restraint in cohabitation. For they include not only men but also women who refrain from cohabiting all through their lives; and they also number individuals who in self-discipline and self-control in matters of food and drink, and in their keen pursuit of justice, have attained a pitch not inferior to that of genuine philosophers.

1. *parables*: this passage came from Galen's lost summary of Plato's *Republic*, of which some quotations survive in Arabic, so it probably refers to such a parable as the Myth of Er (*Republic* 10.164ff.), which is concerned with the after-life. The parenthesis is a comment by the Arabic translator.

EPICTETUS, *c.* AD 50–120, the Stoic philosopher (p. 79) was probably referring to Christian contempt for death in the following. In a chapter on *Freedom from Fear* he had been saying at some length that if a man from madness or despair does not care whether he lives or dies he will not fear a tyrant's guards and that this contempt for death also comes:

Epictetus 4.7.6

§ From habit, as with the Galileans.[1]

1. *Galileans*: this is generally taken as referring to Christians, for there was a Christian church at Nicopolis in Epirus, cp. Titus 3:12, where Epictetus spent his last years. It is a purely incidental reference to what is taken as a well-known fact. Galilean courage is distinguished from the courage of an individual's madness or despair, but by implication it is inferior to that of the Stoic which, as he goes on to demonstrate, is based on rational arguments (cp. Marcus Aurelius p. 176).

LUCIAN, *c.* AD 120 to after 180, born at Samosata, was a Syrian, but had a Greek education, and wrote in Greek. He was a much-travelled, professional rhetorician, celebrated for his witty, flippant short works on a variety of subjects, especially his *Dialogues*. Today he might have been a columnist or one of those television personalities whose stock in trade is to debunk. He gives much valuable information about the Christians of his day, whom he viewed with amused contempt for their naïvety, which left them a prey to any rogue. Most of this comes from *On the Death of Peregrinus*. Peregrinus was a contemporary Cynic philosopher, *c.* AD 100–65, who had made himself conspicuous at the Olympic games by publicly throwing himself on a funeral pyre. Lucian first sketches his early life, how after some unsavoury episodes Peregrinus was suspected of having strangled his father and therefore had fled from his native Greek island of Paros, then wandered from place to place.

*On the Death of Peregrinus 333–8; 341*

❡ At this time he also became thoroughly versed in the astonishing lore of the Christians through consorting with their priests and scribes in the neighbourhood of Palestine. What then? He soon showed them up as children by comparison, for he alone in his own person was prophet, leader of the company, convenor of the congregation, the lot. Some of their books he used to expound and explain and many he even composed himself. They thought of him as a god and treated him as a lawgiver and registered him as their patron. That great man[1] who was crucified in Palestine they still revere, because he introduced this new cult into the world.

1. *great man*: this is probably to be taken as a typical example of Lucian's irony.

¶ Next Proteus[1] was arrested for this and thrown into prison, which in itself brought him no small reputation as regards the future course of his life and the legendary tales and fame which he passionately desired. When he was imprisoned, the Christians took this as disastrous and left no stone unturned in their attempts to get him out. When this was impossible, every other care was taken for him, not in a cursory way but zealously. From dawn old hags, widows and orphan children could be seen waiting by the prison and those in authority among them used even to bribe the jailers and sleep inside with him.[2] A variety of foods used to be brought in and their sacred discourses were recited. The noble Peregrinus – for he was still called this – they dubbed a new Socrates.[3]

    1. *Proteus*: Peregrinus gave himself the name of Proteus, that minor sea-god who could change his shape at will and, if seized, answer any questions.
    2. *old hags* ... : Celsus (cp. p. 182) had also noticed the numbers of women and children among the Christians.
    3. *Socrates*: he was the imprisoned wise man par excellence, put to death by the Athenians in 399 BC.

¶ Moreover envoys came from Christian communities in some of the cities of Asia[1] to aid and advise and comfort him. In any such common emergency they act with amazing speed. In a word, they spare no expense. At that time a lot of money came to Peregrinus from them because of his imprisonment and this brought him in a large income. For the poor wretches have persuaded themselves as a general principle that they will be immortal and will live for all time to come, so that they both despise death and give themselves up of their own free will. Next the first lawgiver persuaded them that they were all brothers one of another, when once they have transgressed by renouncing the Greek gods and worship that crucified sage of theirs and live according to his laws. They despise everything and think everything common property, accepting such teaching without any accurate proof. So if any charlatan and trickster and business-man comes among them, straightway he becomes very rich and sneers at their naïvety.

    1. *Asia*: cp. the way in which the churches of Asia had ministered to Ignatius early in the second century on his way to Rome for martyrdom (p. 153).

¶ But Peregrinus was released by the then governor of Syria, a devotee of philosophy,[1] who understood his madness and that he would accept death, in order to leave behind a glorious name on this account, and released him, thinking that he was not even worth punishing.

1. *philosophy*: the tolerant governor exercised his discretion, regarding Peregrinus as a philosopher, even if a misguided one.

Peregrinus then returned to Paros, but found that accusations were still hot against him.

¶ He left and set out on his wanderings a second time. The Christians furnished him with abundant supplies and as long as he was under their protection he wanted for nothing. For some time he was maintained in this way, then because he committed some offence against them too – for he was seen, I fancy, eating some of their forbidden foods – they no longer accepted him.

1. *forbidden foods*: this may refer to meat offered to idols.

Lucian's two other references to Christians show how firmly established they were in Asia. They come from *Alexander or the False Prophet*. In this Lucian had set out to expose a contemporary charlatan called Alexander (pp. 216ff.) from Abonutichos in Paphlagonia (map 2), who had established an oracle of Asclepius with himself as the god's mouthpiece and had won a great reputation.

*Alexander or the False Prophet* 232.25; 244.38–245

¶ But when many men of sense as if recovering from a deep bout of drunkenness began to band together against him, and especially the followers of Epicurus, who were numerous, and the trickery and contrived stage-effects were by now being gradually detected, to scare them away he issued a proclamation against them. He said that Pontus was full of atheists[1] and Christians, who had the effrontery to utter the vilest slanders about him and he ordered men, if they wanted to retain the god's favour, to stone them and drive them out.

1. *atheists*: this refers to the Epicureans (p. 200), who did not deny the existence of gods, but thought that serene in their own calm abode they took no interest in men. The Christians are distinguished from them, but it is taken for granted that they would be opposed to Alexander and his pagan oracle.

¶ He instituted an initiatory festival[1] with offices of torchbearers and initiating priests, covering three consecutive days. On the first day there was a proclamation like that at Athens: 'If any atheist or Christian or Epicurean has come to spy on our rites, away with him, but let believers in the god be initiated and good fortune attend them.' Then, to begin with, there used to be an immediate expulsion. He would lead off, saying: 'Christians out!' and the whole congregation would respond: 'Epicureans out!'

    1. *festival*: the whole festival with its dramatic representations of incidents connected with the god was modelled on the famous Eleusinian Mysteries (p. 224); the proclamation there simply excluded murderers and those who could not speak Greek.

To sum up, by AD 200 Christianity was a well-known cult with an ever increasing number of adherents, regardless of class, age and sex. They made no secret of the fact that their founder was one of that despised race the Jews and had been crucified like any common criminal; in fact they actually gloried in this. They claimed that he was the Son of God and rose from the dead, a resurrection in which his followers would one day share, at a conflagration of the world, when the dead would rise from their tombs to face God's judgement, assigning to them either Hell-fire or eternal blessedness. This God was the only God and worship, without temples and without sacrificial victims, was due to him alone. This much seems to have been common knowledge. They held meetings behind closed doors and this led to monstrous allegations of infanticide and sexual abominations. They must have been disloyal citizens because they would not accept the conventional tokens of respect towards the great and beneficent Emperor as a divine being. These were the kind of views that led to prejudice against Christians, even to mob violence and bloodlust when they bravely faced or even courted death on occasions of official persecution.

    To others the fact that Christ walked the earth as a carpenter, a man subject to the sufferings and temptations of ordinary humanity, identified him with themselves. They would receive a ready welcome from Christians and behind those closed doors could find teaching to give them joy and hope in believing. Even the sight of courage under unspeakable tortures could move some to investigate a faith which inspired such bravery. In the memorable phrase of TERTULLIAN, c. 160–220 (African church father and author of many influential works):

Tertullian *Apology* 50

¶ The blood of the martyrs is the seed of the church.

What of the moderates, the betwixt and betweens, neither positively anti-Christian nor professed Christians, the great inarticulate majority? By now there were second- and third-generation Christians, neighbours, acquaintances, known from childhood; decent, honest folk, even if they did keep themselves to themselves. Could there really be any harm in such poor simpletons? One may surmise that they would have agreed with Pepys, the seventeenth century diarist, when he wrote in reference to the Nonconformists of his own day: 'While we were talking, came by several poor creatures, carried by by constables for being at a conventicle. They go like lambs, without any resistance. I would to God they would either conform or be more wise and not be ketched.'

# PART III

## The Pagan Background

# The Pagan Background

It is a commonplace that we are conditioned, to a greater or lesser extent, by our heredity or environment. What we are taught in childhood colours our beliefs later, whether we espouse them all the more firmly or react against them violently or sink into an apparently agnostic apathy. So it is worthwhile to examine the pagan background of the Graeco-Roman world, although no all-embracing generalizations are possible. The word *pagan* itself simply means 'countryman', i.e. the type of man least likely to come into contact with either Jew or Christian, a conservative believer in the gods of his own country and countryside.

## Greek and Roman Cults

Greek religion was well developed long before there was any contact with Rome. Every boy was brought up to know Homer. From him and from the Greek cults he knew that there were twelve great gods, all with their own separate functions. When the Romans came to know Greek literature and culture they identified the Greek Pantheon with their own gods, using identity of function as a rough and ready guide. In the following list Latin names are put in brackets and only the most important functions are given.

There were twelve Olympians, great gods:

*Zeus* (Jupiter), father of gods and men, was all-powerful and from his abode in Olympus (earlier the Greek mountain, later located in the heavens), wielded the flashing thunderbolt. He was a notable philanderer and there were many tales of his amours with nymphs and mortals.

*Hera* (Juno), the jealous wife and sister of Zeus, was the goddess of marriage.

*Poseidon* (Neptune), brother of Zeus, was the lord of the sea.

*Athena* (Minerva), a virgin goddess, sprang fully armed from the head of Zeus. She was the goddess primarily of wisdom, also of war, the patroness of craftsmen.

*Apollo* (Phoebus), son of Zeus and Leto, was the god of music and poetry, the sun god, the god of prophecy, as at Delphi and elsewhere.

*Artemis* (Diana), the twin sister of Apollo, was a huntress, also a moon goddess and helper of women in childbirth. At Ephesus she was equated with a local fertility goddess.

*Aphrodite* (Venus), daughter of Zeus and Dione, was the beautiful and seductive goddess of love.

*Ares* (Mars), son of Zeus and Hera, was the god of war.

*Hephaestus* (Vulcan), the lame son of Zeus and Hera, was a skilled smith, the patron of all ironworkers.

*Hermes* (Mercury), son of Zeus and Maia, was the messenger of the gods, guide of the dead to the underworld, a crafty god, patron of business-men and orators.

*Demeter* (Ceres), sister of Zeus, was the goddess of agriculture and fertility. She was the mother of Persephone (Proserpina), who was carried off by Pluto to become queen of Hades.

*Hestia* (Vesta), sister of Zeus, goddess of the hearth, was important symbolically, but had little personality.

To the great twelve may be added:

*Pluto* (Dis), brother of Zeus and Poseidon, was the mighty lord of Hades, the underworld, by his very nature not a dweller in heavenly Olympus.

*Dionysus/Bacchus* (Liber), son of Zeus and the mortal Semele, was the god of wine. Attended by his frenzied female worshippers (Maenads or Bacchantes) he had made his victorious way into Greece from the East and established his own peculiarly orgiastic rites.

Two other gods, originally just heroes, were fully venerated in our period:

*Heracles* (Hercules), son of Zeus and the mortal Alcmene (Alcumena), because of his twelve labours on behalf of mankind, after death received the entrée into Olympus.

*Asclepius* (Aesculapius), son of Apollo and the mortal Coronis, was a skilled physician. Because he brought a dead man back to life he was killed by a thunderbolt from Zeus, but later deified as the god of healing.

These major Greek gods were completely anthropomorphic and their statues were of beautiful and idealized types, some well known throughout the Graeco-Roman world, such as the majestic Zeus of Praxiteles, *c.* 490–432 BC, at Olympia and his famous statue of Athena in the Parthenon, her temple at Athens. Men could picture the gods as superhuman in beauty and stature, but in mythology they were subject to all human frailties: lust, jealousy, greed for power, petty vendettas. Within this rich and varied mythology were a whole host of minor gods, often sketchily characterized and worshipped in special localities. The only ones that need be mentioned here are the powers of nature, venerated by all primitive peoples, whom the Greeks personified by giving individual names to rivers and various nymphs, of streams (Naiads), of mountains (Oreads), of trees (Dryads), of the sea (Nereids). The educated Greek had grown up with these stories, which he knew from Homer, from the rich storehouse of Greek poetry and from the role of the gods in Greek drama.

The Greek countryman had his rustic festivals, but his life was bound up with his city and its civic religious celebrations. The number of temples would vary according to the wealth and size of the city, but each of the larger cities usually had its own special cult of its patron god or goddess, who was supposed to protect it and regard it with particular favour, e.g. Athena at Athens and Artemis at Ephesus. One feature all had in common: although some families might be associated with certain cults, there was no theocratic priesthood. The State organized public ceremonies such as the Panathenaea, the great procession in honour of Athena which is depicted on the Elgin marbles. (These were originally part of the Parthenon frieze and are now in the British Museum.) Often a magistracy might include the temporary holding of a priesthood. The State offered public sacrifices and festivals, so making sure that the city was offering to the gods their due tribute in gratitude for past favours and in the hope of their continued protection. For much the same motives individuals would offer sacrifices, bringing the victim to the god's altar so that the due portion might be dedicated; then they could celebrate by eating what was left over, 'meat offered to idols'. The last words of SOCRATES were to his friend Crito:

Quoted by Plato, *Phaedo* 118

¶ 'Crito, we owe a cock to Asclepius; be sure you don't forget to pay it.'

In this case the cock was a recognized offering for a cure accomplished and is due because Socrates' death will have brought him a release from the malady of life.

The Romans too had their major functional gods, but for them in theory a whole host of minor godlings presided over every act of daily life, e.g. Limentinus who guarded the threshold (*limen*), Cardea who presided over the door-hinge (*cardo*), Cunina who watched over children in the cradle (*cunae*). Priestly colleges, with the Roman love of systematization, busied themselves in drawing up codified lists of such little gods, their proper names and functions, long after the Romans had become an urban folk and little concerned with agricultural activities. With true Roman conservatism however many rituals originally connected with agriculture continued to be practised even in urban surroundings, e.g. the State sacrifice of a red dog to Robigo (blight). The poet OVID, 43 BC–AD 17/18 (p. 64) found them rich material for his story-telling genius in twelve books (six extant) of *Fasti*, a religious calendar for all the festivals and holy days of the year.

In the early days of Rome the household gods were part of the family. As Ovid said:

Ovid *Fasti* 6.305–6

¶ Once upon a time it was usual to sit on long benches in front of the fire and to believe that the gods were present at table.

A prayer was offered to Vesta as goddess of the hearth, mainstay of the family, before the chief meal of the day, and a little cake was thrown into the fire. Vesta herself, not anthropomorphized into an image, also presided over the State hearth and had her temple in Rome, where the Vestal Virgins tended the sacred flame, symbolic of the well-being of Rome, which must never be allowed to go out.

Other family gods were the Lares, deified spirits of dead ancestors or, according to another theory, gods of the farmland. These were honoured with small offerings and sometimes just called collectively the Lar. With them are often coupled the Penates, by derivation 'gods of the pantry (*penus*)', who were also publicly revered as guardians of the Roman State. Hence the expression 'lares et penates' has crept into English to signify one's cherished household possessions.

In public worship Jupiter, with his temple on the Capitol, was the greatest of the gods and the special protector of Rome. He was often linked with Juno and Minerva, a triad worshipped by the Etruscans, who had an early influence on the religion of their Roman neighbours. Mars, god of war, father of Romulus the traditional builder of Rome, was an old fertility god and more important for the Romans than his counterpart Ares was for the Greeks.

Roman priesthoods were essentially secular, steps in a political career. Apart from individual priesthoods and minor priestly colleges, there were the colleges of the pontiffs (presided over by the pontifex maximus) and augurs. The latter classified and interpreted auguries so that public business might be conducted only if the omens were propitious. The former were concerned with maintaining a right relationship between gods and men by ensuring that the correct procedure should be followed in ritual. The formula had to be exactly right; the god had to be addressed by his proper titles and the ritual carried out precisely to the letter, for deviation or error even by a single word involved repetition of the whole. This appealed to the best legal minds. CICERO, 106–43 BC (p. 117), was very gratified at becoming a member of the college of augurs, not only because of its political prestige but because of the nature of the subject; he wrote a treatise *On Divination.*

Before going on to consider the religious beliefs of Cicero and his contemporaries, who were responsible for upholding these State cults, we should take into account the influence of Greece. When the Romans came into contact with Greek literature and thought in the third century BC they embraced it with avidity, taking the Greeks as models. As HORACE, 65–8 BC (p. 65) remarked:

Horace *Epistles* 2.1.156–7

¶ Captive Greece took her barbarous conqueror captive and brought the arts into rough Latium.

Greek slaves captured in the wars leading to the complete subjugation of Greece in 146 BC became tutors in Roman households. Roman boys became bilingual and were well versed in Greek literature. By Cicero's time young Romans went abroad to study under recognized masters in such centres as Athens and Rhodes. The budding politician wanted to study rhetoric but, in order to rank as an educated man and make effective use of rhetoric, he would also require some knowledge, if only a smattering, of philosophy. This latter was more than is implied by the modern term philosophy, which academically can be a completely intellectual and sometimes sterile discipline, divorced from the everyday world. To the ancients, philosophy was more of an ideology, for adherence to a particular school could involve commitment morally, perhaps spiritually, to a whole way of life.

Conventional religion with its unedifying mythology was not likely to supply the needs of thinking men, and the Greeks with their enquiring minds had long been engaged in the study of philosophy. After a period in which they were mainly concerned with the physical nature of the universe their thoughts turned more to the moral, metaphysical and theological. The following main schools emerged, connected with their founder's name but never remaining completely static, here of necessity only briefly characterized.

*Platonism* (from Plato *c.* 429–347 BC, disciple of Socrates, 469–399, both Athenians), posited the existence of *Ideas*, perfect, changeless, invisible, the originals of things as we know them, the highest being the *Idea* of the Good, the ultimate cause. Plato's name is forever linked with the Socratic dialogue, conversations in which Socrates sought to elicit the truth by means of question and answer. The Platonic school was called the Academy, taking its name from its meeting place. For Plato the soul was immortal.

*Peripateticism* (school of Aristotle, 384–322 from Stagira in Macedon), took its name from a covered walk in Athens. Aristotle himself, tutor of Alexander the Great, was a great polymath and treated many branches of learning. He had a scientific mind and, as a philosopher, diverged from his master Plato in positing a life-process of nature in which everything works towards the completion of the ends required by the *Forms* imprinted in matter. God keeps this process in activity but is completely self-contained and has no care for the world. In ethics Aristotle, whose *Nicomachean Ethics* makes very interesting reading, taught the doctrine of the *Mean*, true virtue lying between the extremes of excess and deficiency in any quality.

*Scepticism* (from a Greek root meaning 'examine') was founded by Pyrrhon, *c.* 365/60 to *c.* 275/70 BC, from Elis in the Peloponnese. Its main tenet was that all arguments should be carefully weighed, with the recognition that it was impossible to arrive at absolute knowledge of the truth. This school later became known as the New Academy, so called because its adherents emphasized the Socratic element of examination and dialectic associated with Plato's Academy.

*Cynicism* (literally 'dog-like') got its name from Diogenes, *c.* 400– *c.* 325 BC from Sinope in Pontus. He was the philosopher who lived in a tub in Athens and was nicknamed 'dog' because he snarled at accepted conventions. They were not an organized school, but had certain basic principles of living a life of simplicity and independence. In the first two centuries of the Christian era, they began to proliferate as itinerant beggars with stick and knapsack, teaching and preaching.

*Epicureanism* was founded by Epicurus, born in Samos 341 BC, died in Athens 270 BC. From the fifth century philosopher Democritus he took over and elaborated an atomic theory. Nothing exists but space and matter. The latter consists of atoms, imperishable and indissoluble, continually borne through the void to collide and form combinations. When these combinations, e.g. our own bodies, break up, the atoms go on to form other unions. Atoms fall downwards because of their weight, but not straight, for in that case they would never meet. They swerve at random in order to collide, so there is no determinism and men have self-will. Gods do exist, but serene and apart and have no care for our universe.

LUCRETIUS, probably 99–55 BC, the Roman poet and philosopher, in his great didactic poem *On the Nature of Things* described the Epicurean gods:

Lucretius *On the Nature of Things* 2.646–51

¶ The whole nature of the gods must of necessity enjoy an everlasting life in perfect peace, secluded and far removed from our world. For free from all grief, free from danger, strong in its own resources, needing nothing from us, it is neither won over by deserving service nor touched by anger.

Ethically Epicureanism has incurred a bad reputation which it does not deserve. Epicurus did preach the pursuit of pleasure, but for him pleasure was the avoidance of pain, so no pleasure is to be pursued to excess, as this would entail a disproportionate pain. The philosopher should seek to attain a calm serenity, untroubled by fear of death or of the gods, aloof from ambition and the stress of public life, free from the emotional disturbances associated with sexualism. Great virtues are continence and loyalty and one of life's greatest pleasures is friendship.

*Stoicism* originated *c.* 300 BC with Zeno of Citium in Cyprus. It got its name from a lecture hall in Athens, as there is a Greek word *stoa* meaning 'portico', a colonnade like the Italian 'piazza', sometimes translated rather misleadingly as 'porch'. Its basic doctrines, though revised and developed in course of time, were: *Logos* (reason) is the formative principle of nature, a fiery breath permeating the whole universe. Man's reason is a spark of this divine fire and after death is re-absorbed in it. Periodically the universe is consumed by fire and a new cycle of existence, reproducing the persons and events of previous cycles, starts. The traditional worship of gods may be maintained, for the *Logos* is pantheistic and embraces all manifestations of deity. To be virtuous is to live in harmony with reason or nature and this is the only good; not to be virtuous is the only evil. The wise man, carrying out rationally apprehended obligations, can alone be good. For him everything else is indifferent and he will therefore be independent of external circumstances, absolutely brave, temperate and just. It was this ethical side of Stoicism which appealed particularly to the Romans.

Brief mention may be made of the Neo-Pythagoreans, who had no specific leader or systematic doctrines but were interested in theological speculation and, like Pythagoras (late sixth century BC), in the symbolism of numbers. Neo-Platonism, culminating and becoming dominant in the third century AD, was a synthesis of Platonic, Pythagorean, Aristotelian and Stoic elements, introduced to the Romans in its earliest form by the very influential Posidonius *c.* 135–51 BC (p. 44).

In Greece the study of philosophy had led thinking men to discard traditional ideas about the gods as mere superstition. The crafty politician could see religion as a means of manipulating crowds and Polybius formulated this idea for the Romans.

POLYBIUS, *c.* 200 to after 118 BC, was a Greek deported to Rome as a political hostage. He became friendly with leading Roman statesmen and wrote in Greek a *History of Rome* from the beginning of the Punic Wars in 264 down to 146. He is esteemed as a historian, but not as a stylist.

*Histories* 6.56

¶ In my opinion the chief superiority of the Roman State lies in its conception of the gods. It seems to me that what other peoples consider blameworthy, I mean superstition, is a cohesive factor in Roman affairs; to such an unsurpassable extent has this element been introduced with scenic pomp into both their private and public life. Many would think this surprising, but I fancy it has been done for the sake of the common people. If it were possible to gather together a commonwealth of wise men, perhaps there would have been no need of such a course; but every multitude is volatile and full of lawless desires, irrational anger and violent passion, so it remains for the crowds to be constrained by invisible fears and suchlike theatricalities. For this reason I think that it was not rashly and at random that the ancients introduced among the common folk notions about the gods and ideas of what goes on in Hades, but that the moderns are much more rash and foolish in rejecting these.

This rationalistic approach appealed to the pragmatic Roman mind. The Romans were not themselves originators of philosophical doctrines, but there were keen and knowledgeable amateurs.

CICERO 106–43 BC (p. 117), himself an adherent of the sceptical New Academy as befitted a good lawyer, by his various philosophical discussions in which different speakers propounded different doctrines, did much to disseminate knowledge of these. He was quick to point out inconsistencies and absurdities in augury, but he strongly supported the maintenance of the State cults as an essential bulwark of society.

*On the Nature of the Gods* 1.3.1–2

¶ Moreover in putting on a feigned show,[1] as with the other virtues, in the same way there can be no piety,[2] along with which sanctity[3] and religion[4] must needs be abrogated; if these are gone, the consequence is a life of turmoil and confusion. In fact I am inclined to think that with the abrogation of piety towards the gods good faith and fellowship within the human race and also, that most excellent of virtues, justice are abrogated.

1. *feigned show*: this is a hit at the Epicureans, who avowedly disbelieved that there was any divine interest in human affairs, but had no objection to taking part in ritual.
2. *piety*: the Latin word has no precise equivalent in English. It implies duteous behaviour towards gods, family, State, all to whom one is in any way bound. Virgil's Aeneas gained his title of *pius* because he carried away from burning Troy not only its Penates (cp. p. 198), but also his aged father Anchises on his shoulders.
3. *sanctity*: on the human level this implies moral purity.
4. *religion*: the Latin word has more shades of meaning than the English and is usually to be determined by the context. It may have a very wide sense of awe of the divine; it may be religious belief finding expression in the ritual of a cult. Here in a subjective sense it is more of a feeling of obligation to fulfil one's duties to the gods, but is not necessarily accompanied by any personal or emotional commitment.

VARRO, 116–27 BC (p. 125), is quoted by Augustine as saying in his great work on Roman religion:

Augustine *City of God* 6.5.1–3

❡ 'They call the theology that is used chiefly by poets "mythical", that used by philosophers "physical" and that used by city-states "civil". In the first that I mentioned there are many fictions which are contrary to the dignity and nature of the immortal gods. ...The second kind that I have designated is one on which philosophers have left many books, which are concerned with what gods there are, their origin and their nature, i.e. whether they were born at a certain time or have existed from eternity, whether they are of fire, as Heraclitus[1] believes, or of numbers as Pythagoras[2] thinks, or of atoms as Epicurus[3] says. There are other similar arguments which our ears can endure more easily inside the walls of a school than outside in the market-place.' ...'The third kind', he says, 'is that which citizens within cities, especially the priests, have a duty to learn to know and organize. It tells us what gods the State should worship and what rites and sacrifices the individual should perform. The first theology is chiefly suited to the theatre, the second to the universe, the third to the city.'

  1. *Heraclitus*: this Greek philosopher from Ephesus wrote *c.* 500 BC, at a period when philosophy was chiefly concerned with cosmology.
  2. *Pythagoras*: see above p. 202.
  3. *Epicurus*: see above p. 200.

In defining these three types of theology Varro was echoing Mucius Scaevola, consul 95 BC, d. 82. He was a highly respected lawyer and pontiff who had expressly mentioned, according to Augustine, *City of God* 4.27, among philosophical doctrines which it was expedient to keep from the knowledge of the common folk, the theory that the gods were nothing but mortals apotheosized after their death because of services to humanity during their lifetime. This had been suggested by Euhemerus, late fourth century BC, in a Greek travel novel of which only fragments survive. The much revered poet Ennius, 239–169 BC, who did so much to familiarize the Romans with Greek literature, had based on it a prose work called *Euhemerus*. The doctrine of a 'civil' theology put in its crudest form was neatly summarized by that flippant poet OVID, 43 BC–AD 17/18 (p. 64), in *Art of Love*:

Ovid *Art of Love* 1.645

❡ It is expedient that gods should exist, so let us imagine they do.

Varro however was a religious man. While discounting the mythological accretions introduced from Greece he was convinced that right relations must be maintained with those divinities which controlled all human affairs and the proper ways of doing this be preserved. He voiced his feelings, as quoted by Augustine:

Augustine *City of God* 6.9

¶ Varro distinguishes between the religious and superstitious man on the basis that the latter fears the gods, but a religious man does not fear them as enemies, only views them with the respectful awe due to parents.

Augustine also tells us that Varro gave as his motive for writing on religion that:

Augustine *City of God* 6.2

¶ He was afraid that the gods might perish, not because of an enemy invasion but because of the citizens' neglect. 'From this destruction', he said, 'he wanted them to be saved and to be stored and preserved in the memory of loyal citizens through books like his.'

Certainly Varro had good grounds for his fears. In his own lifetime amid all the turbulent political rivalries of the first century BC, culminating in the bloodshed of the Civil Wars, some priesthoods remained unfilled because no one wanted the irksome obligations involved in performing their ritual, and many temples had fallen into disrepair. Political wrangling, combined with the incompatibility of the solar and the lunar year, had brought the calendar and its seasonal festivals into a hopeless muddle and disrepute. Julius Caesar righted the calendar in 46 BC, in his capacity as pontifex maximus (an office which he had obtained in 63 as a step in his political career), establishing it on a basis which was to last for centuries. His successor Augustus (Emperor 27 BC–AD 14) set himself to rebuild temples, re-establish correct rituals and renew traditional beliefs and morality. He did carry out his building programme and the formal cult ceremonies were maintained by successive Emperors until superseded by the complete triumph of Christianity.

Augustus also enlisted the help of the best poets of his time to popularize the idea of a return to the beliefs and practices which had made Rome great. In 17 BC he held the Ludi Saeculares, a festival supposed to be held once a century and therefore marking the beginning of a new era, for which HORACE, 65–8 BC (p. 65), wrote a hymn to Phoebus and Diana, to be sung by choirs of boys and girls. Horace also wrote some majestic State odes. In *Odes* 3.6.1–8 he emphasized the sense of guilt which many Romans probably did feel and the necessity of making peace with heaven:

Horace *Odes* 3.6.1–8

¶ For the sins of your forefathers, Romans, not for your own deserts, shall you pay retribution, until you have restored the temples and the ruinous shrines of the gods and images befouled with black smoke.

You hold empire, because you walk humbly before the gods: from this everything should start, to this refer every outcome. The gods because they were neglected have imposed much suffering on the sorrowing West.

He also harked back to the good old days when the building of temples took precedence over private luxury, which Augustus was trying to curb by sumptuary laws:

*Odes* 2.15.13–20

¶ Their private store was small, the common stock great. For private citizens no colonnade measured by ten-foot rods faced north to receive the shady breeze nor did the laws allow them to scorn the chance-found turf,[1] but ordered them to beautify cities and the temples of the gods at public expense with freshly cut stone.

1. *turf*: this was used for roofing humble country houses.

VIRGIL, 70–19 BC, was born at Mantua, but went south for education in literature and philosophy. His poetic genius was recognized and he became part of the circle of Maecenas to which Horace belonged. In the *Georgics* he tried to popularize farming, the ancient Roman way of life. In *Eclogue* 4 he signalized the beginning of the new era. The birth of a child would mark a cycle returning to the lost Golden Age. (Later Christians saw in this a prophecy, like that of Isa. 11:6ff., of a new Messianic age and in Virgil a Christian born before his time; hence the introduction of Virgil as Dante's guide through Hell.) His great poetic achievement was his epic, the *Aeneid*, tracing the fortunes of his hero, the Trojan Aeneas, who after the burning of Troy endured many dangers and difficulties in reaching Italy, where by the will of Jupiter he was destined to become the founder of the Roman race. This sense of Rome's divine destiny is emphasized all through the poem and culminates in 12.839 when Jupiter tells Juno, hitherto the jealous enemy of the Trojans, that she shall see this people of mixed Italian and Trojan stock:

Virgil *Aeneid* 12.839

¶ surpass men, surpass the gods in their piety

When peace returned after the Civil Wars and life once more became stable there was a deep sense of gratitude to Augustus as the author of this restored prosperity. In the Greek cities of the mainland, the islands, the older Greek colonies of Asia Minor and Alexander's settlements it was natural that they should wish to honour him in their usual way. Cities found no difficulty in adopting new gods, giving them temples, images, altars, priests, processions, games and sacrifices. The individual could either participate or not, as he pleased. Great men, who for their services seemed to have in them something of the divine, could be thought worthy of similar divine honours, particularly if some kind of miracle attested their superhuman status. Three oracles had declared that Alexander the Great was the son of Zeus and there were wonderful stories of his birth. When in 324 BC he demanded that Greece should give him deification, he had no difficulty in obtaining his request, in this case a question of status rather than of any true religious belief, enhancing his might as a conqueror.

After the death of Alexander when his empire was shared out between his generals, the Diadochi, it was natural that Greeks should wish to ingratiate themselves with their new rulers by showing them similar compliments. In Egypt the Ptolemies, like other new dynasties, claimed continuity with their predecessors. They were therefore in the unique position, at least in the eyes of their Egyptian subjects, of being regarded as divine because they were kings. Elsewhere cities continued to administer their internal affairs, but their sovereigns recognized the value of having their dynasty legitimatized and their edicts sanctioned, if they could be thought to exercise some superhuman power. They did not demand deification, but they accepted such titles as *Soter*, Deliverer; *Euergetes, Eumenes*, Kindly. *Epiphanes*, Illustrious, has an additional undertone of 'divinity made manifest'. Indeed the coinage of Antiochus IV, Epiphanes (*c.* 215–163 BC), by its portrayal of him

points to a growing emphasis on his divine status. Such outward signs
of veneration, shrines and offerings etc. as individual cities might care
to give were admissible. These honours all refer to the benefits which
rulers had conferred on communities and are not marks of personal
devotion. They reflect the degradation of divinity to the human level
which accompanied the growing scepticism among politicians.

As Rome's overseas dominion expanded and Roman provincial
governors superseded previous Greek rulers similar fulsome compliments were paid to them. Even Verres, whose rapacity and abuse of
power as proconsul of Sicily (73–71 BC) have made his name a byword
(thanks to Cicero's brilliant speeches in prosecuting him), was given
the title of *Soter*. Augustus really had earned the gratitude of his
subjects, but he was chary of accepting divine honours, which at Rome
might have led to the suspicion that he wanted to establish a kingship
on the hellenistic model, the very suspicion which had brought about
Caesar's murder. There were precedents. Caesar himself had laid stress
on his own descent from Venus through Iulus, son of the Trojan
Aeneas and grandson of Venus and the mortal Anchises. He had even
built a temple to Venus Genetrix. When a comet appeared after his
death this was taken to signify his entry to heaven, just as Romulus was
thought to have joined the gods, and the senate in 42 BC gave him the
title of *divus*, divine. Sextus Pompeius, son of Pompey the Great, in
an abortive bid for maritime power after Caesar's death, had proclaimed
himself son of Neptune. Antony, whose mistress Cleopatra could
already claim divinity by virtue of being queen of Egypt, had styled
himself a New Dionysus and the two of them had made a triumphal
oriental progress in Asia Minor. Neither of these two latter precedents
was popular at Rome, where Augustus was trying so hard to conciliate
the senate and to represent himself as the restorer of temples and
traditional forms of worship. He therefore allowed provincials to
dedicate temples to Dea Roma, the city personified as a goddess, as some
had already done under the Republic, along with his own *genius* (cp.
p. 157), but permission had to be sought and obtained.

In Rome he styled himself 'son of the divine (*divus*) Julius', for
though he was actually Caesar's great-nephew he had been adopted as
his son. In this way he could be thought to have some tincture of his
divinity. On his death it was claimed that he had been seen ascending
into heaven and on him too the senate bestowed the title of *divus*. From
now on, except in the case of bad or unpopular Emperors, this
posthumous deification was regularly accorded. In fact the process
became so stereotyped that *divus* was almost equivalent to 'late', as

Vespasian (Emperor 69–79) on his deathbed wryly recognized, according to SUETONIUS, late first century AD (p. 84):

Suetonius *Life of Vespasian* 23

¶ 'Alas and alack, I'm becoming *divus*.'

Temples, shrines and altars were now dedicated to dead Emperors, singly or linked, or to their *numen* (divine power), as many inscriptions show, or to the *genius* of the reigning Emperor. Only exceptionally did an Emperor claim divine honours for himself during his lifetime, as did Gaius (37–41) and Domitian (81–96). They paid for this by not being recognized as *divus* after being assassinated. There was no imperial rescript to establish Emperor worship everywhere nor any decree that every citizen must take part. For the most part it seems to have risen from spontaneous outbursts of loyalty, especially in parts which had long been Romanized, though in some newer provinces a governor might organize it as a cohesive and stabilizing factor. Drusus, for instance, established a great festival at Lyons in 12 BC, to which the various tribes of Gaul sent delegates. The average citizen would accept, in some cases welcome, this public imperial cult and as an individual show his respect by some conventional gesture such as offering a pinch of incense or kissing his hand as he passed by the altar. He might also enhance the sanctity of an oath through swearing by the *genius* of the Emperor.

When Pliny (p. 149) was confronted with the problem of the growth of Christianity in Bithynia, where he was sent as governor in AD 110, he knew no recognized procedure. Some means had to be found for differentiating between true Christians and the victims of informers who might be professional blackmailers. So he hit upon the expedient of requiring the offering of incense and the taking of an oath by the Emperor's *genius*, actions utterly abhorrent to Christians with their total repudiation of any god but God revealed in Christ. No evidence of crime was required; their refusal showed them to be disloyal subjects and the sect already had a bad reputation, having been held responsible for the Great Fire at Rome in AD 64. Trajan approved and there things stood. There was no imperial decree to exact uniformity until Decius (Emperor 249–51) enacted that all his subjects should take this test and obtain an official certificate to attest their conformity. Meanwhile in our scanty evidence for the second century this seems to have become the standard test, but put into force only locally and on the basis of information received.

Apart from religion in the public sphere there were certain doubts and problems which, then as now, beset all men alike, whatever their status or nationality. One was the question of the after-life, if indeed there was one to be expected at all. In Greek mythology traditionally the ferryman Charon rowed the phantoms of the dead across the river Styx into Hades. There exemplary punishments were suffered by great and legendary sinners, Tantalus for ever reaching out for food and drink which eluded his grasp, Ixion bound to an ever-revolving wheel, Sisyphus always trying to roll a boulder uphill. For the most part it was a gloomy and miserable abode, not unlike the Hebrew Sheol. Grave-offerings, ancient festivals connected with remembrance of the dead, all bear witness to concern with death. As late as the first century BC Lucretius (p. 201) wrote his poetic exposition of Epicureanism with the avowed object of freeing men from the fear of death by showing that death brought total extinction. In time, of course, less credible features were discarded. JUVENAL (p. 32) could write towards the end of the first century AD:

Juvenal *Satires* 2.149–52

¶ That there are such things as spirits of the dead and underground realms and the punt-pole and black frogs[1] in the Stygian pool and that so many thousands cross the stream in one boat not even boys believe, except those who don't yet pay their copper for admission to the baths.

1. *frogs*: this refers to *The Frogs* of Aristophanes, the Athenian comic playwright, which was staged in 405 BC. In this delightful play set in Hades a chorus of frogs greets those crossing the river.

This negative comfort however could not cause men to shed their fears. Many turned for reassurance to the Mystery religions. For others the epitaph often found for gladiators and slaves expresses a bleak pessimism:

¶ I was not. I was. I shall not be. I do not care.

Or there was the rueful whimsicality of an educated man such as Hadrian (Emperor 117–38):

Scriptores Historiae Augustae *Hadrian* 25.9

¶ Soul, little wanderer, little sweeting, guest and companion of the body, to what regions will you now depart, little one stiff and pale, little one naked, without your usual jests?

Then there was the uncertainty of everyday life. Social and economic conditions in the Graeco-Roman world as a whole, emigration, deportation, wars leading to captivity and enslavement, had led men to venerate Fortune, 'Lady Luck', a goddess with no mythology. On a higher plane she could be seen almost as Fate. Polybius had seen the Fortune of the Roman people as the destiny which had led her to acquire an empire. More often she was viewed as blind, capricious, more often malignant than beneficent. Apuleius' hero Lucius constantly blamed her for his manifold vicissitudes and, after his transformation back to human shape, the priest of Isis expressly contrasted her with that kindly goddess (p. 243). In Greek romantic novels apostrophes to cruel Fortune became a rhetorical commonplace. She could also be the deity linked with the fortunes of a city and, as such, temples were dedicated to her in some cities. Similarly she could be the fortune of an individual, presiding over him from the cradle to the grave, like the Latin *genius* for whom her name Tyche was the Greek equivalent.

Divination in its various forms provided a means of foreseeing and guarding against the twists of Fortune. Omens were a well-known sign of what was to come and were relevant both for the State and the individual. Some were very simple and their meaning well known, as the sight of a black cat might be taken today. The Romans had their college of augurs, skilled in interpreting signs. Sacrificial victims too could be ominous. The Romans in particular, taught by the Etruscans, maintained professional diviners (*haruspices*), skilled in interpreting the divine will as shown by inspection of the victim's entrails.

Dreams and visions had portents. There is a good example of a vision combined with rather an abstruse omen given by T A C I T U S, born *c*. AD 56 (p. 16) in his *Histories* (also told with some variations in detail by S U E T O N I U S, *Life of Vespasian* 7):

Tacitus *Hist.* 4.82

¶ After this Vespasian had a stronger desire to apply to the shrine[1] for advice on imperial policy. He ordered that all should be kept away from the temple. When he had entered and his attention was fixed on the deity he looked round and saw behind him one of the foremost of the Egyptians, called Basilides who, he was well aware, was at a distance of many days from Alexandria and detained by illness. He asked the priests whether Basilides had entered the temple that day. He asked men in the street whether he had been seen in the city. Finally he despatched men on horseback, whose enquiries confirmed that at that very time he had been eighty miles away. Then he recognized the apparition as divine and gathered the meaning of the answer from the name Basilides.[2]

1. *shrine*: the was the famous temple of Serapis (p. 248) at Alexandria. Vespasian had recently cured two sick men who had been advised by this god to apply to him for help (p. 221).

2. *Basilides*: the Greek root of *Basilides* means 'king', so Vespasian took this as showing the god's approval of his assuming the Emperorship. Vespasian's supporters had already overcome Vitellius and in AD 70 the senate had granted him the usual imperial prerogatives (title of Augustus, tribunicial right of veto, control of the army and finance and of the imperial provinces), but he still had to go to Rome to take up power.

There were popular handbooks for the interpretation of dreams. On the lowest plane fortune-tellers such as Juvenal's palsied old Jewess (p. 34) would interpret dreams for a few pence. On a higher plane dreams were a favourite means whereby a god would communicate with an individual. In particular, the sick used to sleep in the temple of a god of healing in the hope that the god would appear to them and heal them. So common was the practice that there was a technical term for it, *incubatio*, for which there is no equivalent term in English, as 'incubation' would be totally misleading. There are many inscriptions from such great centres as Epidaurus in Greece, Smyrna and Pergamum in Asia Minor to attest the gratitude of those who had been healed in this way. One from the temple of Asclepius at Epidaurus is especially interesting because of the parallelism with the account of the healing of the blind man at Bethsaida (Mark 8:22–5):

*Inscriptiones Graecae (IG)* 4.951.120–1

¶ Alcetas of Halice being blind saw a vision in which the god, he thought, came to him and with his fingers went over his eyes, and the first things which he saw were the trees in the temple precincts.

One of our main sources for the importance attached to dreams of this nature is AELIUS ARISTIDES, AD 117 or 129 to 181. He studied rhetoric, but when on a visit to Rome at the age of twenty-six was struck down by some malady which afflicted him for the rest of his life. This debarred him from a public career, but he wrote model discourses and essays and was much admired for his style. Most interesting for us are his *Sacred Teachings*. Because of his bad health, coupled with a certain amount of hypochondria, he spent a lot of time in visiting temples of gods of healing, in the hope of dreams which would prescribe treatment advised by the god himself. He composed the *Sacred Teachings* at the command of Asclepius, who had ordered him to write an account of his dreams and the action which he had taken in each case. In some cases he is writing years after the dream, so the accounts are often vague and diffuse, but it is clear that for him every dream had its interpretation, not always obvious at first, but ultimately elucidated after consultation with the priests. Chronic invalids, as at any spa, would meet every day and compare their illnesses, often pool their dreams in the hope of interpretation. When he had been so ill that he could hardly speak, the god (Asclepius is often simply *Soter*, Deliverer) urged him to oratory again. For instance he dreamed of a certain Rhosandrus, a philosopher and himself a zealous worshipper of the god, who standing by his bed told him that in his estimation he surpassed Demosthenes, so that not even the philosophers themselves could scorn him. Again he had a very vivid dream, which he remembered in detail, of being present at a meeting between the Emperor Antoninus Pius and the Parthian king Vologeses, when he was called upon to exhibit his skill in oratory. At another time he had orders in dreams to compose hymns to the gods and would wake up with the first line of the hymn in his mind, divinely given.

These were highly individual dreams, but more interesting as typical of the dreams experienced at a medical spa are those concerned with his health. Sometimes a man would be informed in a dream of treatment prescribed for another. Whatever the treatment, Aristides accepted the prescription in blind faith, often recording with satisfaction that he carried it out against all the advice of friends and medical men, for of course there were also professional physicians in such centres. He sets down in detail the emetics, the purges, the hot baths, cold baths, abstaining from baths altogether, dieting. Sometimes his obedience to the god drew a crowd. For instance, once at Smyrna he saw a vision of a composite god, at once the Apollo of Clarus and the Asclepius of Pergamum, who said: 'You have ten years from me and three from Serapis.' At the same time the god reckoned the years on his fingers, but by this reckoning made the years seventeen. Then he ordered him to go and bathe in the river flowing before the city. To quote Aristides himself:

*Sacred Teachings* 47.18ff.

¶ It was the middle of winter and a black north wind and very cold,

and the stones were so bound together by the frost that they were like
a sheet of ice, and the water matched the climate! When
the story of the divine vision was reported, my friends escorted me,
also doctors, some of them my intimates, some from anxiety and others
for the sake of the story. There was also another large crowd – for it
happened that there had been a distribution outside the gates – and
everything was in view from the bridge. There was one doctor,
Heracleon, a friend of mine, who confessed to me next day that he
had gone fully persuaded that, at the very best, I should be seized by
cramp or the like.

To cut a long story short, Aristides dived in without hesitation, found
the water delightful, and all the rest of the day experienced a warm
glow.

The god, or gods, for Serapis and Athena also appeared to him, often
gave him warnings of impending dangers and the means of escaping
from them. When the end of the allotted span of years promised him
drew near, he began to grow anxious and fell sick of a disease then
epidemic at Smyrna, but the gods saved him by detailed prescriptions.
About the same time he lost a slave, so he complacently thought that
the slave's life had been taken instead of his own. It is only fair to say
that Aristides really had a strong commitment to the gods and was
vouchsafed personal religious experience. When the god gave him what
sounds a peculiarly horrible prescription of wormwood mixed with
vinegar, Aristides writes:

*Sacred Teachings* 48.32

¶ He appeared with the greatest vividness, for countless details vividly
manifested the appearance of the god. For I could fancy that I touched
him and perceived that he had come himself and that I was betwixt
sleeping and waking and wished to look and was anxious lest he should
slip away too soon and pricked up my ears and listened, partly as if
in a dream, partly as if awake, and my hair stood upright and I wept
with joy and my mind was over-burdened, and what man could
describe this in words? If there is any one who has been initiated, he
knows and understands.

Oracles were another means of probing into the future. There had
long been famous oracles in Greece, such as those of Apollo at Delphi

and of Zeus at Dodona in the north (map 1), along with other oracles of more local repute both in Greece and in Asia Minor. There was also the oracle of Ammon in Libya, famous because it was consulted by Alexander the Great, but too remote to become popular. The means whereby the gods communicated their will varied. Best known perhaps was the frenzy of the Delphic prophetess whose unintelligible utterances were interpreted by the priests. In its heyday Delphi had been a great international centre, but in hellenistic times was losing its influence. Individuals found it easier and less expensive to forego travel to Greece and to consult local or more accessible oracles.

In Rome great importance was attached to the sibylline books. The name of Sibyl, in itself a Greek word, was almost a generic name for a prophetess and mention is made of Sibyls at various times and in various places. For us it has come to refer to the Sibyl of Cumae, who in the *Aeneid* acted as Aeneas' guide through Hades when he wanted advice as to his future course. The sibylline books contained a collection of oracles, said to have been acquired by one of the ancient kings of Rome, Tarquinius Priscus. They were preserved in the temple of Jupiter on the Capitol and were in the charge of a special priestly college, which could consult them only on the orders of the senate. When the Capitol was burnt in 83 BC the sibylline books also perished and a new collection was made from various sources. They were consulted in times of emergency, e.g. after the Tiber had flooded with great loss of life and destruction of property or after the Great Fire of Rome, not to obtain practical help, but to discover means whereby the gods might by propitiated; this might entail bringing in the worship of a foreign deity, in order to enlist additional aid. For instance, the books were consulted in 205 BC, when there were great showers of stones, when too Rome desperately wanted an end to the Second Punic War. It was prescribed that the worship of Cybele should be introduced (see p. 229). The importance of the oracular books is brought out by the fact that historians in their annals recorded occasions when they had been consulted.

By the first century AD oracles seemed to be losing their attraction. At Delphi, where there had once been three prophetesses, two on duty and one held in reserve, there was only one priestess. Plutarch, late first century AD (p. 72), wrote a little treatise called *On the Obsolescence of Oracles*, in which he named various lesser oracles which had ceased to function. He was himself a priest at Delphi and a deeply religious man, but he was not worried by this apparent breakdown between gods and men. It could be explained, he thought, by the fact that the population had diminished and fewer oracular shrines could meet their needs.

In Asia Minor the ancient oracles of Apollo at Didyma near Miletus and at Clarus near Colophon (see map 2) continued to flourish. Individuals still wanted to have access to the will of heaven. Aelius Aristides tells of his personal consultations and how, when there were earthquakes, constant appeals were made to Apollo's oracle at Clarus. Indeed there was even the deliberate institution of a new one in the second century, described by the contemporary L U C I A N (p. 187) in a piece of investigative journalism. In *Alexander or the False Prophet* he tells how a certain Alexander determined, in conjunction with a partner who soon died, to found an oracle at Abonutichos in Paphlagonia (map 2). First they buried bronze tablets at Chalcedon, which stated that Asclepius and his father, Apollo, would settle in Abonutichos. When these tablets were found, the people of Abonutichos at once set about building the foundations of a new temple, although they had one already. Alexander dressed himself up like Perseus (a legendary Greek hero, son of Zeus and slayer of the Gorgon, Medusa), and produced a sibylline prophecy to support his activity, foaming at the mouth and prophesying in unintelligible jargon. He then buried in the foundations a goose egg in which he had inserted a baby snake, and in the guise of a prophet led the citizens to the spot. The baby snake was hailed as a manifestation of Asclepius, for snakes were associated with this cult. Previously Alexander had procured a large tame snake and now proclaimed that the god had grown to maturity in a few days. Crowds poured in to see the new god. They filed in at the front and out at the back, passing through a dimly lit room where Alexander received them. He sat there with the snake embracing his body, its own head hidden in his bosom, and protruding instead a linen head with human features, which had a mechanism whereby the mouth could be operated to open and shut, as if speaking.

The next step was to declare that the god, henceforth to be known under the new name of Glycon, would make prophecies. Scrolls were sent in with enquiries, then returned apparently unopened, with the answer appended. Lucian gives details of the trickery with which it was managed and gives some of the ambiguous oracles. Alexander, appreciating the value of propaganda, would even give unsolicited oracles or send to cities and warn them of impending calamities. The vested interests of older oracles, such as those of Apollo at Didyma and Clarus, were conciliated by his sometimes bidding individuals to consult them instead. He even sent an oracle to the Emperor Marcus Aurelius, when the latter was engaged against the Marcomanni, a tribe by the Danube, ordering him to throw two lions and various aromatic herbs into the river. This was duly done, but the lions swam across and were clubbed to death by the enemy, who next inflicted a savage defeat on the Romans.

Alexander must have been a very plausible charlatan, for in spite of all this adverse publicity he won over Rutilianus, the governor of Asia, to whom he married his daughter. He also instituted Mysteries (see p. 225). The cult did not dwindle with the death of Alexander, but continued until the downfall of paganism.

Astrology too was thought to give man foreknowledge. This was confused with science. Astronomy had discovered fixed rules governing the movements of the stars and the Chaldaeans in the first place had related the movements of the planets to human life and cast horoscopes. In its full elaboration the universe was envisaged as one sympathetic whole, so that humans, animals, plants and stones were all linked together and operated under the domination of the stars. Various attempts had been made by the authorities to expel soothsayers from Rome, but all failed. T A CIT U S, *c*. AD 56 to after 115 (p. 16) described them as:

Tacitus *Hist*. 1.22

¶ A species of men treacherous to the powerful, tricking the hopeful, which in our State will always be both banned and retained.

Tacitus made this remark immediately after describing how Otho in AD 68 had been encouraged by the hopeful prognostications of an astrologer to murder Galba in order to become Emperor himself. In fact it was no wonder that astrology could not be expelled, when it was practised in high places. According to S U E T O N I U S, the late first century biographer (p. 84):

Suetonius *Life of Tiberius* 69

¶ Tiberius was rather careless about the gods and religious observances, for he was addicted to astrology and was fully persuaded that everything was determined by fate.

J U V E N A L (p. 32), that jaundiced late first century AD satirist, included addiction to astrology and fortune-telling among the vices of women.

Juvenal *Satires* 2.6.553–6

¶ They will put more trust in the Chaldaeans and will believe that whatever the astrologer says has been brought from the spring of Ammon, since the Delphic oracle is dumb and the human race condemned by darkness as to the future.

*Satires* 2.6.572–91

¶ Remember to avoid even meetings with the woman in whose hands you see an almanac rubbed with use like unctuous amber,[1] who consults nobody and by now is a consultant. If her husband is on his way to military service or his native land, she will not go along with him if she is detained by the calculations of Thrasyllus.[2] When she decides to journey as far as the first milestone [i.e. the very short distance of one mile], the hour is taken from the book. If the corner of her eye itches when rubbed, she consults her horoscope before asking for eye-salve. Suppose she is lying sick; the only hour suitable for taking food is the one prescribed by Petosiris.[3]

If she is middle class she will haunt the space on each side of the turning posts[4] and draw lots[5] and show her forehead and her hand to the fortune-teller, who tells her to keep on smacking her lips.[6]

To the rich, Phrygian and Indian augurs will give answers and, for hire, an expert on the stars and sky and some senior official, who expiates lightning flashes[7] on behalf of the State.

But the fate of the common folk lies in the *Circus* and the Embankment.[8] The woman who displays a long gold chain[9] on her bare neck enquires in front of the pillars[10] and the columns with their dolphins whether she should leave the huckster and marry the slop-seller.[11]

1. *amber*: it was fashionable for Roman ladies to carry balls of amber in their hand, because when warm these exuded an agreeable scent.

2. *Thrasyllus*: he was an astrologer, died AD 36, who had been intimate with Tiberius and had written books of astrological calculations.

3. *Petosiris*: he was an Egyptian priest who was said to have been one of the founders of astrology. Books ascribed to him were current at this time.

4. *turning posts*: these, like the pillars, were features of the *Circus*, the race-course lying between the Palatine and Aventine hills.

5. *lots*: wooden counters with words inscribed on them were drawn at random.

6. *smacking her lips*: she is to keep up an accompaniment to his reading her forehead and hand.

7. *lightning*: if anything was struck by lightning, this was ominous, and there was a State obligation to bury anything that was left, a ritual to be carried out by a professional.

8. *Embankment*: this was an ancient earthwork, which was a favourite walk.

9. *gold chain*: the Latin reads simply 'gold' and the allusion is unintelligible. Perhaps the most probable explanation is that such a woman would convert any cash into gold, to be carried about on her own person.

10. *pillars*: see n. 4.

11. *slop-seller*: this means a man who dealt in the rough blankets and cloaks used by soldiers.

Astrology, if a man's fate is determined by the stars from birth to death, logically leads to a bleak and pessimistic determinism. In practice, means were found to circumvent Fate by prayers, according to due formulas, amulets (hundreds of which have been found in graves) and charms and incantations for which there is abundant evidence in Egyptian magical papyri. Agrippa, Augustus' trusted chief minister, had issued an edict to ban both astrologers and magic from Rome in 23 BC. It will be remembered that at Ephesus many Christian converts publicly burned their books of magic spells, valued at a total of fifty thousand pieces of silver (Acts 19:18 19), cp. p. 139.

There were spells against malignant spirits, the bogeys who were part of hellenistic folk-lore, such as Empusa who could change her shape at will and Onoskelis, Donkey-Shanks, who was a very beautiful woman with a fair complexion, but who had the legs of a donkey. She dwelt in holes and caves and cliffs, and men, particularly the dark-skinned, were attracted by her and she lay with them and either strangled them or drove them mad.

From such spells designed for men's protection it was an easy step to black magic, whereby a man for his own ends tried to bend heavenly powers to do his will. There is the familiar love charm of Virgil's Eighth Eclogue, based upon a Greek original by the third century BC poet Theocritus, in which a wife tries to rekindle her lover's dwindling affection, each spell followed by the haunting refrain:

(cp. Theocritus *Idyll* 2)

❡ Bring, magic songs, bring Daphnis home from town.

More sinister is one from Africa. The dead were thought to have peculiar efficacy, particularly those who had died a violent death or perished as infants, and lead tablets inscribed with prayers were inserted in their graves. This is one:

From *Defixionum Tabellae* (ed. A. Audollent, Minerva, GmbH, Frankfurt/Main, 1967) 265

❡ Alimbeau, columbeu petalimbeu, make Victoria, daughter of Suavulva, madly in love with me. Let her not see sleep until she comes to me, the ladies' delight. Besides let Ballincus be unable to get in ahead of me; and thou, whoever thou art, demon, I pray thee to force her to come to me, for love and desire of me.

Lead tablets were also a suitable medium for curses and this one gives evidence of the popular passion for racing:

From *Defixionum Tabellae* 234

❡ I conjure thee, demon prematurely dead, whoever thou canst be, by the names of power [magical names follow], bind the horses the names and pictures of which I set for thee on this tablet [names of horses follow by stables]. Paralyse them on the way, break their strength, their spirit, their dash, their speed. Rob them of victory, hamper their feet, weaken them, so that today in the hippodrome they can neither run nor walk nor win nor emerge from the doors, from the stables, nor traverse the arena nor turn the posts, but fall with their drivers [further magical names follow].

Another type, if one wanted to render one's adversary dumb in court before the judge, was to tear the tongue from a living cock in a cemetery by night, then write the enemy's name on a lead tablet along with a picture of the cock and insert it in a tomb.

In the second century AD Apuleius (p. 56) was accused of using magic to obtain a woman's affections and thereby her property on apparently rather trivial grounds, as described in his *Apology* (Defence). He had bought certain fish for magical purposes, it was alleged. Certainly the fish was in Africa and in the East a creature of religious significance, but Apuleius explains that like Aristotle he was interested as a zoologist in the structure. Then he was accused of having caused a slave to fall into a trance from which he awoke knowing nothing of what had passed – obviously the spiritualistic trance of a medium is implied. Apuleius explains this simply as an epileptic fit, which had often happened to the boy whether he was there or not. He was accused of keeping certain objects hidden in a napkin, presumably for magical purposes; he explains these as sacred objects, relics of Mysteries in which he had been initiated during his travels abroad. He was also accused of keeping a skeleton statue, which he had had made specially, and which he worshipped under the title of *Basileus*, King. This he explains instead as a statue of Mercury made of ebony. Apuleius was acquitted, yet after his death he enjoyed a great reputation as a magician, perhaps because of the familiarity with the legendary magic which he showed in his romance, *The Golden Ass* (see in particular 2.6ff.).

A belief in miracles was to be expected in such a world and miracles are on record. There could be a straightforward miracle of healing, accomplished with divine sanction, as in the tale told by both SUETONIUS, *Life of Vespasian* 7, and TACITUS:

Tacitus *Hist.* 4.81.1–7

¶ During those months while Vespasian was waiting for the stated days[1] for the summer breezes and for surety at sea, there were many miraculous events by which the favour of heaven and some inclination of the gods towards Vespasian were displayed. One of the common folk of Alexandria, a well-known sufferer from ophthalmia, fell at his feet and lamenting prayed that he would cure his blindness, on the advice of Serapis,[2] a god to whom a people addicted to superstitions pays special honours. He begged the Emperor to deign to bedew his cheeks and pupils with spittle.[3] Another with a disabled hand, on the authority of the same god, begged that he might be trampled under the soles of his feet. At first Vespasian laughed and rejected them. When they persisted he was by turns afraid for his reputation and led on to hope by their entreaties and the voices of flatterers. Finally he ordered doctors to estimate whether such blindness and disability could be overcome by human means. The doctors put forward various points: in the one case the eyesight had not been utterly destroyed and would return if the obstructions were removed, in the other the limbs had grown out of shape and, if some health-giving force were applied, could be restored. Perhaps, they said, that was the gods' will and the Emperor had been chosen as the divine agent, finally if the cure were accomplished it was Caesar who would be glorified, if it were ineffectual it was the poor wretches who would be mocked. In the end Vespasian thinking that everything lay open to his destiny[4] and nothing more was incredible, while the crowd of bystanders were on tiptoe with expectation, put on a cheerful look and carried out the commands. Immediately the hand returned to use and the light of day dawned again for the blind man. Those who were present tell both stories even now,[5] after there is nothing to be gained by lying.

1. *stated days*: there were strong and perilous winds usually until 26 May.

2. *Serapis*: see pp. 213, 238.

3. *spittle*: cp. the use of spittle to cure the blind man at Bethsaida, Mark 8:23; John 9:6.

4. *destiny*: Vespasian might indeed think himself incredibly fortunate in that his supporters had secured the Emperorship for him, while he was still abroad.

5. *even now*: Tacitus was writing in the time of Trajan (Emperor 98–117), when the Flavian dynasty had become extinct.

Individuals could be credited with miraculous powers. A notable instance was Apollonius of Tyana, the wandering first century AD philosopher and sage. PHILOSTRATUS (p. 114) in his *Life of Apollonius of Tyana* tells many stories about him. For instance:

Philostratus *Life of Apollonius of Tyana* 4.145

¶ This too is one of Apollonius' miracles. A girl was thought dead just at the time of her marriage and the bridegroom was following the bier[1] and lamenting for his unconsummated marriage and all Rome joined in the mourning, for the girl was of consular family. Apollonius happened to witness the calamity, so he said: 'Put down the bier, for I will stop your tears for the girl.' At the same time he asked her name. Most people thought he would deliver an oration such as is usual at funerals and excites lamentation, but by simply touching her and whispering something secretly he woke up the girl from her seeming death. She spoke and returned to her father's house, like Alcestis[2] brought back to life by Heracles. The girl's family wanted to give him one hundred and fifty thousand sesterces, but he said he would contribute them to her dowry. Whether he found some spark of life in her which her physicians had not detected – for it is said that, although there was a drizzle of rain, a vapour rose from her face – or whether life was extinguished and he warmed and restored it is a mystery, incomprehensible not only to me, but to the bystanders too.

    1. *bier*: cp. the raising to life of the son of the widow at Nain, Luke 7:11–15. There is also some similarity with the raising of Jairus' daughter, Mark 5:22–43.

    2. *Alcestis*: Alcestis, wife of Admetus, had volunteered to die in his stead. When Heracles, an old friend of Admetus, learnt that Alcestis had died he kept watch by the tomb. Death arrived to claim his victim and Heracles wrestled with him and overcame him and so brought Alcestis back to life.

    Apollonius had prophetic powers too. He foretold a pestilence that was to come upon Ephesus and the means of averting it (*Life* 4.4.10). Another sign of his power was that when he was brought to trial before Tigellinus, the corrupt and unpopular minister of Nero (Emperor 54–68), the prosecutor on opening his carefully prepared brief found that the sheet was completely blank (*Life* 4.44). Apollonius did not work for money and was much revered during his lifetime and after his death. In fact, Alexander Severus (Emperor 222–35) is said to have had his bust (along with those of Abraham, Orpheus and Christ) in his Lararium or private chapel.

## Mysteries and Oriental Religions

In the ancient world life was lived against a background of superstition combined with religious pomp and show maintained at public expense to preserve for the State a right relationship with the gods. In such a world where man's destiny was either rigidly ruled by the stars or at the mercy of a capricious and sometimes malignant Fortune, men might well feel afraid.

    For some there was the comfort of gods familiar from childhood. For others the campaigns of Alexander, the Civil Wars and similar upheavals had brought the loss of home and property, emigration to repair their fortunes or enforced exile because of enslavement. Merchants and artisans settled in alien lands, soldiers might find themselves transported from the deserts of the East to the cold fogs of Britain, slaves in large households might have no compatriot among fellow-slaves who were of disparate nationalities too.

Attempts were made to keep up a connection with native gods. There are dedications by guilds of foreign merchants and by soldiers bearing witness to minor Oriental gods. Too often however a god was indissolubly linked with his or her own locality. Hence the appeal of great gods such as Isis and Mithras whose power transcended all human boundaries.

This was one reason for the growing popularity of the Oriental religions in Rome. Another was men's need for a more personal relationship with the divinity to relieve their loneliness and to comfort their fears. This could be sought in the Mystery religions. The moment of initiation could bring ever-memorable exaltation. Moreover these religions were not mutually exclusive and men and women could be initiated in several.


### I   Mysteries

The word *Mystery* comes from a Greek verb meaning 'to keep one's mouth shut' and that is precisely what the initiates did. Consequently we are still ignorant of much that happened. There is little literary evidence, although some initiatory formulas have been preserved, usually by Christian authors. However archaeology has discovered frescoes on the walls of houses, objects buried with the dead, statues, altars, dedicatory offerings, carvings and epitaphs, which supplement these scanty sources, especially with regard to Mithraism.

Among Greek Mysteries the most venerable and respected were the Eleusinian, originally a local Athenian fertility ritual, later thrown open to all who could speak Greek and had pure hands, i.e. were not murderers or the like. Underlying the Mystery was the myth of Demeter, the corn goddess, her search for her daughter abducted by Pluto and how she brought her up from the underworld to live for six months on earth every year. Initiates bathed in the sea en masse and then went in merry procession to Eleusis. There they did not receive instruction in any esoteric creed, but did things, handling sacred objects, and saw things, probably ancient statues unveiled and some dramatic re-enactment of the myth. At some point too the initiate was given a drink. It is summed up in the formula:

Clement *Exhortation to the Greeks* 2.21

⁋ I have fasted, I have drunk the posset,[1] I have taken from the chest and put into the basket and out of the basket into the chest.

1. *posset*: this was an ancient Greek word. In Homer it meant a drink of wine mixed with barley groats and grated cheese, but honey and other ingredients could also be used, not excluding drugs.

One who had been initiated need not fear a grim and cheerless after-life, such as lay in store for others. The Eleusinian Mysteries enjoyed an international reputation and many came from many lands to be initiated. Augustus was an initiate and set a precedent followed by his successors, including the philosopher Marcus Aurelius (Emperor 161–80).

Such a Mystery cult, even without any sanction of antiquity, could draw the crowds, for the charlatan Alexander instituted one on the Athenian model, according to his contemporary LUCIAN, born *c.* AD 120 (p. 187):

*Alexander or the False Prophet* 38

¶ He instituted an initiation ceremony and rites by torchlight and divine appearances, lasting for three successive days. On the first there was a proclamation like the one at Athens: 'If any atheist or Christian or Epicurean has come to spy upon our rites, out with him; but let those who believe in the god be initiated and good fortune be with them.' Then at the very beginning there was an expulsion. He led off saying: 'Christians, out!' and all the congregation responded: 'Epicureans, out!' Then there was Leto giving birth to Apollo and his union with Coronis and the birth of Asclepius. On the second day there was the manifestation of Glycon[1] and birth of the god. On the third day there was the marriage of Podaleirius[2] and Alexander's mother. She was called Dadis and torches [*dades*] were kindled. Finally there was the love of the Moon and Alexander and the birth of Rutilianus'[3] wife.

1. *Glycon*: see above p. 216.
2. *Podaleirius*: he was a son of Asclepius; a skilled physician, who took part in the siege of Troy. He had no claim to divine status except what Alexander seems to have fabricated for him.
3. *Rutilianus*: he was the gullible governor of the province, to whom Alexander had succeeded in marrying his own daughter.

Greek too were the Dionysiac Mysteries, though sometimes combined with worship of the equally frenzied Phrygian god Sabazius, connected with the myth that the infant god had been torn to pieces and brought to life again. After the scandal of the Bacchanalia (see below) in 186 BC there was a recrudescence in the imperial period, with associations meeting in private houses for joyful banquets and dancing. Frescoes found in a great dining-room at Pompeii show an initiation ordeal involving flagellation. Reliefs showing the winnowing fan (*liknon*), ivy-wreathed wand (*thyrsus*), phallus, drums and wine attest the popularity of the cult in Italy and the Western provinces. In particular, after burial began to supersede cremation about the middle of the second century AD beautifully carved sarcophagi are found with reliefs symbolizing an after-life, often with Bacchic emblems. This is explicit in a Latin inscription from Philippi. The dead woman is welcomed by a festal procession of Maenads and the inscription runs:

¶ While we, overcome by our loss, are in misery, you in peace and once more restored live in the Elysian[1] fields.

1. *Elysian*: Elysium or the Elysian fields was the legendary abode of the blessed and the Maenads, the god's female attendants, indicate a continuation of the revelry enjoyed on earth.

This cult with its underlying note of real ecstasy had become a sort of early Mafia in the notorious Bacchanalia unmasked in 186 BC at a time of great social unrest in both Rome and Italy. The consequent suspicion and dread coloured Roman attitudes towards foreign religions for a long time to come and LIVY (p. 124) a century and a half or so later devoted twelve vivid chapters to it (39.8–19) summarized as follows:

The initiation cult was started by a Greek in Etruria and spread and degenerated into all kinds of immoral and criminal practices. Of course initiates were bound by a strict oath of secrecy, but discovery came about through a curious chain of circumstances. A certain Aebutius, a young man of good family, had a mistress called Hispala, a freedwoman who had previously been a slavegirl. His widowed mother had married again and the stepfather had squandered Aebutius' patrimony, for which he would have to give account when his ward came of age. He therefore wanted either to procure the youth's death or get some blackmailing hold over him. So Aebutius' mother told him that when he had been ill she had vowed to initiate him in the Bacchic cult; now that he had recovered she must perform her vow. He agreed and she prescribed a preparatory period of purification, ten days without sex.

When Aebutius told Hispala that she would not be seeing him for the next ten days, she asked the reason. On learning it she was much perturbed and told him in strict secrecy that as a slave she had accompanied her mistress to the rites and that all kinds of abominations took place. She begged him to refuse to be initiated. When he did so, his mother and stepfather taunted him with being unable to live without his mistress for ten days and turned him out of the house. Aebutius consulted his aunt and on her advice disclosed everything to the consul Postumius. The latter investigated his bona fides and then sent for Hispala. She reproached Aebutius for his betrayal and said:

Livy 39.13.1–8; 13.18

¶ She was much afraid of the gods whose secret mysteries she was divulging, much more afraid of men who, if she turned informer, would tear her to pieces with their own hands. [On being assured of protection she went on:] 'At first it was a women's ceremony and it was a rule that no man was admitted. There were three fixed days a year on which Bacchic initiations were held by day. Matrons were appointed priestesses by turns. Paculla Aunia, a Campanian,[1] when priestess, had changed everything, as if by divine admonition. She was the first to initiate men, her own sons. The initiations were performed at night instead of by day and instead of three days a year on five days every month. From the time that the rites became promiscuous and men mingled with women, with the added licence of the dark,[2] every kind of criminal and disgraceful act had been committed; there was more lewdness between men than between men and women. If any shrank from vice or were reluctant to commit crime, they were sacrificed as victims. The sum total of their religion was to consider nothing wrong.'

    1. *Campanian*: there was an Italian region, not far from Rome, called Campania.
    2. *dark*: compare the similar accusations of immorality in the dark brought against Christians by Fronto (p. 175 above).

¶ Men, as if out of their minds, ranted, throwing themselves about fanatically. Matrons in Bacchic garb and with flowing hair ran down to the Tiber with burning torches, plunged them into the water and, because they contained natural sulphur along with lime, brought them out with flame unharmed. Men were said to be carried off by the gods when they had been bound to a machine and hurled out of sight into hidden caves. They were ones who had refused to join in the oath or take part in crimes or submit to lewdness. There was an enormous host, now almost a second populace, and among them were some men and women of noble birth. For the last two years it had been a rule that no one over the age of twenty should be initiated. Those were entrapped who were of an age to go astray and to submit to lewdness.

The two consuls with the approval of senate and people took swift measures against what was seen as a public danger. Rewards were offered for information. Exits from the city were barred; many were caught trying to escape and some committed suicide. Assizes were held throughout Italy. More than seven thousand were said to be involved. Those who had taken the oath, but had committed no crime, were kept in prison; the rest, including the four male ringleaders, were executed. Women, if condemned, were handed over to their kinsfolk to be punished in private (cp. p. 147 for the similar procedure in the case of Pomponia Graecina).

¶ Then the consuls were given the task of pulling down all Bacchic premises first in Rome, then throughout Italy, unless there were any ancient altar or consecrated statue. Precaution was taken for the future by a senatorial decree: 'There were to be no Bacchic premises at Rome or in Italy. If anyone thought such a rite was solemn and necessary and that he could not omit it without feeling scruples and making expiation he was to make a statement to the city praetor, who was to consult the senate. If permission were given (a senatorial quorum of one hundred being necessary) he was to conduct the rite with the stipulation that no more than five were to be present at the sacrifice, there was to be no communal fund, no master of ceremonies and no priest.'

There is an inscription extant (*Corpus Inscriptionum Latinarum* (*CIL*) 1.96) which contains this edict and corroborates Livy. What is noteworthy is the Roman care to preserve anything ancient and not to offend the gods by omitting any kind of religious observance which even an individual might think obligatory.


## II   *Oriental Cults*

The great Oriental divinities were Cybele and Attis from Phrygia, Isis and Osiris and Serapis from Egypt, Mithras from Persia and Atargatis

from Syria. These had their Mysteries but, with the exception of
Mithras, also public rites.

*Cybele and Attis:* Cybele was a fertility goddess from Phrygia, the Great
Mother, mistress of mountain, forest and wild creatures. She drove in
a chariot drawn by lions and on her head wore a crown of towers to
signify her power over cities too. She was accompanied by a noisy escort
of priests (*galli*) who in the frenzy of their worship had emasculated
themselves. Often she was associated with a young man called Attis,
though she was always the dominant partner. There were many
ramifications of mythology, but basically the story was that Cybele
loved a young shepherd called Attis. He forsook her for a mortal love,
so the goddess in her anger drove him to a frenzy in which he castrated
himself beneath a pine tree and bled to death. His resurrection seems
to have been a later addition to the story.

In 204 BC there were showers of stones and also the State was
suffering grievously from the protracted war with Hannibal. So the
sibylline books were consulted and, with hints that a foreign invader
would be driven out, prescribed that the Black Stone, symbol of the
Great Mother, should be brought from Pessinus in Phrygia (map 2)
and her cult established in Rome. The Stone was duly brought and in
202 Hannibal was decisively defeated. Credit for the victory went to
the goddess and a temple was built for her on the Palatine. Ludi
Megalenses (Games of the Great Mother) were established every year
from the 4th to the 10th of April. These were on a Roman model,
theatrical performances for which a theatre was specially built,
sideshows and general festivity, but this was the only Roman
participation in her worship. Priests and priestesses were imported from
Phrygia and Romans were forbidden on pain of death to emasculate
themselves and join them. At the culmination of the festival the priests
in noisy procession carried the image through the streets to the river
Almo, where it was bathed and after this purification taken back to
the temple. The priests were also allowed on fixed days to go about
to collect alms for the maintenance of the cult. It remained alien, quite
contrary to Roman sobriety, a little enclave of orgiastic worship on
Roman soil.

In the eastern parts of the Mediterranean her worship had spread
and even at Rome she excited fear and honour. The different attitudes
of the nobility and of at least some of the common folk are illustrated
by an anecdote about an event in 102 BC told by DIODORUS
SICULUS (*fl.* in the second half of the first century BC p. 46):

*World History* 36.13

¶ A man called Battaces, a priest of the Great Mother of the Gods, arrived from Pessinus in Phrygia. Alleging that he had come at the command of the goddess, he had an audience with the consuls and senate and declared that the temple of the goddess had been polluted and a ritual of purification must be carried out at Rome in the name of the State. His clothing and the rest of his outfit were outlandish and unacceptable by Roman standards, for he wore an enormous golden crown and a brightly coloured robe threaded with gold, emblems of royal status. [After addressing the people in such a way as to excite their superstitious fears he was granted hospitality at public expense. One of the tribunes, Aulus Pompeius, forbade him to wear his crown and treated him contemptuously, so he took umbrage and would not stir from his lodging, claiming that both he and the Great Mother had been insulted.] Pompeius was immediately seized by a violent fever; after this he lost his voice, had an attack of quinsy and died two days later. The masses thought that he had lost his life by divine providence because of his offences against the priest and the goddess, for the Romans are very addicted to superstitious fears. Accordingly an agreement was reached about his sacred robe and outfit and he was honoured with notable gifts. When he left the city to return home he was escorted on his way by throngs of both men and women.

Some fifty years later two Roman poets show the fascination of the exotic cult. CATULLUS, 87 to *c.* 47 BC, best known for his passionate love lyrics, wrote a long poem of ninety-three lines, a tour de force in an unusual metre called galliambics, which has an exciting rhythm. He tells how a young Greek called Attis (no relation to the god) sailed with a band of companions to Phrygia to worship Cybele. They rushed into the forest and there under the stimulus of the ecstatic band of devotees and the orgiastic music he castrated himself. Next day he woke to find himself alone and realizing what he had done he bitterly lamented the loss of his manhood. When he would have returned home the goddess sent one of her lions to chase him back into the forest and there he remained until he died. The poem ends with a poignant invocation from the poet. The first line is given here in Latin, so that the force of the alliteration and the strong beat of the rhythm may be appreciated.

Catullus 63.91–3

❡ dea, magna dea, Cybelle, dea domina Dindimei

Goddess, great goddess, Cybelle,[1] goddess, mistress of Dindimus,[2] far from my home, lady, be all your fury! Drive others frenzied, drive others mad.

    1. *Cybelle*: the poet spelt the name in this way to suit his metre.
    2. *Dindimus*: this was a mountain in Phrygia.

LUCRETIUS, 99–55 BC (p. 176), describes the procession when the goddess's image was carried through the streets, as would happen in many cities where she was worshipped. This might seem irrelevant in a didactic poem on the atomic theory, but Lucretius excuses the insertion on the grounds that the Great Mother symbolizes the earth, which contains the atoms of all animals and plants. Clearly his poetic imagination had been inspired by the sight.

*On the Nature of Things* 2.618–28
Referring to the *galli*:

❡ The taut tambourines thunder beneath their palms and all around are the concave cymbals and the horns menace with their harsh-sounding note and the hollow flute excites the mind with its Phrygian rhythm. They brandish weapons in token of their violent frenzy, in order to terrify the unthankful souls and impious hearts of the common folk with fear of the goddess's divinity. Therefore as soon as she is carried through great cities and silently blesses mortals with mute salutation, they strew all her passage through the streets with bronze and silver, enriching her with bounteous gifts and snow down rosebuds, overshadowing the Mother and her attendant host.

The constant influx into Rome from the Levant brought in more who already worshipped Cybele and others who were devotees of minor Oriental deities. Finding in Rome a well-established cult with the inestimable advantage of official recognition they had little difficulty in accommodating their own worship, so that their own gods became absorbed. Ma for instance was assimilated with Cybele and Men with Attis. This increase in popularity is reflected in the re-organization of the cult under Claudius (Emperor AD 41–54), although there was probably also a political motive – to counterbalance the favour shown by Gaius, his predecessor, to the worship of Isis. The festival now took place from the 15th to the 27th of March, marking the return of the spring equinox, while the emphasis on Attis and his death and resurrection has the nature of a fertility ritual.

The programme ran as follows:

15 March: *Entrance of the Reed* (*canna intrat*). The Company of Reedbearers (*cannephori*) brought bunches of reeds from the river Almo to the temple on the Palatine. There is doubt about the nature of this rite, but a probable explanation is that it recalled how Cybele found the infant Attis (one ramification of the myth) in a bed of reeds by the river Sangarius in Phrygia. These then aided the high priest (*archigallus*) in sacrificing a six-year-old bull. Then there was a week during which there was abstinence from certain foods for the initiates.

22 March: *Entrance of the Tree* (*arbor intrat*). The Company of Treebearers (*dendrophori*) cut down a pine tree and carried it in procession to the temple. It symbolized the dead Attis and was decked with woollen fillets and crowned with violets.

23 March: *Day of Mourning* (*tristitia*). This was given up to mourning and lamentation for the dead Attis.

24 March: *Day of Blood* (*sanguis*). Those already initiated scourged and wounded themselves until the blood came. The neophytes in a frenzy of enthusiasm used sharp stones to castrate themselves. The pine tree was carried into the inmost sanctuary of the temple, where it remained until the following year. Fasting and lamentation continued all through the night.

25 March: *Day of Rejoicing* (*hilaria*). The high priest announced the resurrection of the dead Attis and there were scenes of wild rejoicing and feasting.

26 March: *Day of Rest* (*requietio*).

27 March: *Day of Lavation* (*lavatio*). The silver statue of the goddess, which had in place of a head the Black Stone originally brought from Pessinus, was carried in triumphant procession, accompanied by the *galli* and their noisy music and a whole host of clergy and temple officials and the general public down to the river Almo, where it was bathed and purified before being returned to the temple.

Claudius, when he re-organized the cult, also relaxed the ban on Roman participation, although castration remained unlawful for citizens. The Companies of Reedbearers and Treebearers, for instance, need no longer be foreigners. Although the new *galli* in their castration underwent a kind of initiation, after which they were totally committed to the service of the goddess, this was not in itself a Mystery, as there was nothing secret about it. Equally public was another ritual, first attested in the West at Puteoli in Italy in AD 143, but becoming increasingly popular for the few who could afford the expense. This was the *taurobolium*. The meaning is unknown, but it could be derived from its two component roots to mean originally 'lassoing of the bull', though this was no part of the developed ritual. The ceremony was also more cheaply performed with a ram, when it was known as *criobolium*.

A detailed description has been left by the Christian poet PRUDENTIUS, 348 to after 405, in his *Crown of Martyrdom*, which relates in Latin verse the stories of various martyrs in earlier centuries. After telling how a Christian called Romulus had his tongue excised so that a flow of blood gushed out, the poet then compared this with the blood that bespattered the man taking part in the *taurobolium*.

Prudentius *Crown of Martyrdom* 10.1011–50

¶ The high priest, to be sure, after a pit has been dug underground, descends into the depths to be consecrated. He wears a strange headband, his temples bound with ritual fillets, then his hair combed back under a golden crown. His silk toga[1] is held up by a Gabine[2] girdle.

    1. *silk toga*: the toga was the conventional Roman robe, but it was normally made of wool. The use of expensive Oriental silk strikes an exotic note.
    2. *Gabine*: the derivation is unknown, but it was a way of wearing the toga on sacrificial occasions.

¶ Above they construct a platform from a layer of planks with gaps where the boards are loosely joined. Then they cut or bore through the floor, using awls to make many perforations in the wood, so that it is opened up by a large number of small holes.

Hither a great bull with a savage and shaggy brow is led, its shoulders or horns garlanded with wreaths of flowers. The victim's brow also gleams with gold and the glitter of the plating colours his bristling hide.

When the beast has been stationed here for sacrifice, they cleave his breast with a consecrated hunting-spear. The wide wound spurts out a tide of boiling blood and pours a steaming flood onto the framework of the underlying bridge and sends out its billows far and wide.

Then the shower makes its way through the many passages of a thousand chinks and rains down its foul dew. This the priest immured below receives, holding his head beneath to catch every drop, so that corruption covers his clothing and his whole body.

Nay more, he bends back his face, offers his cheeks, submits his ears, presents his lips and nostrils and bathes even his very eyes with the flood. Now he does not spare his mouth either and wets his tongue until the whole of him has drunk in the dark blood.

After the blood has been drained and the priests have dragged the stiffening carcass away from the scaffolding, the pontiff comes forth, a horrible sight. He displays his dripping head, his sodden beard, his dank fillets and his soaking clothes.

Defiled as he is with such pollution, filthy with the putrid gore of the victim freshly slain, all hail and reverence him from afar, because the paltry blood of a dead ox has bathed him while he lay concealed in a loathsome pit.

This ceremony was performed for an individual or sometimes 'For the well-being of the Emperor.' In the case of an individual he could regard himself as 'reborn for ten years' or sometimes the inscription runs 'reborn for ever'.

There were also Mysteries proper of which little is known, connected specifically with Attis. CLEMENT OF ALEXANDRIA, *c.* AD 150–215 (p. 59), preserved a formula in his *Exhortation to the Greeks* (cp. the very similar Eleusinian formula quoted on p. 224):

Clement *Exhortation to the Greeks* 2.15

¶ I ate from the tambourine, I drank from the cymbal, I carried the vessel, I entered the bridal chamber.

So like this is the formula preserved in reference to Attis that they probably refer to the same ritual. This is quoted by FIRMICUS MATERNUS, who wrote in AD 347 a Latin treatise, *On the Error of Pagan Religions*, appealing to the Emperors Constantius and Constans to destroy the pagan idols by force. The author is not concerned to give an exhaustive account of paganism, but simply picks out various myths and practices in order to confute them by an appeal to reason and by lengthy quotations from scripture.

Firmicus Maternus *On the Error of Pagan Religions* 18.1

¶ In a certain temple in order that a mortal man may enter the inner sanctum he says: 'I have eaten from the tambourine, I have drunk from the cymbal[1] and I have learnt the religious secrets,' which is in Greek:

'I have eaten from the tambourine, I have drunk from the cymbal, I
have become an initiate of Attis.'

1. The tambourine and cymbal were among the musical instruments
of the cult and therefore fit vessels for a symbolic meal.

Firmicus also describes another ritual of mourning followed by joy,
which may refer to Attis:

*On the Error of Pagan Religions* 22.1

¶ On a certain night a statue is laid face upwards on a couch and is
mourned with lamentations rhythmically uttered by turns. Next, when
they have had their fill of the feigned wailing, a light is brought in.
Then the throats of all the mourners are anointed by the priest and
after this anointing he whispers in a slow murmur:

> 'Take heart initiates; the god has been delivered.
> For we shall have deliverance from troubles.'

Terracotta statuettes of Attis have been found in tombs and it may
reasonably be supposed that the initiate shared in his resurrection.
Cybele, apart from her grim aspect, had the ever popular appeal of
a Mother Goddess. Attis, as time went on, even became a solar deity
and increased immensely in importance under the later period of the
Empire. Both had their worshippers throughout the Empire and
survived until paganism was completely extirpated.

There is much archaeological evidence, coins, remains of temples,
reliefs showing Cybele and her attendant lions and as a fertility goddess.
Attis, always recognizable by his Phrygian cap, is shown as a simple
shepherd or in various poses as a beautiful, effeminate youth. Later both
of them appear in conjunction with heavenly signs and inscriptions
which show the wide dispersion of the cult and how it was favoured
even by the highest in the land.

On the human side there are inscriptions with portraits of priests.
One especially fine example from a small town near Rome is in the
Capitol Museum there. It shows the half-figure of an *archigallus*. The
face is smooth, calm and feminine. The dress is feminine, delicate
swathes of some fine material with long sleeves. Like an Indian sari
it is draped over the head, revealing carefully arranged waves of hair.
Long fillets hang down on either side. There is a headband with a
medallion of Jupiter in the centre and medallions of Attis to right and

left. He wears a necklace and on his breast hangs a pectoral, an image of Attis inside a shrine. In one hand is a pomegranate with three shoots rising from it, in the other a plate of fruit. Over the left shoulder hangs a scourge. In the background are a tambourine and cymbals, a flute, a horn and a casket. This cultic apparatus is counterbalanced by the dispassionate serenity of one wholly committed to the worship of the divinity.

### III   *The Egyptian Cult*

Egypt with its strange tongue, its mighty monuments, its hieroglyphics and animal-headed gods had been alien to the Greek world at large, although it was respected for its antiquity and the reputed learning of its sages. When Ptolemy I, one of Alexander's generals, became its ruler he transferred the capital from Memphis to Alexandria, founded by Alexander in 332 BC. There he wished to organize some common focus of worship for both his Greek and his Egyptian subjects. He therefore imported a new god, not a difficult thing to do, for Egyptians were familiar with the idea that new dynasties favoured each their own special gods. Greeks too, as shown by the ease with which Alexander of Abonutichos introduced a new deity (see p. 216), were not likely to cavil.

TACITUS, late first century AD (p. 16), gives an account which emphasizes the miraculous element necessary to accredit the god.

Tacitus *Hist.* 4.83–4

¶ Where the god came from is a subject that has not yet been treated by Roman authors. According to Egyptian priests, Ptolemy,[1] the first of the Macedonians to consolidate the resources of Egypt, as soon as he had founded Alexandria wanted to add walls and temples and religious cults. In his sleep there appeared to him a youth of outstanding beauty and superhuman stature, who advised him to send his most trusty courtiers to Pontus and fetch his statue: that would bring prosperity to the kingdom, and the habitation which received him would be great and famous. Straightway the youth appeared to rise into heaven surrounded by flames.

1. *Ptolemy*: this was Ptolemy I (*Soter* or Deliverer), who ruled Egypt

from 305 to 282 BC. Tacitus thought of him as the founder of Alexandria because he had done so much to enhance the prestige of the city.

¶ Ptolemy was disturbed by the miraculous omen and revealed his nocturnal vision to the Egyptian priests, who are used to interpreting such things. They had little knowledge of Pontus[1] and foreign parts. So he asked the Eumolpid[2] Timotheus, whom he had brought in to oversee ritual, what cult it was, what deity. Timotheus made enquiries from travellers to Pontus and discovered that there was a city called Sinope and a temple not far off, long famous among the inhabitants, which belonged to Zeus of the underworld; close by there was also a female statue commonly called Proserpina.

Ptolemy however, though easily alarmed as is the nature of kings, when he was released from anxiety gave more heed to his pleasures than to religion. Gradually he thought less of it and turned his mind to other business, until the same apparition now more terrible and more menacing threatened him and his kingdom with destruction, if his commands were not carried out. Then he ordered arrangements to be made for an embassy and gifts to king Scydrothemis and, when the envoys were just about to embark, instructed them to consult Pythian Apollo. They had a prosperous voyage and there was no ambiguity in the answer of the oracle: they were to go on their way and bring back his father's statue and leave behind his sister's.[3]

1. *Pontus*: this kingdom lay on the south coast of the Black Sea.
2. *Eumolpid*: the Athenian clan of the Eumolpidae held the hereditary priesthood which organized the Eleusinian Mysteries.
3. *sister's*: Proserpina was the half-sister of Apollo. Zeus here is thought of as reigning both in the underworld and above, just as Serapis was to combine features of Osiris and Zeus. Pythian Apollo was the god of the Delphic oracle.

¶ When they reached Sinope, they brought to Scydrothemis their king's gifts, entreaties and mandates. He kept on changing his mind, now dreading the divinity, now terrified by threats of popular opposition, often swayed by the envoys' gifts and promises. Meanwhile for a space of three years Ptolemy did not relax his exertions and his entreaties.

He continued to enhance the status of his envoys, the number of ships and the weight of gold. Then Scydrothemis encountered a threatening apparition, forbidding him to delay the god's purpose any longer. While he hesitated, he was harassed by various calamities and diseases and the manifest anger of the gods, from day to day more grievous. He called a public assembly and set forth the god's commands, his own and Ptolemy's visions and the increasing troubles. The common folk repulsed the king, begrudged Egypt, were afraid for themselves and picketed the temple. From this point on, the story is more marvellous, that the god himself embarked of his own accord on board the fleet, which was moored near the shore. Then wonderful to relate, after covering such a vast expanse of sea they reached Alexandria in three days. A temple befitting the greatness of the city was built in a place called Rhacotis, where there had long been a shrine dedicated to Serapis and Isis.

This is the commonest story about the origin and conveyance of the god. I am aware that some say that he was brought from the Syrian city of Seleucia, in the reign of Ptolemy the third.[1] Some ascribe the act to the same Ptolemy, but give Memphis, once famous as the capital of ancient Egypt, as the place from which the god was transferred. Many identify the god himself as Aesculapius, because he heals the sick, some as Osiris, a very ancient divinity of those peoples, a larger number as Jupiter because he holds power over all things, the vast majority as father Dis[2] because of the attributes[3] with which he is symbolically depicted.

1. *Ptolemy*: this was Ptolemy III who reigned from 246 to 221 BC.
2. *Dis*: this old Latin name for God came to be attached to the god of the underworld.
3. *attributes*: he was sometimes depicted with a dog (Cerberus, guardian of Hades) and a snake.

PLUTARCH, first century AD (p. 72) contemporary with Tacitus, told the same tale in *On Isis and Osiris* 28, but in his version two courtiers, when they heard of the dream, went to Sinope and simply stole the statue. Also, according to him, Ptolemy took counsel with Manetho, the Egyptian priest and historian (p. 38). So he had the benefit of advice from experts in both Egyptian and Greek ritual. The new god, Serapis or Sarapis, took over the attributes of both Zeus and the Egyptian Osiris. A magnificent statue by the Greek sculptor Bryaxis acted as model for countless others, such as the majestic head found in the London Mithraeum and now to be seen in the Museum of London. The god is bearded and carries on his head a *modius*, a basket filled with fruits and wreathed with olive branches. Another innovation was that hymns in honour of the gods were now composed in Greek.

The native gods, except for Anubis, the faithful retainer of Isis, who always kept the head of a dog or jackal, were either passed over or completely anthropomorphized and so became more acceptable in a Greek environment. The chief of these were Isis and Osiris. Plutarch wrote a treatise *On Isis and Osiris*, which is a vast and rambling compilation of complicated learning. FIRMICUS MATERNUS, fourth century Christian (p. 234), gives a simpler account of the mythology in *On the Error of Pagan Religions*:

Firmicus Maternus *On the Error of Pagan Religions* 2.1–3

❡ The inhabitants of Egypt, receiving the benefits of water, worship water, pray to water, venerate water with continuous and superstitious supplications. But in their sacred rites which they call Mysteries they add tragic deaths and deadly quarrels ending in fearful calamity, incest committed with a sister and adultery and the husband's punishment of this crime with severe penalties. Isis is the sister, Osiris the brother, Tyfon the husband. When he learnt that Isis had been seduced by her brother's incestuous passion he killed Osiris, tore him limb from limb and cast forth the quivering limbs of the wretched corpse all along the banks of the river Nile. Isis deserted Tyfon and in order to bury one who was both her lover and her husband she enlisted the help of her sister Nepthus and the hound Anubis, who was given a dog's head because he found the parts of the torn body by the craft of a dog on the trail. When Osiris had thus been found Isis buried him. These [Osiris and Tyfon] were indeed alike in exercising kingship and dominion over Egypt, but Osiris was righteous apart from that offence with his sister, Tyfon was furious, uncontrolled and arrogant. Therefore the former is revered and the latter shunned.

Firmicus does not mention that Osiris then reigned as king among the dead nor that Isis bore a son, Horus or Harpocrates. He is a minor figure, but sometimes appears as a child or as a babe in arms.

Long before Rome had much contact with Egypt these deities were revered in Greece and the Greek cities of Asia Minor, where their worship was spread by traders, mercenaries, priests and travellers. The cult had spread to the Greek cities of Italy in the second century and at last reached Rome. Here Isis soon became popular, especially with ladies of the demi-monde. Many of these would be freedwomen or of freedwomen stock, without links with the gods of the Roman establishment. In a man's world they were doubtless attracted by a kindly, motherly, powerful goddess, whose support could be assured by adhering to all the purificatory rituals prescribed (see below).

OVID, 43 BC to AD 18 (p. 64), advising a young man where to look for a girl wrote in *Art of Love*:

Ovid *Art of Love* 1.77–8

❡ Do not shun the Memphian temple of the linen-clad heifer;[1] she makes many women what she herself was to Jupiter.

    1. *linen-clad heifer*: the epithet describing her priests has been transferred to the goddess, whom Ovid has confused with the Greek Io, as Isis was sometimes depicted with horns. Io was loved by Zeus, but was transformed by his jealous wife into a white heifer and goaded on by a gadfly, until her frenzied wandering ended in Egypt. There she was turned back into human shape and bore him a son.

JUVENAL (p. 32) too, almost a century later, wrote:

Juvenal *Satires* 2.6.487–9

❡ Suppose that she has made an assignation and wants to be decked out more becomingly than usual and is in a hurry and is expected already in the gardens or, more likely, in the temple of the Isiac bawd.

Because of this connection the goddess had an unsavoury reputation and there was also the political prejudice excited by Cleopatra VII, so that four times between 58 and 48 BC the senate ordered her shrines and statues in Rome to be destroyed, but they always re-appeared. Augustus (Emperor 27 BC to AD 14), that staunch conservationist of traditional Roman religion, no doubt applauded the patriotic fervour of VIRGIL (p. 206), when in the *Aeneid* he depicted on Aeneas' shield the future battle of Actium:

Virgil *Aeneid* 8.696–700

¶ In the centre the queen[1] with her native rattle[2] calls upon the ranks and does not yet see the twin snakes behind her. Monstrous gods of every kind and barking Anubis are in arms against Neptune and Venus and Minerva.

    1. *queen*: Cleopatra and Antony were decisively defeated by Octavian at Actium in 31 BC and after fleeing to Egypt she committed suicide from snake-bite.
    2. *rattle*: this was a bronze instrument, like the rattle of a football fan, whirled in accompaniment of ritual. It is often known by the technical term *sistrum*.

    Under Tiberius too the nasty scandal of an Egyptian priest who had tricked a noble Roman lady (p. 103) had led to government action. Gaius however (Emperor AD 37–41), probably sensing popular demand, built a great temple for the goddess in the Campus Martius, which was further embellished by Domitian (Emperor 81–96). JUVENAL (p. 32) described the hold which by now the cult had obtained even over respectable Roman ladies, in his catalogue of the frailties of women:

Juvenal *Satires* 2.6.522–41

¶ In winter she will break the ice and go down into the river. In the early morning three times will she immerse herself in the Tiber and bathe her timid head to the tips of her hair. Then stripped and trembling she will crawl on bleeding knees the whole length of the proud king's[1] field. If white Io commands, she will go to the land of Egypt and bring warm water sought from Meroe,[2] to sprinkle it in the temple of Isis, which rises next to the ancient sheepfold.[3] She believes that she is advised by the voice of the queen herself. A likely sort of soul and intellect for the gods to converse with by night! Therefore he earns the chief and highest honour who speeds surrounded by a herd linen-clad and bald, Anubis[4] mocking the mourning[5] throng. He begs pardon, as often as the wife does not abstain from sex on days to be observed as sacred and a great penalty must be paid for profanation of the coverlet and the silver serpent has been seen to have moved its head. His tears and studied mutterings prevail upon Osiris not to refuse pardon for her guilt, Osiris bribed[6] forsooth by a big goose and a little cake.

1. *proud king*: the Campus Martius, where the temple stood, was said to have been occupied by the legendary 'Tarquin the Proud'.

2. *Meroe*: this was an island in the Nile.

3. *sheepfold*: in early days under the Republic this was a voting enclosure for the common folk.

4. *Anubis*: he was impersonated by a priest wearing the mask of a dog. Linen garments and shaven heads were a distinguishing mark of the Egyptian priesthood.

5. *mourning*: Isis was supposed to be mourning for the death of Osiris.

6. *bribed*: the priests would receive gifts on the god's behalf.

The cult was meticulously organized, as in Egypt, with a hierarchy of full-time priests and priestesses and minor temple attendants. The priests alone knew the proper litany, which was an essential part of the service. Every morning there was a ceremonial opening of the temple, the sacred fire was kindled, there were libations of Nile water and hymns were sung to the accompaniment of flutes and rattles. The officiating priest invoked the god in the Egyptian tongue. Next came the robing and adornment of the statue by special bands of *dressers* and *adorners*, for devotees contributed rich robes and jewels. All day spectators could enter and stand in mute adoration until the ceremonial closing of the temple.

There were other more public rites on fixed days in the year. Apuleius gives a most vivid description of the *Ship of Isis* at Corinth on 15 March at the start of the sailing season, when a ship was hauled in procession down to the sea with pageantry and revelry and carnival.

There were Mysteries too, on a Greek model, for the ancient Egyptians were more concerned with rites to be performed with the mummification of the corpse and the provision of grave furniture to serve in the after-life.

APULEIUS, AD 123 to *c*. 185 (p. 56) in Book 11 of his *Metamorphoses* (*The Golden Ass*) is our chief source for the Egyptian Mysteries.

*Metamorphoses* 11.5; 15; 23–5

Lucius, the ass, had been brought by his master to Corinth for the great festival of Isis, when, to mark the beginning of the sailing season, there was a procession through the city and a ship was dragged down to be launched. He had managed to get away by night to the lonely beach and there prayed to Isis, who rose from the waves in full splendour, crowned with flowers, wearing a multi-coloured robe under a dark iridescent upper-garment. In her right hand she carried a bronze rattle, in her left a small golden cup. Her feet were shod with sandals made from leaves of victorious palm. She addressed him:

¶ 'Lo, here I am, Lucius, moved by your prayers, begetter of the universe, mistress of all the elements, original offspring of the ages, greatest of divinities, queen of the dead, first of the heavenly beings, one uniform shape of gods and goddesses, governing by my nod the luminous heights of heaven, the health-giving sea breezes, the dreadful silence of the underworld. My sole divinity is worshipped under many forms by the whole world, with varying ritual and under manifold names.'

A catalogue, similar to others found elsewhere, follows of the different goddesses with whom she is identified by different nations. She tells him that next day in the procession her priest, forewarned by her, will carry a wreath of roses – Lucius had known from the beginning of his enchantment that a rose was the antidote, but had never been able to find one. He is to eat one and will regain his natural shape. All falls out as she had foretold. The priest had brought a garment to cover his nakedness and then addresses him:

¶ 'After experiencing many sufferings of various kinds, driven by great storms of Fortune and mighty gales, you have at last, Lucius, reached the haven of Quiet and the altar of Mercy. Neither your birth nor your status nor the very learning by which you have made your mark have availed you at all, but in the prurience of your green and tender youth you stooped to slavish pleasures and obtained a hurtful recompense for your unfortunate curiosity. The blindness of Fortune, while tormenting you with the worst of dangers, by her unforeseeing malignity has brought you to a religious blessedness. Let her now depart and rage with her utmost fury and seek another object for her cruelty. Hostile chance has no scope against those whose lives our majestic goddess has claimed for her service. What profit to nefarious Fortune[1] were bandits, wild beasts, mazes of the roughest of roads returning to their starting point, fear of death every day? You have now come under the protection of a Fortune, but a Fortune that has sight, who by the splendour of her light illuminates the other gods also. Now put on a gladder look to match your white clothing and with fresh gait[2] accompany the procession of the saving goddess. Let the irreligious see, let them see and recognize their error: "Lo and behold, Lucius freed from former woes by the providence of great Isis triumphs over his Fortune." However, in order to be safer and better fortified, enrol yourself in this sacred army, whose oath of fealty you were not previously invited to take. Now dedicate yourself to allegiance to our religion and willingly submit to the yoke of its service. For when you begin to serve the goddess, you will better appreciate the enjoyment of your freedom.'

1. *nefarious Fortune*: this brings out poignantly how a man might feel himself utterly at the mercy of an irresponsible and even malignant Fortune, which had subjected him to the bandits etc. described in the preceding account of Lucius' adventures while he was an ass.

2. *fresh gait*: i.e. no longer an ass but as a man.

Lucius now hired a lodging inside the temple precincts and every morning joined the throng of worshippers who hymned the goddess when the white curtains had been pulled back to disclose her statue and the priest was going round tending her altars. In nightly visions the goddess urged him to take the further step of being initiated in her Mysteries. At first he hung back, but gradually became more and more eager, until at length he approached the priest. The latter told him he must wait until the goddess herself designated a particular day and a particular priest and the expenses necessary for the ceremony. Eventually both Lucius and the priest received the divine sanction in dreams on the same night. The priest showed him certain books in hieroglyphics in an inner shrine and told him what to buy for carrying out the initiation.

¶ Then at the due time, as the priest said, he led me attended by a crowd of the faithful to the nearest baths. First he consigned me to the usual bath, after praying for the divine favour, then besprinkled[1] and cleansed me most purely and brought me back to the temple. Two-thirds of the day were now over. He stationed me at the very feet of the goddess and after secretly giving me certain instructions, surpassing utterance, he clearly commanded me, with all to witness, all through the next ten days to hold in check the pleasures of the table, to eat no animal flesh and drink no wine. These I duly observed with reverential continence. Now the divinely appointed day was at hand and the curved sun was entering evening. Then behold! crowds of the faithful thronged on every side honouring me by ancient ritual, each with various gifts. Next after all the profane² had been removed to a distance the priest clothed me in a simple linen garment, took my hand and led me into the inmost part of the actual sanctuary.

1. *besprinkled*: in this ritual cleansing and other preparations the Isiac Mysteries resembled others (p. 232).
2. *profane*: this does not mean expulsion of the impious, but a proclamation ordering the uninitiated to depart.

❡ Perhaps you may ask with some anxiety, zealous reader, what was said next, what done; I would say, if it were permissible to say; you should know, if it were permissible to hear. But ears and tongues would both suffer alike for their rash curiosity. Yet I will not torment you with protracted torture, when you are perhaps in suspense through a religious longing. So hear, but believe, what is true. I approached the border of death and after treading the threshold of Proserpina¹ and passing through all the elements I returned. At midnight I saw the sun gleaming with bright light, I publicly approached the gods below and the gods above and worshipped them at closer quarters. Behold! I have told you what, although you have heard it, you must yet needs fail to understand.

1. *Proserpina*: this was the Latin name of Persephone, carried off by Pluto to become queen of the underworld.

❡ Therefore I will tell you what alone can without guilt be reported for the understanding of the uninitiated. By early morning it was over and after the solemn rites I came forth consecrated by twelve robes, a garb that was religious enough, but there is nothing to prevent me from speaking of it, because at that time many spectators were present. In the very middle of the temple a wooden dais was set up before the statue of the goddess. Under orders I kept my linen garment, but was conspicuous because of my brightly embroidered vestment. From my shoulders over my back a precious cloak hung down as far as my heels. Wherever you looked, I was distinguished by animals of various colours depicted around it; on this side were Indian serpents, on that side Hyperborean[1] griffins,[2] which another world produces in the likeness of a feathered bird. The devotees call this the Olympian robe. In my right hand I carried a torch in full flame and my head was garlanded with a beautiful wreath of shining palm leaves projecting like rays. When I had been adorned in this way like the Sun and set up like a statue, the curtains were suddenly drawn back and the public wandered round to look. Next I celebrated my festive birthday within the sacred rites and there was a delightful dinner and merry feasting. The third day too was celebrated with a similar ceremonial ritual. There was a religious morning meal and the appointed completion of the initiation. After this I stayed there for a few days enjoying the inexplicable pleasure of the divine image.

1. *Hyperborean*: these were a legendary people, supposed to live a life of great blessedness in the far north.
2. *griffins*: these too were imaginary, generally depicted with a lion's body, but an eagle's beak and wings.

Eventually he went to Rome and then:

¶ My chief pursuit was to offer daily prayer to the greatest divinity, the power of queen Isis who, under the name of *Campensis*[1] because of the situation of the temple, is worshipped with the utmost veneration. In short I was an assiduous worshipper, a foreigner indeed to the shrine, but a native in religion.

1. *Campensis*: this means *of the plain*. Her old temple in Rome was in the Campus Martius, the plain of Mars, which contained many temples.

After about a year and a half he received divine admonition that he ought also to be initiated in the rites of Osiris. Even though he had to sell his clothes to defray the necessary expenses he complied. After a little while he was ordered to become an initiate of Isis yet again and this time he jibbed, doubting the good faith of the two former priests who, he felt, must have left something undone, but a vision of the goddess reassured him. (These two later initiations are not described in any detail.) Thanks to the gods' care he now had a successful legal practice. Finally even the great god Osiris himself appeared in a dream and singled him out from the common throng of worshippers by giving him a minor office in his entourage.

*Metamorphoses* 11.30

¶ In short I shaved my head and, for all to see, did not conceal or cover my baldness,[1] but continued in the joyful performance of the duties of that most ancient college,[2] founded in the famous days of Sulla.[3]

1. *baldness*: these words, the last in the book, recognize a minor inconvenience. Full-time Egyptian priests were conspicuous because of their typically Egyptian linen clothing and shaven heads and probably received the respect due to holy men. The ordinary worshipper was not subject to food restrictions and had no distinguishing outward mark, but a lay-brother, so to speak, was recognizable by his shaven head. This did not carry the same social stigma as circumcision. By the second century AD Isiac religion was widespread and enjoyed imperial favour. The initiate had no difficulty in accepting the traditional state religion and imperial godhead as well, since he believed that the great gods Isis and Osiris subsumed in themselves all minor manifestations of divinity.

2. *college*: this refers to the college of *pastophori*; their function was on certain occasions to carry around miniature shrines of the goddess.

3. *Sulla*: he was born about 138 BC and died in 78, well known as a most successful general, also a statesman and for a time Dictator.

These initiations were selective. There is not only the evidence of Apuleius, but inscriptions on temple walls record that initiations took place, 'from a vision' or 'from an intimation'. In any case expenses had to be incurred. There was that festive meal, a very enjoyable social occasion for others than the one who had just been initiated.

A ritual in connection with Osiris, which by its content was originally esoteric, had by the time of Plutarch in the late first century AD become a recognized public ceremonial. It was held from 26 October to 23 November every year and was described by FIRMICUS MATERNUS, writing in the early fourth century:

*On the Error of Pagan Religions 2.3*

❡ This is the sum total of Isiac ritual. In the shrine they have an idol of
Osiris entombed. This they bewail with annual mourning, shave their
heads in order to lament the pitiable fate of their king by shamefully
disfiguring their head, beat their breasts, lacerate their arms and cut open
the scars of old wounds so that by the annual mourning the hurt of
his deadly and pitiable slaughter may be renewed. When they have done
this for a certain number of days, then they pretend to look for the
remains of the torn body and when they have found them they rejoice
as if their mourning had been set at rest.

[The author after a long polemic urges his readers to seek the way
of true salvation and then, like the worshippers of Osiris, cry aloud:]
'We have found, we rejoice together.'

Osiris was essentially the god of the underworld, reigning as he had
reigned in life, and could give his devotees life too, not as pale shades,
but sharing life with him. There are many tomb inscriptions such as:

From Kaibel, *Inscriptiones Graecae* 14.1488, 1782

❡ Take courage with Osiris.
May Osiris give you cold water.[1]

1. *cold water*: an inestimable boon to desert travellers.

Serapis, so confusingly blended with Osiris, was like him shown as
the consort of Isis. He was a god who not only had healing powers,
but also could be identified with Zeus/Jupiter himself. Isis was the great
goddess who had bands of hymn-writers attached to her temples to
detail her virtues. She was a 'lady of countless names', 'one who is all
things'. In literature and statuary she was sometimes identified with
Fortune, but a kindly Fortune. Usually the emphasis is on her role as
a mother, sometimes a nursing mother. She and Serapis lent themselves
to syncretism. Archaeological evidence shows that the Egyptian cults
were widespread, both in the West and the East. They reached the
height of their importance towards the end of the second century AD,
after which solar monotheism came to the fore; but their appeal
continued until the end of paganism, when the destruction of the great
temple of Serapis in Alexandria in 391 was a landmark in the campaign
of militant Christianity.

## IV  *Mithraism*

Mithras was originally a minor Persian deity. He fought on the side of Ahura-Mazda, the great and good god of light, in the eternal battle against Ahriman, the evil one who was the god of darkness. As such, he figured in the hymns of Sanskrit scriptures. His cult spread in Asia Minor, as is shown by the use of his name as an element in the names of kings of Pontus, Cappadocia, Armenia and Commagene, e.g. the notorious Mithridates of Pontus, 120–63 BC. In the first century BC he was depicted, among other greater deities, on a bas-relief of the mausoleum of Antiochus I of Commagene at Nemroud Dagh in the Taurus mountains as shaking hands with the king over an altar.

He is first mentioned in the West by PLUTARCH, second half of the first century AD (p. 72):

### Plutarch *Life of Pompey* 24

¶ They themselves[1] offered strange sacrifices on Mount Olympus and conducted certain secret rites or religious mysteries, among which those of Mithras have been preserved to our own time, after being previously instituted by them.

   1. *They themselves*: this refers to the Cilician pirates whom Pompey rooted out in 67 BC.

No more is heard of Mithras until the time of STATIUS, *c.* AD 45–96. In his epic poem *Thebais*, written in Latin on the expedition of the Seven against Thebes, he followed a common literary device and invoked Phoebus, asking the god by what name he should be called:

### Statius *Thebais* 717–19

¶ Or is it better to be addressed as Osiris, bringer of harvest, or as Mithras who beneath the rocks of a Persian cave twists the unyielding horns?

   Clearly Statius assumes that this reference to Mithras and his slaying of the bull (see below p. 251) would require no explanation for his readers. From this period dates the first known inscription to him. Literary evidence is scarce and comes largely from prejudiced Christian sources. Christians however, if writing before the downfall of paganism, could have got their information from pagan converts, who thought themselves absolved from their oath of secrecy; in any case they were unlikely to indulge in the wilder flights of fancy, as later writers did, while there were still influential Mithraists extant to rebut them. As it was truly a Mystery cult, there were no public celebrations or processions to elicit incidental comment.

There is an abundance of archaeological evidence. When all the data are compared the following general conclusions emerge. Mithraic temples were small, windowless and rectangular, a long narrow nave with stone benches along the walls to right and left, often with an apse at one end. There might also be one or two smaller rooms. There was an altar and sometimes a spring. The ceiling was vaulted and might be painted to represent the vault of heaven. When possible, the shrine was in an actual cave or at least underground. The focal point was a representation on the rear wall of Mithras killing the bull, carved in stone or painted or moulded in stucco. This was accompanied by scenes of other exploits of the god or external mythological events which had made their way into the cult. Usually the decor was austere and simple, but there could be frescoes on the side walls and mosaic on the pavement.

The following cycle of events (not all found everywhere) can be traced:

1   Creation of the universe.
2   Reign of Saturn/Kronos, often shown holding a sickle.
3   The war of Jupiter against the Giants.
4   Jupiter enthroned among the other Olympians.
5   The birth of Mithras. This was celebrated every year on 25 December, after the winter solstice. The god is born from a rock, sometimes as a child, sometimes as an adult carrying a torch or a knife. He is also shown emerging from an egg; there are examples of this at Gloucester and at Housesteads on Hadrian's Wall. Shepherds may be spectators of the birth. This was an important event and is often found in a prominent position.

JUSTIN, c. 100–65 (p. 160) referred to it in his *Apology*:

Justin *Apology* 1.66.4

¶ Those who transmit the mysteries of Mithras say that he was born from a rock and call the place where they traditionally initiate those who believe in him a cave.

FIRMICUS MATERNUS (p. 234) in his *On the Errors of Pagan Religions* (c. 347) quoted an invocation:

*On the Errors of Pagan Religions* 20.1

¶ 'God from the rock.'

> 6 Mithras standing or seated upon a rock shoots an arrow towards a rock or cloud. From this there pours a shower of water into the cupped hands of two men below. The beneficent god is delivering mankind from a drought.
> 7 Preparation for the bull-slaying. Mithras is shown hunting the bull, finally catching it and riding it.

FIRMICUS MATERNUS referred to this:

*On the Errors of Pagan Religions* 5.2

¶ Worshipping a cattle-rustler they transfer his rites to the power of fire, as his prophet has handed down to us, saying:

'O novice in the theft of the bull, initiate of the glorious father.'

Him they call Mithras and they hand on his rites in hidden caves so that always sunk in the concealing squalor of the darkness they may avoid the loveliness of the shining and serene light.

> 8 Mithras carries the bull on his shoulders to a cave.
> 9 The bull-slaying. This was the most important event in the series. Details vary, but Mithras always wears Persian dress (a cap or tiara like the Phrygian cap of Attis, long trousers and tunic and mantle). His clothing is often red and the bull white. He has two attendants similarly dressed named Cautes and Cautopates, who stand cross-legged, one on either side of him. Cautes holds a flaming torch upwards symbolizing sunrise, Cautopates a torch pointing downwards to symbolize sunset. There is a similar symbolism in heads of Sun and Moon to right and left above.
> Mithras kneels upon the bull and plunges his knife into it. He looks sorrowful as he does so. Sometimes a raven in the region of the Sun is a messenger from the Sun. A dog and a snake are licking up the bull's blood and sometimes an ear of corn springs from his tail. An evil scorpion attacks the bull's testicles. It is deduced that Mithras by his unwilling slaughter of the bull has released fertility and new life. Spiritually this could mean new life in the hereafter, as attested by a verse from the Sancta Prisca Mithraeum in Rome, AD 202:

From Vermaseren *Corpus Inscriptionum et Monumentorum Religionis Mithriacae* (*CIMRM*) 1.485

¶ And you saved us by having shed the eternal blood.

This scene, carved in relief, was found in the Wallbrook excavations in the Mithraeum there and may be seen in the Museum of London. It contains the essential features described above, but the bull-slaying is enclosed in a circular band containing the signs of the Zodiac. The four corners of the rectangular slab are occupied at the top by Sun and Moon driving chariots, the former upwards and the latter downwards, at the bottom by busts of two wind gods. There is also in the Museum of London an exceptionally fine marble head of Mithras.

> 10   Treaty between the Sun and Mithras. Sometimes the former kneels before the latter, sometimes they pledge with a handshake.
>
> 11   A sacred meal of the Sun and Mithras in a cave, an important event. This may also be symbolized by human participants wearing masks. Lower grades of initiates. Ravens and Lions, wait upon them.

JUSTIN knew of this too, for in his *Apology* he writes in reference to the Christian Eucharist:

*Apology* 1.66.4

¶ In imitation of this the evil demons have made it a traditional rite in the mysteries of Mithras. For you either know or can learn that bread and a cup of water are set out in the initiation rites along with various explanations.

> 12   Ascent into heaven. The Sun helps Mithras to mount into his chariot and both leave the earth together.
>
> The last three episodes can be seen beneath the weathered relief of the bull-slaying found at York and now in the Yorkshire Museum.

Mithras is sometimes also shown as a hunter. With faithful animals such as the lion and dog he hunts down hurtful animals that could be associated with evil. A relief from a Mithraeum in Germany brings in the myth of Phaethon who, driving the chariot of his father the Sun, could not control the fiery horses so that the earth would have been burnt up, if Zeus had not intervened by killing him with a thunderbolt. From this it has been deduced that Mithraism had been influenced by Stoicism and had introduced a final conflagration into its mythology. Two lines from Santa Prisca in Rome run:

From Vermaseren *CIMRM* 1. 485

¶ Accept, O Holy Father, accept the incense-bearing Lions,
Through whom we offer the incense, through whom we ourselves are consumed.

Initiation was confined to men, who knew each other as *brothers*. There were seven grades, each associated with a particular heavenly body. JEROME, *c.* 342–420, the Christian saint and scholar who compiled the Latin Vulgate, in a *Letter to Laeta*, 107, listed these and his list has now been confirmed by the archaeological evidence. What is given below is based on the frescoes at Santa Prisca and the mosaic floor of the Mithraeum of Felicissimus at Ostia, which shows the symbols associated with each grade.

> 1  Raven (*corvus*) has the emblems of a cup and a *caduceus*, the staff entwined by a serpent which is the attribute of Mercury. The cup is there because it was his function to serve this at the banquet. In the fresco his picture has been lost.
>
> 2  Bride (*nymphus*) has a long yellow veil over his head and carries a lamp. His emblems are a lamp and a decorated diadem, symbolizing Venus.

A formula quoted by FIRMICUS may refer to him:

*On the Errors of Pagan Religions* 19.1

¶ 'Hail bride, hail new light.'

The Greek feminine noun for *bride* has been given a masculine ending. The initiate wears a bridal veil and under the auspices of Venus, goddess of love, is entering into a closer relationship with Mithras.

> 3  Soldier (*miles*) is dressed in brown and has a soldier's knapsack slung over his left shoulder. At Ostia his emblems are a knapsack, a helmet and spear to signify Mars. Some inscriptions call one who had reached this grade 'pure' or 'devout' or 'loyal'.
>
> 4  Lion (*leo*) wears a long scarlet cloak. His emblems were a fire shovel, a rattle (probably to whirl during rites) and a thunderbolt, the symbol of Jupiter.
>
> 5  Persian (*Perses*) is dressed in a grey tunic and carries long twigs, perhaps ears of corn. His emblems were a sickle and a scythe. A star in an inverted crescent symbolized the Moon.
>
> 6  Courier of the Sun (*heliodromus*) wears a red garment with a yellow belt. In his hand he clasps a blue globe. His emblems were a lighted torch, a radiate crown and a whip. He is under the protection of the Sun.
>
> 7  Father (*pater*), like Mithras, wears a red robe and a pointed cap. His emblems were the Phrygian cap of Mithras, a staff and ring and a sickle, symbol of Saturn. From various inscriptions we learn that he has been chosen by his fellow initiates, dispenses initiation, is the high priest, has studied astrology, is 'most pious', 'most worthy', 'A Father of the Fathers from amongst the ten superiors'.

As for the process of initiation, it seems that those who wished to undergo it had a period of instruction first. TERTULLIAN, *c.*

160–220, the African scholar and author of many theological works, himself a Christian convert, stated:

*To the Gentiles* 1.7

¶ There is no doubt that those who wish to be initiated first approach the Master of Sacred Rites or Father.

A papyrus reveals that before initiation the novice took a solemn oath to reveal nothing. Certainly ordeals of some kind were involved, as witness *Suidas*, the tenth century lexicon (p. 61), under the heading *Mithras*:

*Suidas* M 1045

¶ Nobody could be initiated if he did not undergo a number of ordeals and show himself sanctified and thus impervious.

In the wall-paintings of the Mithraeum at Capua, preserved in a rather fragmentary condition, an initiate may be seen naked and blindfolded. He kneels and another figure stands over him and a sword or stick lies on the ground. This is perhaps to be linked with the information given by the PSEUDO-AUGUSTINE fourth century work, *Against the Pagans*:

*Against the Pagans* 5

¶ What sort of mockery is it that is played out blindfold in a cave? They are blindfolded that they may not shrink in horror from their shameful degradation. Moreover some flap their wings like birds and mimic the sound of a raven; others growl like lions; some have their hands tied together with chicken guts and are thrown down upon small pits full of water. Somebody approaches with a sword and cuts through the guts mentioned above, calling himself a liberator.

There may have been a mock murder. In the *Life of Commodus* (Emperor 180–92), included in the fourth century compilation, SCRIPTORES HISTORIAE AUGUSTAE (p. 84) it is stated:

*Life of Commodus* 9

¶ He defiled the Mithraic rites with a genuine murder when in the rite something is regularly represented by word or deed so as to inspire a kind of fear.

A sword had some part in the initiation of the grade of Soldier, according to TERTULLIAN:

*On the Crown 15*

❡ His [i.e. Christ's] fellow-soldiers should blush, for they are now to stand condemned not by him, but by a Soldier of Mithras. When he is being initiated in a cave, the very camp of darkness, a crown is offered to him on the point of a sword and, as if in mimicry of martyrdom,[1] he is instructed to push it away just when it is being fitted to his head and to transfer it as if by chance to his shoulder, saying that Mithras is his crown. After this he never wears a crown again and has this sign as evidence if there is any test in connection with his military oath, for he is immediately recognized as a soldier of Mithras if he rejects the crown, saying that it rests in his god.

1. *martyrdom*: this treatise had been written because a Christian soldier had refused to wear a laurel wreath which soldiers wore when they were about to receive an imperial bounty. He had explained this by declaring that he was a Christian, which had led to his trial and martyrdom.

Branding was one part of the ordeals. GREGORY OF NAZIANZUS, 329–89, the Cappadocian saint and theologian, in *Against Julian I*, reproached Julian (Emperor 361–63, 'the Apostate') for admiring:

Gregory of Nazianzus *Against Julian I 97*

❡ The ordeals in Mithraic ritual and the due branding of the initiates.

TERTULLIAN may refer to this:

*On the Prescription of Heretics 40*

❡ Mithras seals his soldiers' foreheads.

There is archaeological evidence from portraits showing brand or tattoo marks on the forehead. Whether this occurred specifically in the initiation of the Soldier is debateable. Tertullian may have been referring to Mithras' soldiers in general, for initiation by fire seems more applicable to the grade of the Lion. He wore a red cloak and a fire shovel was among his emblems. There is also the evidence of

PORPHYRY, AD 232/3 to *c.* 305, the very influential Neo-Platonic scholar and mystic, who wrote:

### On the Cave of the Nymphs 15–16

¶ The theologians employ honey for many varied symbols, because it consists of many powers, especially of the power to cleanse and preserve. By means of honey many things remain uncorrupted and lingering wounds are cleansed by honey. It is sweet to the taste and gathered from flowers by bees which, as it happens, are generated from cattle. Therefore whenever in the initiation of Lions they pour honey for washing the hands instead of water, they order them to keep their hands clean from all that is painful, hurtful and vile. As becomes an initiate, fitting ablutions are used, since fire is cleansing, and water is rejected because it is hostile to fire. They also cleanse his tongue with honey from all that is sinful. But whenever they bring honey to the Perses as a guardian of fruits, they symbolize its preservative quality.

The connection of Mithraism with astrology has already been shown. It seems that in initiation the soul was to pass through the seven spheres each connected with a planet. Ascent was by a kind of ladder, composed of a different metal in each stage, until the supreme heaven was reached. In its passage the soul divested itself of the passions and faculties peculiar to each planet, which it had gathered in its original descent from the heavens to earth at birth. Bronze amulets in the shape of ladders have been found in tombs and Porphyry described the Mithraic worshippers in the cave:

### On the Cave of the Nymphs 6

¶ Bearing symbols of the planets and of ladders.

The chief literary evidence comes from CELSUS, late second century AD (p. 60), quoted by Origen:

### Origen *c. Celsum* 6.22

¶ Celsus, wishing to show off his erudition in his treatise against us, also describes certain Persian mysteries. 'This is the riddling meaning of the Persian teaching and of the Mithraic initiation which they practise. In the latter there is a kind of symbol of the two celestial orbits, one stationary and the other assigned to the planets, and of the soul's passage through them. There is a ladder with seven gates and at the top an eighth gate. The first of the gates is of lead, the second of tin, the third of bronze, the fourth of iron, the fifth of an alloy, the sixth of silver, the seventh of gold. They assign the first to Kronos [Saturn], symbolizing by the lead the slowness of the star, the second to Aphrodite, comparing with her the brightness and softness of tin, the solid one with a bronze base to Zeus, the fourth to Hermes, since both Hermes and iron can stand all kinds of work and promote commerce and are hardened to toil, the fifth, the uneven and variable product of mixing, to Ares, the sixth, the silver one, to the Moon, the seventh, the golden one, to the Sun, in imitation of their colours.

Another sign of the close connection of the cult with astrology is the statue, often found in Mithraea, of Aion (infinite time), an originally Persian figure, hellenized as Kronos or Saturn. He generally appears with a human body, but a lion's head, and with four wings, symbolizing the winds. A snake, sometimes decorated with the signs of the Zodiac, entwines his body. This snake is sometimes found entwining the body of Mithras.

Mention should be made of a magical papyrus, which the German scholar A. Dieterich identified as a *Mithras Liturgy*. He did not deny that many magical terms had crept in, for the appendix in particular is pure magic telling how to obtain fortune-telling from the god when once he had appeared, but he maintained that it represented the initiation whereby a man came to apprehension of Mithras. It starts with an invocation by the man who is about to perform the initiation:

### From the *Mithras Liturgy*

¶ Be gracious to me, Providence and Fortune, if I describe these first traditional Mysteries, immortality for my son alone, a worthy initiate in this power of yours, which the great god, the Sun Mithras, gave orders should be imparted to me, so that I alone, an eagle, might traverse the heavens and look down on all things.

First the initiate must utter an invocation to the four elements, all interspersed with much unintelligible gibberish, of a type usual in magical papyri, then continuing:

¶ For I, born mortal of a mortal womb, sublimated by mighty power and an imperishable right hand, today with immortal spirit am going to view with immortal eyes the immortal Aion,[1] Lord of the fiery crowns, when I am sanctified with holy sanctification and my mortal spiritual power is sanctified for a little while, which I shall receive back again after the present bitter necessity[2] which besets me. ... Draw a breath three times, as deeply as you can, and you will see yourself levitating and rising on high, so that you will think yourself in the midst of the air. You will hear no man or beast, nor in that hour will you see anything of things mortal on earth, but all that you will see is immortal. For you will see the divine ordering of that day and hour, the presiding[3] gods rising into heaven and others descending. ... You will see the gods gazing intently at you and advancing towards you. Immediately put your right finger on your mouth and say.... Then whistle.... Then hiss.... Then you will see the gods eying you kindly and no longer advancing towards you, but going about their own business.

    1. *Aion*: see above (p. 257) for the connection of Aion with Mithras.
    2. *necessity*: this is the constraint of life in the body.
    3. *presiding*: this refers to the astrological belief that planets in the ascendant rule the destiny of each day.

After this there is a clap of thunder and fiery doors open in heaven:

¶ You will see the world of the gods, which is inside the doors, so that for the pleasure and joy of the sight your spirit will follow and rise up. Immediately avert your eyes from the divine and draw breath. When your soul has regained its composure, say: 'Approach, Lord....' When you have said this, rays will turn towards you and you will be in the midst of them. After doing this you will see a young and beautiful god with fiery hair, who wears a white tunic and scarlet cloak, with a fiery crown.[1] ... When you have said this he will enter the firmament and you will see him in motion, as if keeping to a course.

Fix your eyes and utter a long hornlike bellow at full breath, pressing your flank. Groan and kiss your amulets and say first to the right: 'Protect me.' When you have said this, you will see doors opening and seven maidens coming from the deep; they are clad in linen and are snake-headed. These are called the Fortunes[2] of the heavens and they hold golden sceptres. Greet them.... .

Another seven gods also come forward. They have the faces of black bulls and wear linen girdles and seven golden diadems. These are the so-called rulers of the heavenly pole. Greet them in the same way.

1. *fiery crown*: this figure has the attributes that might be expected of the Sun.

2. *Fortunes*: this is the word that is used for the goddess Fortune (Tyche).

¶ When they stand in position on this side and that, gaze into the air and you will see lightnings coming down and lights flashing and the earth quaking and a god immensely great coming down, with shining face, young, golden-haired, wearing a white tunic, a gold crown and trousers.[1] In his right hand he holds the golden shoulder of a calf, which is the Great Bear that sets the sky in motion and reverses it, rising and setting according to season. Then you will see lightnings springing from his eyes and stars from his body. Immediately press your stomach hard and bellow loud as long as you can to stimulate your five senses. Kiss your amulets again and say:...'Remain with me in my soul, do not leave me....' Letting out a long bellow fix your eyes on the god and greet him thus: 'O Lord, hail master of water, hail ruler of earth, hail sovereign of spirit.... Lord, reborn I die, while growing and after growing I come to an end, born from life-giving birth I am dissolved and go my way to death, as you established, as you ordained and conducted your Mystery.'

1. *trousers*: it is this Persian dress that essentially identifies the god as Mithras.

For men, particularly for soldiers, Mithraism had a great appeal. Mithras had undergone great toils to capture the bull and, subordinating his own wishes, had slain it in order to gain benefits for mankind. He inculcated the soldierly virtues of courage, hardihood and loyalty. His initiates were assured of brotherhood and fellowship in this world and, after death, of an ascent into the heavenly regions. Moreover Mithras was not a jealous god; his worshippers were often initiated into other rites too. Small wonder then that his cells were to be found all over the world, particularly in districts occupied by the army, and that some of the later Emperors proclaimed their allegiance to him.

## V  Syrian Cults

There was no one national cult as in Egypt, no one type of initiation as in Mithraism. Instead originally the various tribes each had their own Baal or Bel with his consort, whose powers extended only to the protection of their territory. Immigrants to the West brought in and maintained the worship of their own special god, as is shown by dedications. Gradually the name Syrian came to be applied in the West to any cult from Syria itself, Phoenicia, Assyria and such neighbouring small kingdoms as Commagene.

The first cult to make any impact in Italy was that of the 'Syrian goddess'. This was her usual name in the West instead of the more Oriental Atargatis, so common in fact that *dea Syria* became vulgarized as one proper name *Iasura*. She was brought in by Syrians enslaved as a result of Rome's wars with Antiochus the Great (*c.* 242–187 BC).

FLORUS, early second century AD who was born in Africa and wrote an *Epitome*, an abridgement of Roman history up to Augustus (Emperor 27 BC to AD 14), records with reference to the destructive Sicilian Slave Revolt of 134 BC:

*Epitome* 2.3

¶ Numerous prisons for slaves employed in tilling the land and chain-gangs of farm-labourers provided forces for the war. A certain Syrian called Eunus (the greatness of our defeats preserves his memory), simulating an inspired frenzy and wildly tossing his hair in honour of the Syrian goddess, incited the slaves to arms and liberty under pretext of a divine command.

The goddess was in many ways akin to Cybele, for she had her castrated devotees who like the latter's were called *galli*, and a noisy type of worship.

APULEIUS, AD 123 to *c.* 185 (p. 56), gives a vivid picture of her mendicant priests operating in Greece.

*Metamorphoses* 8.27–8

Lucius in his ass's shape had been bought by a band of eunuch priests of the Syrian goddess to carry her image on his back when they went out on their begging expeditions:

¶ Next day they came forth clad in various colours and with hideous make-up, their faces smeared with grease paint and their eyes black with mascara. They wore headbands and yellow robes of linen and silk and some had white tunics, held up by a girdle and painted with zigzag purple stripes like small spears. On their feet they had saffron-yellow shoes. The goddess they clothed in a silk cloak and put her on my back for me to carry. They bared their arms up to the shoulder and brandishing huge swords and axes and excited by the music of the pipe they bounded with frenzied cries in a frantic dance.

After passing through a few hamlets they reached the house of a wealthy landowner. From their first entrance they raised a din with discordant shrieks and whirled around like madmen and for a long time they bent down their heads and twisted their necks with sinuous movements so that their dangling hair spun round in a circle. At times they bit their own flesh and finally with the two-edged swords that they carried they each cut their arms. In the course of this one of them raved more wildly, heaving many a deep sigh from the depths of his heart, and as if he were filled with divine spirit he feigned sickness and madness, just as if by the presence of the gods men were usually not made better but weak and sickly.

Note then what just reward he received by divine providence. Making up a false tale he began with noisy prophesying to reproach and accuse himself, as if he had committed some act against the sanctity of religion. Moreover he demanded just punishment at his own hands for the noxious crime. Finally he snatched up a scourge,[1] such as those that eunuchs carry, with numerous twisted knots and tassels of wool and edged with many a sheep's knucklebone. With its knotted thongs he scourged himself violently, marvellously fortified by obstinacy against the pain of the blows. You might have seen the ground wet with the eunuchs' blood because of the sword-cuts and the blows of the scourge.

1. *scourge*: this is just like the scourge carried by a priest of Cybele (p. 236).

¶ When they were wearied out at last or certainly had their fill of lacerations and stopped mangling themselves, many vied in offering contributions in coppers and in silver too. These they received in the wide-open bosom of their dress and also a vessel of wine and milk and cheeses and some spelt and wheat; some brought barley for the goddess's bearer. Greedily they raked it all in, stuffed it in sacks[1] prepared beforehand on purpose for these acquisitions and loaded them on my back.

1. *sacks*: a Greek inscription found in Syria (*Bulletin de Correspondence Hellénique* 21, ed. Ch. Fossey, 1897) records the begging expeditions of a 'slave of the Syrian goddess', each of which brought in seventy bags.

It is easy to imagine how poor folk, unable to maintain a temple of their own, would welcome visits from such itinerant showmen, bringing a touch of colour into their drab lives, especially as fortune-telling was sometimes one of their sidelines.

LUCIAN, *c.* AD 120 to after 180 (p. 187), wrote a piece *On the Syrian Goddess*, a parody of Herodotus in its dialect and catchphrases and fondness for erotic and miraculous stories, which gives some superficial information. He describes the great temple at Hierapolis, Holy City (Bambyce), and its statuary:

*On the Syrian Goddess* 31

¶ In this chamber sit the statues, one of Juno[1] and the other of Jupiter, whom they call by another name.[2] Both are of gold and both are seated, but lions support Juno and the other is seated on bulls. Certainly the image of Jupiter is like Jupiter in every respect, head and garb and throne and, even if you wanted, you could not compare him to anything else. But when you look at Juno, she will show great diversity in her appearance. On the whole she is truly Juno, but she has something of Minerva and Venus and the Moon and Rhea[3] and Nemesis[4] and the Fates. In one hand she holds a sceptre, in the other a distaff and on her head she wears rays and a tower and she wears the girdle which is the attribute only of Heavenly Venus. Outside she is decked with more gold and precious stones of great value.

1. *Juno*: Lucian writing in Greek calls her Hera, but translators generally replace the Greek names by the Latin equivalents, which would be found on monuments in the West.

2. *another name*: he was the god Hadad, consort of Atargatis and less important than the goddess.

3. *Rhea*: in Greek mythology she was the wife of Kronos, therefore mother of the gods, but her name is often given to Cybele, who is probably meant here.

4. *Nemesis*: in Greek mythology she was a goddess of retribution, but could also be identified with the better known Fortune (Tyche).

Later Lucian describes the organization of the temple:

*On the Syrian Goddess 41*

¶ In the courtyard great cattle graze freely and horses and eagles and bears and lions and they never hurt men, but are sacred and tame. Many priests are appointed, some of whom slaughter the victims, others bear libations, others are called fire-bearers and others altar-attendants. When I was there more than three hundred used to come to the sacrifice. Their clothing is entirely white and they have a felt hat on their heads. A different high priest succeeds every year; he alone wears purple and binds his head with a golden headband. There is also another multitude attached to the temple, flute-players, pipers and *galli*, also frantic women out of their wits. A sacrifice which all attend is offered twice a day. To Jupiter they sacrifice daily without song or flute, but when they are sacrificing to Juno they sing and pipe and clash cymbals.

There was one particularly grim and primitive ritual:

*On the Syrian Goddess 49–51*

¶ Of all the festivals that I know they celebrate the greatest at the beginning of spring. Some call it the fire festival, some the torch festival. The sacrifice is as follows. They cut down great trees and set them up in the precincts. Then they collect goats and sheep and other domestic animals and hang them alive from the trees; among them are also birds and clothing and objects of gold and silver. When all is ready they carry the sacred objects round the trees and throw in a burning brand and straightway everything is burnt up. To this festival many come from Syria and from all the surrounding countries and they each bring their own sacred objects and carry tokens made in their likeness.

On fixed days the crowd gathers in the temple areas and many *galli* and the temple attendants whom I mentioned celebrate their rites. They cut their arms and lash one another's backs. Many stand beside them and play the flute, many beat the tambourines and others sing inspired and sacred songs. This takes place outside the sanctuary and those performing these acts do not enter the sanctuary.

On these days too men are made *galli*. For when the others are piping and carrying out their rites, many are seized by hysteria and many who came as spectators perform the act.

A description of the castration follows. The whole is very similar to the procedure at the imperial festival of Attis and Cybele at Rome (p. 232).

Syrians were excellent business-men and spread all over the Empire, in all walks of life. Even court circles were affected and Nero (Emperor 54–68), according to S U E T O N I U S, late first century AD (p. 84):

*Life of Nero* 56

¶ despised all religions, except that of the Syrian goddess alone. Soon he showed his contempt for her.

Akin to Atargatis was the Phoenician Astarte. Lucian links her with Adonis in a ritual similar to that of Attis. This was particularly popular with women, who grew little Adonis-gardens of plants which quickly flowered up and withered, symbolizing Adonis' brief resurrection and death. The myth had various versions, but basically Adonis was a beautiful youth, beloved of Venus; he was killed by a boar while out hunting, but once a year came to life again for one day. At Alexandria crowds rushed to view images of Adonis and Venus, lying together to renew their love for the one day of his resurrection, after which his image would be carried down to the sea amid general lamentation and set adrift. There is a vivid and very amusing poem by the third century BC Greek poet Theocritus (*Idyll* 15) describing two women at this show, too long to quote, but well worth reading.

Lucian's description runs:

Lucian *On the Syrian Goddess* 6

¶ I also saw in Byblus a great temple of Aphrodite[1] of Byblus, in which they carry out the sacred rites of Adonis, and I learnt these rites. They say that the business of Adonis and the boar took place in their country and in memory of the disaster they mourn and lament every year and perform sacred rites and there is great grief throughout the land. When they have stopped mourning and weeping, first they offer sacrifice to Adonis as dead, but afterwards on the next day they tell a story that he is alive and they bring him into the open and shave their heads, as the Egyptians do for the death of Apis.[2] All women who are unwilling to be shaved pay the following penalty. They stand for one day offering their beauty for sale.[3] The market is open only to foreigners and the price provides for sacrifice to Aphrodite.

    1. *Aphrodite*: Lucian had earlier identified her as Astarte.
    2. *Apis*: strictly speaking a bull sacred to Osiris, but often synonymous with the god himself (p. 43).
    3. *sale*: this custom of sacred prostitution, common in the East, was not acceptable in Rome nor did the rites of Adonis, although known (p. 64), make headway there. In this respect Venus differed from Aphrodite, who did have this in common with Astarte, cp. S T R A B O, 64/3 BC to AD 21 (p. 50), who wrote in *Geographica* in reference to Corinth:

Strabo *Geographica* 8.6.20

¶ The temple of Aphrodite was so wealthy that it possessed more than one thousand temple-slaves, courtesans, whom both men and women had dedicated to the goddess. Therefore because of them the city was crowded and became rich.

In other Syrian cults gods played the major role alongside their female consorts. Local Baals were equated with Jupiter in the West and differentiated by place-names, e.g. Jupiter Damascenus, who had a shrine at Puteoli as early as the second century BC. In Syria itself the greatest of these was Jupiter of Heliopolis, City of the Sun (Baalbek). He was worshipped as chief of a triad, the other members of which were Venus-Atargatis and their son Mercury-Semeios. Antoninus Pius (Emperor 138–61) enlarged an existing temple and its magnificent ruins can be seen today. Also in the Antonine period a sanctuary of this same triad was built on the Janiculum hill in Rome.

Most popular however in the West was Jupiter Dolichenus, the Baal of Doliche, an insignificant place in Commagene (see map 1). He was essentially a military god and his worship was carried by soldiers to the furthest corners of the Empire. Monuments show him in military dress standing on a bull, while his consort Juno sometimes stands on a hind. He brandishes a double axe and lightning. Inscriptions in his largest sanctuary at Rome on the Aventine hill and in that of the Heliopolis triad mentioned above show that there were dining-clubs of devotees, but no details of any secret rites or initiation ceremonies are known.

From the literary evidence it is clear that primitive Syrian religion was closely associated with natural objects such as animals and trees; a particular sanctity was attached to fish and doves. It retained some grim and repulsive features of ritual, which were not exported. At the same time there was a professional priesthood, strongly influenced by astrology and the learning of neighbouring Babylon. Each Baal, like the Roman Jupiter, had dominion over the sky. As the Sun came to be recognized as the greatest of the heavenly bodies, so the Baals were seen as manifestations of the Sun, the supreme god. This aspect came into prominence in the second century AD and, although outside the limit of our period, AD 200, it is worthwhile to trace its development. Julia Domna, second wife of Septimius Severus (Emperor 193–211) was a Syrian and promoted her own religion. Her grandson Elagabalus (Emperor 218–22) was hereditary priest of the sun-god of Emesa, Elagabal, and fanatically devoted to him. He imported from Emesa the sacred Black Stone associated with the god (like the Black Stone of Cybele from Pessinus p. 229) and built two great temples for the god in Rome. After his assassination there was official revulsion against this State support of the cult. Aurelian (Emperior 270–5) however in 274 established a cult, with an image imported from Palmyra, of the Invincible Sun, as patron of the State. By that time a strong tendency towards syncretism was promoting the idea of one supreme god merging in his own person lesser manifestations of the divine and, without opposition, he took his place in the official Roman pantheon.

The native religions of the far western provinces may be left out of our account. We do know something of them from Caesar and Tacitus and from archaeological evidence, but as Romanization advanced, at least in urban centres, they tended to become identified on functional grounds with Roman gods. Their impact on the Graeco-Roman world was negligible.

## Conclusion

From this brief survey of the pagan background the following generalizations may be made. Whether priesthoods were political or professional, liturgy and ritual were conservative and followed fixed patterns. Sacrifices were an essential part of the system, whether at public expense or offered by the individual. Statues gave mental pictures of the gods to their worshippers and functional gods reflected men's various needs, especially the Great Mother who appears in the oriental cults under so many names. Public processions and rituals could satisfy a desire for colour and pageantry and participation.

' Apart from the guilt of crimes generally recognized as heinous, such as murder and perjury (likely to bring down divine wrath), it is doubtful whether individuals had any particular sense of sin. Ritual purifications were certainly enforced and the superstitious thought it necessary to do penance if taboos were broken. There were no divine scriptures within reach of the ordinary man, even if priests had arcane books. Cultivated philosophers discussed high problems of ethics, but everyday moral teaching, if any, came from itinerant Cynic preachers.

Initiation in Mystery religions could bring mystical exaltation at the time, a sense of community and of being accepted and, above all, the assurance of a better after-life. For those who could afford it initiation in several cults was possible. If some regarded one deity, Mithras or Isis or the Sun as supreme, the existence of others was not denied and they were given due respect.

Over against this background Judaism (after the fall of the Temple) and Christianity stood out in stark relief. Neither had sacrificial system nor statues. For them the heathen gods were all alike simply idols or demons. There were no public processions and pageantry to catch the eye. They had holy books which gave them a theology and inculcated a strict morality. They also formed closely-knit groups giving mutual help and security.

In other features they differed. Judaism was intensely nationalistic, the religion of a chosen people, marked by such peculiarities as circumcision and food laws, to all of which the proselyte had to submit. It was fiercely monotheistic. At the same time it was legally recognized and, in spite of occasional troubles, could rely upon the protection of the law. Christianity transcended all racial barriers and imposed no irksome ritual taboos. Its missionaries evangelized strenuously and publicly and made many converts. On the other hand the doctrine of a Messiah might seem to infringe the purity of a strict monotheism and there was always the stumbling block of the crucifixion, that ultimate degradation for one who was acclaimed as the Son of God. There were slanderous stories current and they lived under the constant threat of persecution.

To conclude, there is a fitting defence of polytheism, such as would have been acceptable to any religious and educated pagan, especially a Stoic, given by PLUTARCH, late first century AD (p. 72), in *On Isis and Osiris*:

Plutarch *On Isis and Osiris* 67.377

¶ We do not conceive of the gods as different among different peoples, nor as barbarian and Greek, nor as southern and northern; but just as sun and moon and sky and earth and sea are common to all men, but have different names among different peoples, so for that one Reason which sets all things in order and for that one Providence which has oversight over them and for the attendant Powers, which are set over all, different honours and names have come into being among different peoples according to their customs. Men employ consecrated symbols, some obscure, some clearer, in guiding the intelligence towards things divine – not without risk. For some go entirely astray and sink into superstition, while others flying from superstition as if it were a quicksand do not realize that they have fallen over the precipice into atheism.

# Appendix: Chronological Chart

| | | |
|---|---|---|
| 400 BC *Fourth Century*<br>Alexander the Great 356–23 | Hecataeus, historian (G) *fl. c.* 300 | Persian dominion overthrown<br>Alexandria founded by Alexander 332 |
| 300 BC *Third Century*<br>Serapis cult in Egypt | Manetho, Egyptologist (G) *fl. c.* 280 | Ptolemies rule Egypt, also Judaea<br>Antioch founded, *c.* 300 |
| 200 BC *Second Century*<br>Roman dominion extending overseas<br>Temple of Cybele at Rome 191 | Mnaseas, geographer (G) *fl. c.* 200<br>Polybius, historian (G) *c.* 200 to after 118<br>Agatharchides, historian (G) *fl.* 116<br>Lysimachus, Egyptologist (G) (?) | Seleucid rule in Judaea<br>Antiochus IV desecrates the Temple 168<br>Maccabaean rising 168<br>Expulsion of Jews from Rome 139 |
| Bacchanalia 186<br>100 BC *First Century* | Meleager, poet (G) *fl. c.* 100<br>Alexander Polyhistor, historian (G) b. *c.* 115<br>Posidonius, philosopher etc. (G) *fl. c.* 135–51 | Hasmonaean dynasty in Judaea (client kingdom of Rome) |
| Caesar 100–44<br>Pompey 106–48<br>Crassus d. 53<br>First Triumvirate 60–53 | Apollonius Molo, rhetorician (G) *fl. c.* 87<br>Cicero, orator etc. (L) 106–43<br>Varro, antiquary (L) 116–27<br>Lucretius, poet (L) 94–55<br>Catullus, poet (L) 87 to *c.* 47<br>Diodorus, historian (G) d. *c.* 21 | Pompey enters the Temple 63<br>Crassus loots the Temple 54 |
| Mark Antony *c.* 83–30<br>Civil Wars 49–45 | Tibullus, poet (L) b. 55/48<br>Horace, poet (L) 65–8 BC | |

**Rulers and political events**

Caesar murdered 44
Battle of Actium 31

Octavian 63 BC–AD 14
EMPERORS replace Republic
Augustus (Octavian)
27 BC–AD 14  AD 100 *First Century*
Tiberius 14–37

Gaius 37–41
Claudius 41–54
Nero 54–68

Galba }
Otho } 68–9
Vitellius }
Vespasian 69–79

Titus 79–81
Domitian 81–96

**Writers**

Virgil, poet (L) 70–19
Livy, historian (L) 59 BC–AD 12

Ovid, poet (L) 43 BC–AD 17
Nicolaus, historian (G) c. 64 BC–AD 6

Strabo, geographer (G) 64/3 BC–AD 21
Pompeius Trogus, historian (L) *fl.* 27 BC–AD 14

Valerius Maximus, historian (L)
Apion, Egyptologist (G) (*fl.* under Tiberius and Claudius)
Philo, theologian (G) c. 15 BC–AD 45
Seneca, philosopher etc. (L) 4 BC/AD 1 to 65
Petronius, novelist (L)
Persius, satiric poet (L) 34–62
Lucan, poet (L) 39–65
Chaeremon, philosopher (G)
Apollonius of Tyana, seer (G)

Elder Pliny, encyclopaedist (L) 23/4 to 79

Statius, poet (L) 45–96
Josephus, historian (G) 37/8 to 94
Quintilian, orator (L) b. c. 30/5
Martial, poet (L) c. 40–104
Juvenal, satiric poet (L) c. 60–130
Plutarch, biographer etc. (G) c. 50–120
Suetonius, biographer (L) 69 to after 121

**Events**

Herod the Great d. 4 BC – three sons share realm

*Christian Era Begins*
Expulsion of Jews from Rome 19
Pontius Pilate procurator 26–37
Crucifixion of Jesus c. 33
Pogroms in Alexandria 38
Threat to desecrate Temple averted 41
Expulsion of Jews from Rome 49
Christian church expanding
Great Fire of Rome 64
Persecution of Roman Christians
First Jewish Revolt 66–74

Period of Civil War

Jerusalem destroyed 70
Temple tax diverted to Rome

Traditionally time of Christian persecution

| | | |
|---|---|---|
| Nerva 96–8 | Dio Chrysostom, philosopher (G) c. 40–125 | |
| Trajan 98–117 | Younger Pliny, letter writer (L) c. 61–112 | |
| | Tacitus, historian (L) c. 56–115 | Unrest in the Diaspora |
| | Frontinus, military writer (L) c. 30–104 | |
| | Ignatius, bishop of Antioch (G) c. 35–107 | |
| | Longinus, literary critic (G) (?) | |
| AD 100 *Second Century* | | |
| Hadrian 117–38 | Florus, historian (L) | Second Jewish Revolt 132–5 |
| | Epictetus, philosopher (G) c. 50–120 | Foundation of Aelia Capitolina |
| | Arrian, historian (G), edited Epictetus | |
| Antoninus Pius 138–61 | Aelius Aristides, orator (G) 117/129–181 | |
| | Lucian, lecturer (G) b. c. 120 | |
| | Apuleius, novelist (L) 123 to c. 185 | Martyrdom of Polycarp and others |
| | Numenius, philosopher (G) (?) | at Smyrna 155 |
| Marcus Aurelius 161–80 | Justin, Christian apologist (G) c. 100–65 | Martyrdom of Justin and others at |
| | Fronto, orator (L) c. 100–66 | Rome 165 |
| | Galen, physician (G) 129–99 | Martyrdoms at Lugdunum (Lyons) 177 |
| | Celsus, philosopher (G) fl. c. 178 | Martyrdoms at Scillium 180 |
| Commodus 180–92 | Dio Cassius, historian (G) c. 150–235 | |
| Pertinax | Clement of Alexandria, Christian author (G) c. 150–215 | |
| Didius Julius | Tertullian, Christian author (L) c. 160–220 | |
| Septimius Severus 193–211 | Philostratus, biographer (G) c. 170–245 | |

Later writers who provide quotations from earlier writers or attest beliefs and practices, which from archaeological evidence are known to have existed, but for which no earlier literary evidence survives:

| | |
|---|---|
| *Third Century* | Origen, theologian (G) *c.* 150–215 |
| | Minucius Felix, Christian author (L) *fl.* 200–40 |
| | Porphyry, philosopher (G) 232/3–305 |
| | Arnobius, Christian author (L) *fl.* 295 |
| *Fourth Century* | Scriptores Historiae Augustae (L) |
| | Ammianus, historian (L) *c.* 330–95 |
| | Eusebius, church historian (G) *c.* 260–340 |
| | Firmicus Maternus, Christian author (L) *fl. c.* 347 |
| | Gregory of Nazianzus, church father (G) 329–89 |
| | Macrobius, polymath (L) *fl. c.* 400 |
| | Synesius, bishop (G) *c.* 370 to *c.* 414 |
| *Fifth Century* | Jerome, church father (L) *c.* 342–420 |
| | Augustine, church father (L) 354–430 |
| | Prudentius, Christian poet (L) 348 to after 405 |
| | John of Antioch, bishop (G) d. 441 |
| *Sixth Century* | Lydus, antiquary (G) |
| | Digest (L) |
| *Tenth Century* | *Suidas*, encyclopaedia (G) |

# Select Bibliography

Translations of most of the authors quoted are available in the Loeb Classical Library (W. Heinemann, London), which also contains the original text; some are also available as paperbacks in Penguin Classics. An asterisk indicates that a book is illustrated.

*Cambridge Ancient History*, Vols. 7–12, Cambridge University Press (CUP) 1939

*Oxford Classical Dictionary*, Oxford University Press (OUP) 1957, revised edn 1970

*Oxford Dictionary of the Christian Church*, OUP 1957, revised edn 1974

*\*Shorter Atlas of the Classical World*, H. H. Scullard, Nelson 1961

*\*Atlas of the Early Christian World*, F. van der Meer and Christine Mohrmann. Transl. and ed. by Mary F. Hedlund and H. H. Rowley, Nelson 1958

M. M. Austin, *The Hellenistic World from Alexander to the Roman Conquest: A Selection of Ancient Sources in Translation*, CUP 1981

J. R. Bartlett, *Jews in the Hellenistic World* (Cambridge Commentaries on Writings of the Jewish and Christian World 200 BC to 200 AD, vol. 1), CUP (forthcoming)

H. Chadwick, *The Early Church*, Penguin Books 1967
(ed. and trans.) Origen, *Contra Celsum*, CUP 1953, paperback 1980

*\*F. Cumont, *The Oriental Religions in Roman Paganism*, University of Chicago Press (Routledge, London) 1911, Dover Press 1956
*After-life in Roman Paganism*, Yale University Press 1922, Dover Press 1959
*\*The Mysteries of Mithra*, University of Chicago Press 1910, Dover Press 1950

A. Dieterich, *Eine Mithrasliturgie* (text with German translation), Teubner 1910, 1923

J. Ferguson, *Greek and Roman Religion: Source Book*, Noyes Press 1982
*\*The Religions of the Roman Empire*, Thames and Hudson 1970 (This contains an excellent and detailed bibliography.)

A. J. Festugière, *Personal Religion among the Greeks*, University of California Press 1954

W. H. C. Frend, *Martyrdom and Persecution in the Early Church*, OUP 1965
*The Early Church*, revised edn SCM 1982

*\*J. Goodwin, *Mystery Religions in the Ancient World*, Thames and Hudson 1982

W. R. Halliday, *The Pagan Background of Early Christianity*, Hodder and Stoughton 1925

273

M. Hengel, *Jews, Greeks and Barbarians*, SCM 1980
  *Judaism and Hellenism*, SCM paperback 1981
M. A. Knibb, *The Qumran Community* (Cambridge Commentaries on Writings of the Jewish and Christian World 200 BC to AD 200, vol. 2), CUP (forthcoming)
A. R. C. Leaney, *The Jewish and Christian World 200 BC to AD 200* (Cambridge Commentaries on Writings of the Jewish and Christian World 200 BC to AD 200, vol. 7), CUP 1984
H. Lietzmann, *History of the Early Church*, Lutterworth Press 1937, 3rd edn 1960
R. MacMullan, *Paganism in the Roman Empire*, Yale University Press 1981
A. Momigliano, *Alien Wisdom: The Limits of Hellenization*, CUP 1975
H. Musurillo (ed. and trans.), *Acts of the Christian Martyrs*, OUP 1972, reprinted 1979
  (ed. and trans.) *Acts of the Pagan Martyrs*, OUP 1954
A. D. Nock, *Early Gentile Christianity and its Hellenistic Background*, Harper Press Books 1964
  *Conversion*, OUP 1933
R. M. Ogilvie, *The Romans and their Gods*, Hutchinson 1969
J. W. Packer, *Acts of the Apostles* (Cambridge Bible Commentary), CUP 1966
H. W. Parke, *Greek Oracles*, Hutchinson 1967
H. J. Rose, *Religion in Greece and Rome*, Harper Torchbooks 1966
  *A Handbook of Greek Mythology*, Methuen 1972
  *A Handbook of Greek Literature*, Methuen 1965
  *A Handbook of Latin Literature*, Methuen 1966
A. N. Sherwin White, *Racial Prejudice in Imperial Rome*, CUP 1967
E. Mary Smallwood, *Documents illustrating the Principates of Gaius, Claudius and Nero*, CUP 1967
  *The Jews under Roman Rule*, Brill, corrected edn 1981
M. Stern, *Greek and Latin Authors on Jews and Judaism* (ed. with Introduction, Translation and Commentary), Israel Academy of Sciences and Humanities 1974
W. W. Tarn and G. T. Griffith, *Hellenistic Civilization*, 3rd rev. edn Arnold 1958
L. R. Taylor, *The Divinity of the Roman Emperor*. Monographs published by the American Philological Association, No. 1 1931, new edn Arno Press 1975
*Arnold Toynbee (ed.) *The Crucible of Christianity*, Thames and Hudson 1969
*M. J. Vermaseren, *Mithras, the Secret God*, Chatto and Windus 1963
  *Corpus Inscriptionum et Monumentorum Religionis Mithriacae*, 2 vols., Martinus Nijhoff 1956
  *Cybele and Attis: The Myth and the Cult*, Thames and Hudson 1977
R. Walzer, *Galen on Jews and Christians*, OUP 1949
H. R. Willoughby, *Pagan Regeneration*, University of Chicago Press 1920
*R. E. Witt, *Isis in the Graeco-Roman World*, Thames and Hudson 1970

# Index

Capitals are used for names of sources; numbers in bold type refer to their biographical details.